Cartographies
of Knowledge

This book is dedicated to all of the scholars who have labored at the margins of their disciplines to help create more equitable and more effective forms of social research and to you, the reader, in gratitude for your interest and in hopes that you will expand upon and improve all that you find here.

Cartographies *of* Knowledge

EXPLORING QUALITATIVE EPISTEMOLOGIES

CELINE-MARIE PASCALE
American University

Los Angeles | London | New Delhi
Singapore | Washington DC

For information:

SAGE Publications, Inc.
2455 Teller Road
Thousand Oaks,
 California 91320
E-mail: order@sagepub.com

SAGE Publications Ltd.
1 Oliver's Yard
55 City Road
London EC1Y 1SP
United Kingdom

SAGE Publications India Pvt. Ltd.
B 1/I 1 Mohan Cooperative
 Industrial Area
Mathura Road, New Delhi 110 044
India

SAGE Publications Asia-Pacific Pte. Ltd.
33 Pekin Street #02-01
Far East Square
Singapore 048763

Printed in the United States of America

Library of Congress Cataloging-in-Publication Data

Pascale, Celine-Marie, 1956-
Cartographies of knowledge: exploring qualitative epistemologies / Celine-Marie Pascale.
    p. cm.
Includes bibliographical references and index.
ISBN 978-1-4129-5496-9 (pbk.)
    1. Social sciences—Research. 2. Qualitative research. I. Title.

H62.P313 2011
001.4'2—dc22   2010022051

This book is printed on acid-free paper.

10   11   12   13   14   10   9   8   7   6   5   4   3   2   1

Acquisitions Editor:	Vicki Knight
Associate Editor:	Lauren Habib
Editorial Assistant:	Ashley Dodd
Production Editor:	Catherine M. Chilton
Copy Editor:	Megan Markanich
Typesetter:	C&M Digitals (P) Ltd.
Proofreader:	Annette R. Van Deusen
Indexer:	Molly Hall
Cover Designer:	Glenn Vogel
Marketing Manager:	Stephanie Adams
Permissions:	Karen Ehrmann and Adele Hutchinson

BRIEF CONTENTS

DETAILED CONTENTS

PREFACE

——◆•◆•◆——

*C*artographies of Knowledge: Exploring Qualitative Epistemologies examines the theoretical foundations that shape both the premise and logic of qualitative social research. It critiques the politics of knowledge production by exploring some of the ways that a 19th-century philosophy of science both enables and constrains qualitative research in the 21st century. In particular, *Cartographies of Knowledge* illustrates how qualitative social research constructs knowledge that is recognized as credible social science by exploring analytic induction, symbolic interaction, and ethnomethodology.

Arguably, analytic induction is the defining *logic* of qualitative inquiry. It is foundational to qualitative research—including the prominent interpretive strategies of symbolic interaction and ethnomethodology. At the same time, the logic of analytic induction is used frequently with postpositivist and social constructionist research. Consequently, the chapter on analytic induction as a *method* of inquiry (Chapter 3) includes considerations of postpostivism as well as various forms of social constructionism. Further, since analytic induction is frequently practiced as a variation of grounded theory, this chapter also undertakes discussion of the logic and techniques of analytic induction in relation to those of grounded theory.

Symbolic interaction is the earliest form of interpretive research and remains one of the most common styles of interpretive research practiced today. Four variations of symbolic interaction are now embodied in distinct schools of research—the collection of which point to the longevity, intellectual diversity, and prominence of the field. *Cartographies of Knowledge* delineates the history and practices associated with each school as well as their relationships to analytic induction as a method of inquiry. While ethnomethodology is less widely used than symbolic interaction, it is a distinctive interpretive framework and represents the efforts of scholars to systematically challenge the foundations of qualitative research. Indeed the field began with scholars questioning the processes used to create knowledge that is recognizable as "science." Both symbolic interaction and ethnomethodology offer particular insights into how scholars have challenged dominant research paradigms in the past and offer tangible insights into the promise and problems of transforming the practices of qualitative social research today.

Throughout the book, I argue that the philosophical foundations embedded in the premise and logic of qualitative analysis render knowledge that is incomplete and, at times, distorted. As a qualitative researcher, my critique is not intended to find fault with qualitative research (as opposed to quantitative). Rather, I aim to provide deeper understanding of the methodologies I most value in order to suggest alternatives that may be capable of more fully apprehending porous social contexts and routine of relations of power in the 21st century. My critique of qualitative research is both a historical analysis of the limits that are imposed on qualitative research and an experiment with provocations for going beyond them.

Cartographies of Knowledge makes an unusual and practical contribution by combining a study of specific methodologies with corresponding analyses of empirical data. While there are many excellent books on research methodology that offer important critiques of epistemology and ontology (cf. Denzin, Lincoln, & Smith, 2008; Haraway, 1991; Harding, 1987, 1991, 2007; Ramazanoğlu & Holland, 2002; Sandoval, 2000; Smith, 2004), *Cartographies of Knowledge* takes up both theory and praxis by illustrating how the theoretical foundations of analytic induction, symbolic interaction, and ethnomethodology enable and constrain specific empirical analyses. It demonstrates how each framework functions differently in the production of social science knowledge.

Cartographies of Knowledge is substantially different from existing literature in three key ways. First, it provides historical overviews of the development of each framework that are intended to illustrate the theoretical and philosophical assumptions inherent in each. All social research advances not only substantive findings but also an implicit view of the social world that includes a politics of culture, knowledge, and power. Second, *Cartographies of Knowledge* applies each analytical framework to exactly the same set of data, thus more clearly demonstrating how each framework animates social research differently. Collectively, these chapters will demonstrate how analytic strategies elide, as well as produce, knowledge. Third, *Cartographies of Knowledge* has a very specific concern with issues of agency, subjectivity, and experience, and in this sense, it considers the political effects of analytical strategies. Typically discussions of agency and subjectivity are considered to be the domain of critical social theory; they are rarely central points of discussion in social research methods. Yet within every method is a theory of agency and subjectivity. More recently methods books, particularly those concerned with issues of reflexivity, have taken up important issues of subjectivity and agency with respect to the role of the researcher and data collection. However, these books are not focused on issues of ontology and epistemology that underpin social sciences, nor do they consider how social research animates particular conceptions of agency, subjectivity, and experience. I argue that researchers need more explicit understandings of how qualitative strategies themselves animate particular conceptions of agency, subjectivity, and experience. *Cartographies of Knowledge* is rooted to feminist, critical race and poststructural critiques—it was written with the hope of strengthening qualitative social research and encouraging more and different critiques.

ORGANIZATION OF THE BOOK

Despite progressive work on methodology, there is a general disconnect between methodological critiques of epistemology and ontology and discussion of the pragmatics of data collection and analysis. This book sets out to fill that void. *Cartographies of Knowledge* applies each framework to several styles of empirical data to illustrate how the different philosophical foundations of each framework are expressed in the relative abilities of each framework. The analyses demonstrate the effectiveness of each framework with respect to newspaper articles, television drama, and semistructured interviews.

My intention in using three sources of data is to illustrate how analytic induction, symbolic interaction, and ethnomethodology each approach commonly used sources of data in the social sciences. Newspaper articles, television drama, and research interviews also proved to be efficient resources for generating exemplars—as compared with other common forms of empirical research such as ethnography, focus groups, participant observation, and

action research. The variety of empirical data helps to showcase the breadth
and depth of each analytical framework. At the same time, I believe that the
analytical issues illustrated in this book can be usefully translated to other
forms of empirical data derived from qualitative data collection.

All empirical excerpts appear as originally collected; they are not scripted
or edited. Throughout I treat each as analytical exemplars. Specifically, in
each of Chapters 3, 4, and 5, I examine an article from the *New York Times*
about resistance to including Oscar Pistorius ("the fastest man on no legs")
(Longman, 2007) in the 2008 Olympics; an excerpt about same-sex marriage
from the ABC television drama *Brothers and Sisters*; and an excerpt from an
interview that I did with Tony Romero, an Esselen Indian (in the excerpt, he
talks about racialized violence in his youth).[1] The newspaper, television, and
interview excerpts articulate contemporary concerns regarding ability, sexuality, and race, respectively.

Cartographies of Knowledge breaks with what has become the more
expected social science trilogy of race, class, and gender. Analyses of ability,
sexuality, and race—frequently understood as essential categories of identity—
are especially vibrant resources for illustrating the implications of various conceptions of agency, subjectivity, and experience. As a result, the exemplars
offer an effective way to demonstrate how each research framework both
relies upon and generates different understandings of culture, knowledge,
power, and privilege. Overall this focus provides a fresh approach with important and potentially engaging contexts.

Although I treat data excerpts as exemplars, I also offer a necessary
caveat: They do not come from complete research designs and therefore cannot be the basis of a comprehensive analysis. However, by using analytic
induction, symbolic interaction, and ethnomethodology to analyze the same
empirical data, I illustrate the various ways that each framework interprets the
same excerpts and demonstrate how theoretical underpinnings establish commitments regarding the nature and possibilities of agency subjectivity and
experience. In the process, I critically examine the construction of what comes
to be seen as evidence.

Although scholars often use critical race theory, feminist theory, and/or
poststructural theory in combination with analytic induction, symbolic

---

[1]Tony Romero is a pseudonym used throughout the book.

interaction, and ethnomethodology, the ensuing chapters do not. The analyses in Chapters 3, 4, and 5 are not intended to show the creative and complex ways in which scholars incorporate theory and methods. Rather the analyses seek to demonstrate the underlying philosophical premises that shape all qualitative research—despite the various theoretical strategies that scholars might use to compensate for particular limitations. My intention is to produce bare bones analyses that bring the foundational assumptions of qualitative research clearly to the surface. Chapters 3, 4, and 5 collectively demonstrate the significant differences among analytic induction, symbolic interaction, and ethnomethodology; they also demonstrate how these frameworks are constrained in surprisingly similar ways. Collectively, the chapters build as a form of argument that leads to the provocation in Chapter 6 calling for a fundamental change in the philosophical foundations of qualitative research.

OUTLINE OF THE CHAPTERS

Cartographies of Knowledge begins with a chapter that defines the large questions of ontology, epistemology, and social justice that run throughout the book. It also elaborates on the relationship of analytic induction to interpretive research. Chapter 2 examines the historical terrain that shaped qualitative research and situates the development of research paradigms within philosophical debates about the nature of self, society, and interaction. This context establishes the importance and implications of how researchers conceptualize agency, subjectivity, and experience. Chapters 3, 4, and 5 each presents a single analytical framework. These three chapters begin with a general introduction and are then divided into four primary sections.

- The first section provides a historical context and an intellectual trajectory in relation to the key points of the framework. It offers a descriptive (rather than critical) overview of the development of the framework and renders a pragmatic consideration of the theoretical/philosophical foundations that give rise to particular conceptions of agency, subjectivity, and experience. This section concludes by tracing the development of various schools within each framework and fundamental differences/debates among them.

- The second section summarizes the framework's central points to orient the reader to the key distinguishing features of the framework *as it is most commonly used today* and as it will be used to analyze the excerpts.
- The third section systematically analyzes newspaper, television, and interview excerpts. In order to illustrate the power of each framework, the analyses treat the excerpts as exemplars of patterns that articulate substantive findings. Exactly the same configuration of data is analyzed in each chapter, giving readers a clear way to compare how each framework generates different problems, solutions, and conclusions.
  - o Each analysis is followed by a critique that analyzes the possibilities that are opened or foreclosed by the framework. It draws out the implications of the particular conceptions of ontology, epistemology, agency, subjectivity, and experience that are embedded in the framework.

- The fourth section builds upon the critiques of newspaper, television, and interview analyses to explore how "scientific research" is accomplished. It seeks to answer questions such as How does this framework help or hinder understanding of routinized relations of power and privilege? What relations of power and privilege come to be visible? What are the implications for understanding culture, knowledge, and power? In addition, each analytic chapter offers concluding thoughts that emphasize the dilemmas and issues raised in the chapter and closes with suggestions for further reading.

The sixth and final chapter is a provocation toward rethinking the philosophical foundations and implications of empiricism in social research. It joins with, and extends, indispensable critiques of methodology in relation to dominant social research strategies. Chapter 6 draws together, and expands upon, the analyses of earlier chapters to reconsider the purpose of a social science and to argue for social epistemologies. Ultimately, this chapter offers grounds for rethinking social research in relation to the politics of production of knowledge and offers potential solutions to the limitations posed by existing qualitative frameworks.

ACKNOWLEDGMENTS

I owe a special debt of gratitude to my family and friends for their loving support that continues to sustain me. I especially want to thank Mercedes Santos for her love and for being a transformative force in my life. Many people provided critical feedback on earlier drafts of this book. In particular, this book benefitted enormously from the insights and suggestions that emerged from long and ongoing conversations with Ezerbet Barat and John Kelly. Their intellectual contributions vastly improved my work. I want to thank Melanie Heath for generously reading multiple drafts of this manuscript; her comments have been invaluable. Ian Bruff, Shobha Gurung, and Corinne Kirschner also provided thoughtful perspectives and clarifying comments on an earlier draft. I owe Chanda Cook an enormous debt of thanks for the excellent research assistance she provided throughout. In addition, I want to acknowledge rich conversations on epistemology, ontology, and social research that I have enjoyed both with Patrick Thaddeus Jackson and with the doctoral students of the Graduate Research Cluster: Jesse Crane-Seeber, Shaconna Haley, Jacon Stump, Malinda Rhone, Maria Amelia Viteri, Arventia Washington, and Briana Weadock.

I am deeply appreciative of American University for providing institutional support that enabled me to complete this book. As well, I am grateful to my colleagues at American University, the Congress for Qualitative Inquiry, and the International Sociological Association (ISA) for sustained and sustaining conversations on the politics of social research.

I owe a special debt to the editorial staff at SAGE, including Lisa Cuevas-Shaw and Margo Crouppen for their vision and encouragement in the early days of this project and most especially to Vicki Knight, who guided this book to completion. I also want to thank Ashley Dodd, Megan Markanich, and Catherine M. Chilton for contributing their thoughtful expertise to the production of this book. From planning to completion, this book benefitted from 3 review cycles and a total of 18 outside reviews. While this sounds arduous, it was terrifically supportive. I want to thank all of the following reviewers for contributing their time and expertise to help make this a better book.

Ellen M. Broido
Bowling Green State University

Carol Chetkovich
Mills College

Thomas Cushman
Wellesley College

Sarah Amira De la Garza
Arizona State University

Patrick Dilley
Associate Professor of Higher Education and Qualitative Research
Southern Illinois University Carbondale

Marco Gemignani
Psychology Department, Duquesne University

Elizabeth McGibbon
St. Francis Xavier University

sj Miller
Indiana University of Pennsylvania

Patricia Somers
University of Texas at Austin

Elizabeth Adams St.Pierre
University of Georgia

Karen M. Staller
University of Michigan School of Social Work

Of course, the remaining shortcomings are mine alone.

My deepest gratitude goes to the many scholars cited in this book whose critical scholarship has sustained, inspired, and transformed qualitative social research.

ABOUT THE AUTHOR

Celine-Marie Pascale is an associate professor of sociology at American University in Washington, DC, where she teaches courses on language and inequalities. With a doctorate in sociology and a certificate in women's studies from the University of California, Santa Cruz, Pascale pursues research regarding issues of culture, knowledge, and power. In 2008, she received the Distinguished Contribution to Scholarship Book Award from the American Sociological Association Section on Race, Gender, and Class for a distinguished and significant contribution to the development of the integrative field of race, gender, and class for her first book *Making Sense of Race, Class and Gender: Commonsense, Power and Privilege in the United States* (Routledge, 2007). Her third book, *Inequality & The Politics of Representation: A Global Landscape*, is due out from SAGE in 2012. Pascale also has published her research in journals that include *Cultural Sociology, Current Sociology, Qualitative Inquiry, Studies in Symbolic Interactions, Advances in Gender Research, Cultural Studies ↔ Critical Methodologies*, and *Perspectives on Social Problems*. In 2005, Pascale was awarded the American University Multicultural Affairs/International Student Services Award for Distinguished Faculty for scholarly achievements and commitment to the enhancement of cultural awareness and diversity at American University. She is active in the International Sociological Association (ISA) and currently serves as president of the Research Committee on Language and Society.

CHAPTER ONE

INTRODUCTION

———◆———

MAPPING THE JOURNEY

Social sciences encompass technologies for generating knowledge; as such, they shape and are shaped by cultural ideologies, concepts, conditions, and processes. The use of cartography as a metaphor in the title, and throughout the book, alludes to geographies of power expressed in technologies for generating knowledge. Early maps, as a technology for creating knowledge, served merchants engaged in trade as well as nations engaged in the colonial expansion of empire. In both contexts, maps might be understood as textualization of power struggles—maps have supported both real and symbolic forms of control.

Early maps produced not only redrawn boundaries in the service of empire but also *a language of conquest* that was needed to create new social orders through genocide, enslavement, and colonization. Discourses of conquest and discovery provided a means to reduce entire civilizations to "savages" and to define ancient homelands as "new territories." Regardless of real-world knowledge, maps remained Eurocentric ideological expressions of power for centuries. Indeed, maps began to acquire geographic proportion only in a postcolonial world. In the Western traditions of science, where the language of "discovery" has been foundational, maps were an early metaphor for knowledge production.

> Traditional epistemology is consistently defined in geographical terms—knowledge is surveyed and divided into fields, topics (from *topos*, or place), provinces, domains, realms, and spheres. Implied in this subdivision of episte-mological territory is a mastery or dominance over knowledge, as the terms "subject" and "discipline" make evident. Thus knowledge in the Enlightenment tradition is represented metaphorically as a territory that can be unproblemati-cally encompassed, mapped, and viewed empirically and objectively. Moreover, this knowledge can be framed, by the philosopher, in an objective and literal language—a language that denies any difference between the word and thing, between map and territory. (Mitchell, 2007, p. 2)

The classical map metaphor began to shift in the early 20th century. By the late 20th century, it had transformed into a site of poststructural critique of both classical and modernist epistemology. Poststructural map metaphors highlight the subjective and political experience of mapmaking as well as the constructive processes of reading. If sun and light were the primary metaphors of Classical and Enlightenment epistemes—and biological and mechanical tropes definitive of the Modernist episteme—the map becomes a formative and performative metaphor of postmodern epistemes (Mitchell, 2007, p. 26). The map metaphor in this book emphasizes the ways that social research goes well beyond merely representing social realities and suggests both the impermanence of boundaries and subjective nature of understanding. *Cartographies of Knowledge* examines how forms of knowledge are made true by social science—it challenges both the production of knowledge and the meaning of science.

Cartographies of Knowledge begins with a distinction between methodol-ogy (the logical frameworks of research design) and methods (techniques for acquiring data) and presents a critique of method-driven research that is profi-cient at applying techniques for acquiring and analyzing data but not responsi-ble for politics on which those techniques are premised. Despite rich literature in research methodology, it is possible to learn, and to use, social research methods without *ever* considering their philosophical/theoretical foundations—which has profound implications for the production of knowledge.

To the extent that social sciences treat the philosophical foundations of research as tangential abstractions, contemporary research paradigms carry unnoticed historical commitments within them. The analyses in *Cartographies* demonstrate some of these historical commitments. I argue that, despite significant efforts to move beyond the philosophical foundations of the natural sciences, techniques of data collection and analysis have kept analytical processes of qualitative research tethered to a 19th-century philosophy of science.[1] This has created odd analytical crosscurrents in social research and truncated the ability of qualitative research methods to apprehend profound changes in social life and routine relations of power and privilege.

A number of big questions run through this book. The first is the fundamental question of *ontology.* Ontologies are theories about the nature of existence. As such, they address the question of what can be known. Yet ontologies are not motivations or causal explanations for how we develop research methods. Indeed researchers' emotional and intellectual investments often induce particular ontological views about the nature of the social world. It may be helpful to consider a primary ontological change in the social sciences. The pursuit of social laws once served as the intellectual compass that oriented the development of social research—scholars, certain that fixed laws governed social life, borrowed analytic frameworks from the physical sciences that had been used to ascertain laws that govern physical matter. Few social researchers today believe that fixed laws govern social life. Social research has been through an ontological shift. However, methods premised on this earlier ontology remain cornerstones of social science research. What other assumptions about the nature of the self and social life remain sequestered in the methods that scholars use today?

Ontological questions are fundamental to social research. All research is anchored to basic beliefs about how the world exists. For example, to what extent is the world objectively real? Socially constructed? What is the relationship of the unconscious to social life?[2] The answers to these, and other ontological questions, constitute the foundations of social inquiry yet dominant social science protocols generally direct researchers away from such philosophical pursuits and toward more pragmatic concerns of systematic data collection—as if data exist independently and need only to be collected properly.

The neglect of philosophical foundations in social research results in ontological assumptions that function as untheorized truths. Ontological

---

[1]This is a reference to René Descartes, whose philosophy gave rise to logical positivism in the 20th century. Although subsequent scholars, such as those in the First Vienna Circle, elaborated upon logical positivism, the theoretical foundation of logical positivism—indeed of all social science research—can be traced back to the philosophical premises established by Descartes.

[2]Arguably, the most substantial obstacle posed to social research is the unconscious. In order to be ethically responsible scholars, "we cannot be tied to the conceit of a fully transparent self"— our own or others' (Butler, 2005, p. 83). Yet by and large, social sciences have been unprepared to address issues of the unconscious in social life.

assumptions operate as ideologies that construct what can be known and on what terms—they constitute social research through the topics researchers take up. Ontological assumptions are extremely powerful, not just because they shape what counts as valid knowledge, but because they do so in ways that are not explicit and therefore not accountable, and not even easily open to doubt.

The second big question framing this book regards *epistemology*. Epistemology is a branch of philosophy that takes up questions about *how* the world can be known—it concerns the nature, sources, and limits of knowledge. As such, it regards issues of belief—assertions and propositions about how the world can be apprehended. How can we produce knowledge about the social world? Under what conditions can we know what we know? Epistemology can be understood as a *justificatory account* of the scientific production of knowledge. To recognize epistemology as a justificatory account of knowledge production is to recognize as well that values, ethics, politics, and power are intrinsically and inseparably infused in the production of knowledge (Flyvbjerg, 2001).

Yet scholars are seldom well trained in epistemology; rather, in mainstream social science programs, students are likely to study techniques of data collection and analysis but to inherit broad epistemological assumptions that render core aspects of inquiry a matter of common sense. In vernacular usage, common sense refers to sound, uncomplicated judgment. However, Gramsci provided a more critical understanding of common sense as shared knowledge that is so pervasive, so commonly held that it appears only tacitly as shared assumptions.[3]

Commonsense assumptions arise at every step of the research process as seen, but unnoticed, features of research. For example, the concept of evidence as some thing to which one can physically point is just such an assumption. It is an epistemological assumption that is treated as being so obvious that it passes without remark—as a matter of common sense. What other kind of evidence could there possibly be in science? However, for those trained in nonhegemonic social research that critiques epistemology, the notion of evidence is itself extremely problematic.

Processes of research, which are rendered as matters of common sense, are not easily available to doubt or critique. This is true in part because these assumptions are implicit, but also because common sense prepares one to think about the world in particular ways by excluding some topics from consideration, while making others appear obvious (Handel, 1982, p. 56). Historical arguments about the nature and importance of ontology and epistemology are embedded in

---

[3]This is consistent also with an ethnomethodological usage of common sense.

commonsense assumptions about the research process. How each researcher conceptualizes the best way to apprehend the social world is clearly dependent upon what she or he believes about the nature of existence. What constitutes data? What constitutes a pattern in data? What does the pattern mean?

Whether or not researchers use the term epistemology, and regardless of whether or not researchers *understand* epistemology, we all draw from it each time we assert (or assume) that something counts as evidence. Every decision that we make about how to create valid knowledge about the world is an ontological and epistemological issue. There are two broad issues at stake in ontological and epistemological assumptions: One is the reproduction of hegemonic scientific discourse; the other is the production of knowledge about the social world. My intent is not to try to eliminate commonsense assumptions but to transform them into more critical modes of engagement.

The third big question for this book regards the fundamental issue of *how social research relates to social justice*. Even advocates for objective social research (as opposed to activist social research) often are concerned with issues of inequality. Researchers concerned with inequality face a broad range of philosophical questions. To what extent is a concern for issues of inequality the same as a concern for social justice? To what extent is a concern for creating inclusive research projects the same as a concern for social justice? Is social research for social justice simply a matter of exposing inequalities? Is it a matter of supplying remedies for inequalities? Of producing knowledge that empowers people to act in their own best interests? Does social research that is sensitive to issues of social justice require an ethic of transparency? Of co-participation? To what extent does social research for social justice require us to expose the machinations of power? All of these questions about social justice are important and deserve to be answered—multiple times and in multiple ways—yet this book does not take up the kind of analyses needed to answer them. Rather, *Cartographies of Knowledge* takes up a more rudimentary approach to social justice by exploring the politics of knowledge production; it addresses foundational issues that must be reconciled *before* these questions can be adequately addressed by a 21st-century social science.

Cartographies of Knowledge explores the liberatory potentials of social research by contesting the conventional oppositional binary between the philosophical and the practical. There is a tendency among persons concerned with the immediacies of inequality to dismiss philosophical concerns as belonging to the "ivory tower" of academia. However, in very important ways, this binary way of thinking counterproductively separates the techniques of data collection from the philosophical foundations that direct the very possibilities of knowledge production.

If issues of ontology or epistemology seem remote or too erudite to be practical, consider the vast changes in social research that emerged in the 1960s and 1970s from feminist and critical race critiques of social research methods. Scholarship demands not only a thoughtfulness about who or what we study but also insight into the tools we use for conducting research—regardless of whether we care about social justice—yet even more so if we are committed to research that supports social and economic equality. To the extent that contemporary social science holds an emancipatory promise, it is a promise that cannot be fully realized unless it can account for the most intractable forms of privilege that social life produces. At the same time, social science must be able to grasp new forms of social relationships and knowledge that emerge through technological and global changes.

Concerned both with effective research and issues of social justice, I locate the politics of knowledge production in relation to conceptions of subjectivity, agency, and experience. It is important to underscore that I do not attempt to *link* methodology or methods with an external theory. Rather, I work to *excavate* the theoretical foundations that already exist in social research paradigms in order to more fully understand their implications as resources for understanding culture, knowledge, power, and privilege. It is a beginning effort to explore the possibilities and potentials that arise from taking up the uneasy and problematic tensions among methods, methodology, and theory in the service of social research and social justice.

FAMILIAR INTELLECTUAL GEOGRAPHIES

The impetus for *Cartographies of Knowledge* came from three paradigmatic quandaries that arose quickly in my academic career; one regards ethics, power, and knowledge; one regards the study of routine relations of power and privilege; and one regards the relationship between social theory and social research. This nexus of these analytical problems form the intellectual foundation that both motivated and framed my thinking about this book, so they warrant some discussion.

Although discussions of research ethics are generally limited to the concerns of institutional review boards (IRBs), as a graduate student working on my dissertation, the IRB was the least of my ethical concerns. I interviewed a number of people who could not afford housing. In particular, I interviewed a

53-year-old woman who suffered from several serious illnesses and had recently gone through a divorce. As a result of these circumstances, she was unable to work, was living on Social Security, and was sleeping in her car. The combination of the car and Social Security made her both unusually wealthy, and particularly vulnerable, among people on the streets. She was the person everyone went to when they needed a lift to a clinic or money for medicine. At the same time, she was easy prey on the streets—her age, gender, visibly poor health, and comparative wealth marked her as an easy target. Although I did what little I could for her at the time, ultimately I left her to sleep in her car and went home to type up my field notes. If this were my experience with only one person, it would have been hard enough, but I spent long hours talking with people who were much less fortunate than the woman I describe.

I sought advice both from textbooks and a variety of senior scholars. In feminist scholarship, I found critiques of prevailing standards of ethical responsibilities regarding insider/outsider research (Zinn, 1979), critiques of ethnographic processes (Rosaldo, 1993; Smith, 1999), and more general critiques concerning the design of feminist methods (DeVault, 1999; Harding, 1991; Olesen, 1994; Reinharz, 1992; Stanley & Wise, 1983). This literature was both valuable and important but not adequate for addressing the pragmatic, ethical, and methodological quandaries that I faced.

Senior scholars consistently advised me to remember that I was in the field *to collect data* and that I needed to set better boundaries between me and the people I interviewed. Over and again, scholars reminded me that I could not fix the troubles I saw. Of course, I knew that I could not end systemic, chronic poverty—I could not even find affordable housing for one woman. I also knew that I was facing the opportunism of a broader system that actively rewarded researchers for turning away from the suffering encountered in the field. However, I faced more than "simple" careerism.

In the face of seemingly unsolvable conflicts, I began to think seriously about the vision of power I was asked to embody for the pursuit of knowledge. I eventually came to understand that social research ethics were not just a set of rules to protect the people researchers study. It seemed to me then, as it does now, that learning to be a scholar was a process of learning to be accountable to a different set of ethics than those I might use in daily life. Consider that as a researcher I was potentially accountable to the IRB for an ethic of doing no harm, informed consent, and so forth; I might even be called to acknowledge and analyze my research as a subjective process. But I was not ever accountable—in any way—for easing the suffering that I saw, for compensating people for their time, or for contributing to the communities in which I worked. This is striking in two ways. First, it is notable that feminist developments in the ethics of social research have remained marginal to IRB protocols for more or less 50 years.

Second, this lack of accountability was striking because the enlightenment ideals of social progress and betterment were said to have shaped the formation of the social sciences. Certainly, the social sciences have a long and rich history of research of making visible the plights of marginalized people— yet this is quite different from having a rich history of helping to create a level playing field. One might argue that visibility is the first step toward equality; however, the social sciences have intellectual histories that are voyeuristic at times and colonialist at others. I began to think about research ethics not as a set of norms to which one must conform but as a set of conditions that produce the subject position of social researcher—the position from which it becomes possible to produce credible knowledge.

A 19th-century philosophy of social science directed scholars to treat the people they studied as objects—which we did through most of the 20th century. For this reason alone (and of course, there are many others), it should not be surprising that marginalized people developed a deep distrust of social researchers and social research (cf. Denzin, Lincoln, & Smith, 2008; Steinberg, 2007). The notion that scholars should mirror the physical sciences by treating people as objects was critiqued in the 1960s and, by and large, has been abandoned; but in the late 20th century, I found myself wondering about other cultural distortions embodied in the practice of social research. How do other aspects of a 19th-century vision of power remain embedded in contemporary research practices?

In *Cartographies of Knowledge*, I examine how commonsense assumptions embedded in the foundations of qualitative social research embody historical relations of power. Throughout the book, my analyses bring these assumptions to the surface for consideration. This critique joins with, and extends, recent feminist scholarship on social research methodologies (cf. Harding, 2007) by challenging the foundation's knowledge construction in mainstream, qualitative research.

The second intellectual quandary that inspired this book arose from the challenges that I faced when designing a study to apprehend routine relations of power. For example, the routine, or commonsense production of whiteness, as an *unmarked* category, leaves little or no empirical evidence in daily interaction or in media—precisely because it passes without remark. How do social researchers analyze what passes without comment? I consistently found that social science research methods could help me to examine oppression and domination, but were poor tools for understanding the forms of privilege and power that routinely pass without remark in daily life.

A social scientist needs evidence—indeed a particular kind of evidence, something in a specific context to which one can point. While researchers can prompt interviewees to talk about whiteness (cf. Bonilla-Silva, 2003), analyzing whiteness in media and in unprompted conversation or interaction poses an arguably insurmountable challenge within the existing paradigms of science. All routine relations of power and privilege pass without remark—this is the measure of how deeply routinized such relations are in a culture.

Social researchers know that whiteness, as an unmarked category, has profound importance in social interaction and in media representation—yet it consistently escapes empirical analysis. Social science is not prepared to enable scholars to examine the effects of what isn't expressed. On the one hand, a reader must ask, should it be? On the other hand, this problem directs us back to an analysis of the politics of knowledge production. If social research is not yet capable of fully accounting for human experience, there must be something in our assumptions that alienates research processes from aspects of human experiences. In *Cartographies of Knowledge*, I demonstrate the strengths and limits of qualitative frameworks for being able to analyze routine relations of power. In this respect, my analyses join contemporary critical race scholarship on methodology (cf. Bernal, 2002; Denzin et al., 2008; Ladson-Billings, 2003a; Osha, 2005; Smith, 2004; Sullivan & Tuana, 2007; Twine & Warren, 2000; Zuberi, 2001; Zuberi & Bonilla-Silva, 2008).

The third quandary that shaped *Cartographies of Knowledge* regards the relationship between theory and method. As a sociologist, I quickly encountered a schism between empirical studies of talk in the social sciences and theories of language/discourse in the humanities. When writing my first book, *Making Sense of Race, Class and Gender: Commonsense, Power and Privilege in the United States*, I wanted to analyze commonsense assumptions embedded in social interaction and in popular media. The techniques available to me, as a sociologist, all concerned language use in a localized context: ethnomethodology, conversation analysis, and variations of sociolinguistics. All of these analytical frameworks treat the speaker (or writer) as an autonomous individual, free to speak or write as she or he chooses—without considering how both history and culture shape the possibilities for speaking at any moment in time. By contrast, theoretical studies of language (e.g., the variety of styles of discourse analysis) in the humanities illuminate broader structures of language by pursuing the historical and cultural productions of meaning. Consequently these analyses tend to focus on how personal agency is constrained. Theory is not bound to the concreteness of language use in daily life—it does not examine the specific practices through which people variously reproduce and subvert broader cultural discursive paradigms.

This distinction between theories of language and studies of talk, between theory and method, and between social science and the humanities seemed to me both artificial and unhelpful. Language use regards *both* individual agency and social constraint. Studies of agency must be grounded in local, material contexts, yet knowledge/power always exceeds the immediate moment. Knowledge/power is never a local event, although it has local expressions. Knowledge/power needs to be understood through its ability to travel across time and space.

The schism between social theory and social research that I encountered prevented a full analysis of knowledge, power, and agency. At the time, I addressed this problem by taking a heterodox approach that drew from both ethnomethodology and poststructural discourse analysis—other strategies have been effective as well (cf. Van Dijk, 1993; Watson & Seiler, 1992; Williams, 1999; Wodak & Meyer, 2009). Yet the conceptualization of theory and methods as dichotomous binaries remains at the heart of social sciences. The continuing theory and method binary regards more than disagreements about the kinds of problems social theory or social research can solve. The theory/method binaries of existing paradigms and standards have made particular kinds of problems impossible to legitimately investigate. Indeed many researchers attempt to overcome limitations by combining analytic induction, symbolic interaction, and ethnomethodology with analytical frameworks drawn from the humanities. Ultimately, the robustness of social research is dependent upon its ability to allow for a variety of analytical paradigms and explorations. However, the social sciences generally remain reluctant to consider the methodological limitations that are bound to notions of evidence and discourses of science.

My experience in social research brought me to *Cartographies of Knowledge* committed to the belief that the possibilities of democratic knowledge production require analyses that can move beyond the limiting methodological, theoretical, and disciplinary positions that present dichotomous binaries such as theory/method, macro/micro, and structure/agency. In this respect, *Cartographies* contributes to scholarship that challenges traditional boundaries between method and theory in the social sciences (cf. Bjelic & Lynch, 1992; Cannella & Lincoln, 2004; Clarke, 2009; Cruz, 2006; Flyvbjerg, 2001; Holstein & Gubrium, 2000; Lal, 2008; Latour & Woolgar, 1986; Saukko, 2003). *Cartographies of Knowledge* explores and critiques qualitative strategies for producing scientific knowledge within and across the social sciences.

IMPLICATIONS FOR SOCIAL RESEARCH

Scholars' abilities to conduct effective social research—with an eye toward social justice or not—requires a thorough grasp of the theoretical frameworks that direct particular techniques of data collection and analysis. We must understand more than the mapmaker's immediate tools of paper and pen, yet journals and grantors consistently reward scholarship that focuses on findings while completely neglecting the philosophical foundations of research. In dominant research practices, the underlying philosophy of science operates implicitly and unaccountably. This has profound consequences that will be explored throughout the book.

At this juncture, it may be useful to consider the simple observation that ethnomethodology and symbolic interaction are each understood as interpretive forms of research. Interpretive research takes *"human interpretation* as the starting point for developing knowledge about the social world" (Prasad, 2005, p. 13). While scholars often use analytic induction with symbolic interaction and ethnomethodology, analytic induction is not an interpretive framework; nor must researchers use it with interpretive frameworks. Analytic induction stands on its own as a legitimate qualitative method—arguably the most common qualitative method. Consequently, it is particularly important to consider that qualitative research that does not account for the importance of human interpretation in social interaction arguably limits understandings of human behavior to a behaviorist framework of stimulus–response.

It has been a long time since social scientists have accepted a stimulus–response framework for social interaction. Social researchers broadly believe that people do not simply respond to what others say or do but to their *interpretation* of what has been said or done. Therefore it is important to consider the various ways in which standard analytic induction functions as an interpretive framework that is not made to account for its interpretations. To the extent that the social sciences do not acknowledge analytic induction as an interpretive framework, analytic induction is made to appear as an objective (realist) process for apprehending social facts. Yet nothing is less real than "realism." In mapmaking, the most simple distortions can have the most profound and lasting impact.

CONCLUDING THOUGHTS

Cartographies of Knowledge is not intended as a "how to" book, nor is it intended as a definitive exegesis on qualitative research. Rather I intend, and trust, that it will offer some thought-provoking insights with regard to commonsense assumptions that researchers learn to make—and, into how these assumptions map a particular kind of social world by bringing particular relations of power into view while obscuring others.

The framework of the book distinguishes between the range of techniques used for interpreting data and the techniques employed to produce credible social science claims. By breaking research into these dual functions of interpretation and authentication, the differences among analytic induction, symbolic interaction, and ethnomethodology come into sharp relief. At the same time, the assumptions embedded in processes of authentication are so systematic that the analyses may feel surprisingly consistent at places.

Many scholars in the social sciences have tried to achieve sound analytic strategies for apprehending both routine relations of power and the intertextuality of social life by drawing from theoretical frameworks. While this impulse has produced, and continues to produce, important insights, the analyses of *Cartographies* demonstrate why these strategies are not enough. Any mature science needs to include a broad range of strategies and tools in order to be fully capable of responding to contemporary issues. Consequently, it may be useful to read the ensuing chapters, while thinking about potential paradigm shifts in the social sciences. To the extent that maps can never be identical with what they represent, it is important to keep in mind that distortion remains an implicit feature of all maps—including the metaphoric one being constructed in this book.

FURTHER READING

Flyvbjerg, B. (2001). *Making social science matter: Why social inquiry fails and how it can succeed again.* Cambridge: Cambridge University Press.

Harding, S. (1991). *Whose science? Whose knowledge? Thinking from women's lives.* Ithaca, NY: Cornell University Press.

Osha, S. (2005). *Kwasi Wiredu and beyond: The text, writing and thought in Africa.* Dakra, Senegal: Council for the Development of Social Science Research in Africa.

Sandoval, C. (2000). *Methodology of the oppressed.* Minneapolis: University of Minnesota.

Saukko, P. (2003). *Doing research in cultural studies.* Thousand Oaks, CA: Sage.

Smith, L. T. (2004). *Decolonizing methodologies: Research and indigenous peoples.* London: Zed Books Ltd.

⊰ CHAPTER TWO ⊱

PHILOSOPHICAL ROOTS OF
RESEARCH METHODOLOGIES

INTRODUCTION

Historically, Western traditions of social research have taken the methods established in the physical sciences as the model for social inquiry. Auguste Comte (1798–1857), one of the first social researchers, asserted that authentic knowledge came from personal experience rather than from metaphysical or theological foundations. He argued that by "relying solely on observable facts and the relations that hold among observed phenomena, scientific inquiry could discover the 'laws' governing empirical events" (Hawkesworth, 2007, p. 472). Comte is widely accepted as the founder of positivism, a philosophical orientation toward research methodology.[1] Positivism articulated a search for laws of social life that could stand as equivalents to the natural laws of the physical sciences. Consequently, it is anchored to the same ontological premise of the natural

---

[1] Comte is also widely recognized as the founder of sociology.

sciences: The world exists as an objective entity and is (at least in principle) knowable in its entirety; epistemologically, the task of the researcher is first to accurately describe the reality and then to analyze the results (della Porta & Keating, 2008). In this sense, positivism (and neopositivism) mirrors the commonsense ontology of daily life in which things exist as they appear—unless one is dreaming or deceived.

Epistemological realism was "one moment of the general revolutionary progressivism of 18th- and 19th-century science and politics in which societal laws of nature—rather than laws of the state—now explained the social world" (Somers & Gibson, 1996, p. 47). Positivist research can be characterized by a quest for determinacy, expressed through a reductionist impulse to develop precise meanings and operational indicators. By embracing the ontological belief that a single reality exists, and the epistemological claim that this reality can be known objectively, social scientists argued that there was one, and only one, correct logic for scientific inquiry. As a consequence, positivism served as *the* methodological foundation of the early social sciences.

Antonio Gramsci (1995) was an early critic of the trend in social research to use the physical sciences as a model; he described this attitude toward the physical sciences as "science as fetish." Gramsci wrote, "There do not exist sciences par excellence and there does not exist a method par excellence, 'a method in itself'" (Gramsci, 1995, p. 282). Gramsci argued that every process of inquiry needed to be congruent with its own particular purpose.

Despite such critiques, researchers continued to use the scientific discourses of the physical sciences to legitimate all forms of social research. And, as scientific knowledge was idealized, its philosophical underpinnings faded from view. Scholars in the social sciences treated social research as a tool that offered peerless access to the social world; consequently, they tended to focus on improving techniques for more effective data *collection*, while neglecting the theorization of knowledge production, including the creation of data itself. Although positivism still appears to many researchers as the most legitimate form of social research, it also continues to be soundly critiqued.

> Assumptions guiding positivism derive from the study of largely inanimate or biological phenomena that lack the capacity for self-reflection and cultural production. . . . By contrast social sciences are inevitably concerned with social, economic, and cultural worlds that are constituted by the human capacity for meaningful understanding and action. According to Flyvbjerg (2001), this human capacity for interpretation incessantly thwarts the social

science dream of becoming the mirror image of the natural sciences. Furthermore, such a dream is not merely impossible, it is also pointless inasmuch as positivism is ill equipped to answer many questions of interest to social science. These include questions such as why organizational reform efforts are frequently met with resistance; which cultural features are most responsible for the collapse of corporate ethic; or how organizations socialize their members. (Prasad, 2005, p. 5)

The way that power is distributed across social, cultural, economic, and institutional orders strongly influences what we have learned to regard as legitimate knowledge (Northcutt & McCoy, 2004, pp. 3–4)—and as legitimate routes to knowledge. Social sciences emerged as part of a modernist discourse of progress that was concerned with goals of value neutrality and an ever-increasing effort to generate insights into social life that could stand as the equivalents of physical laws. With the benefit of hindsight, social scientists in the 21st century frequently recognize that science has been more than a search for objective knowledge. Consider, for example, that social scientists searched for laws that would explain progress from "primitive" to "advanced" forms of society (Connell, 2010).

The practical work of scientific research necessarily reproduces culturally shared assumptions about how the world exists and how it works. To the extent that social sciences developed alongside the nation-state, they are bound by nationalist assumptions and experiences (della Porta & Keating, 2008). Science, like the concept of modernization, was a tool of colonization, and as such, it contributed to the decimation of cultures. Discourses of science erased important knowledge and useful epistemologies by systematically devaluing entire cultures as well as specific groups of people within cultures.

One does not have to look hard to find scientific research that advanced various forms of bigotry—today such studies clearly reveal more about cultural hierarchies of power than about the people, places, and cultures that were studied. The "ways of knowing" that have been privileged by academics in dominant cultures continue to be a site of contention and resistance—particularly for those who have been constructed as "Other" in their discourses. Linda Tuhiwai Smith (2004, p. 1) wrote, "the term 'research' is inextricably linked to European imperialism and colonialism. The word itself, 'research', is probably one of the dirtiest words in the indigenous world's vocabulary." Researchers in dominant cultures have viewed the social world through classificatory systems that embody a hegemonic view of power. To understand research methods as value-laden relations of power is to make an epistemic break with history.

> The traditional epistemology of the Anglo-American canon was a theory for *knowledge makers*. It was a normative theory that told how knowledge makers ought to reason to reach knowledge of the true or the good or the right. The fact that it was a theory for knowledge makers was covered up by using several clever strategies—including the democratic claim that anyone might have knowledge if only they used the certified method. (Addelson, 2007, p. 265)

Although research is always credited to specific individuals, *knowledge* is never produced by an individual—knowledge is necessarily the product of a cultural community. And every powerful community has its gatekeepers.

In some sense, it has been easy to imagine that the results of earlier research supported bigoted social hierarchies because the researchers themselves held such views. Consequently, contemporary researchers have challenged specific research findings, even as we have advanced 19th-century paradigms of social research—as if prevailing social and political agendas produced good research methodologies and methods that had been put to bad ends. Students and scholars alike tend to look back at the bigotry of the 19th century as the perspectives of individuals, and perhaps of an era; we less frequently acknowledge that the era, and its scholars, shaped what we understand (and continue to use) as the foundations of social research, social theory, and indeed the university system itself. Arguably, the intellectual empires of the 19th century have outlasted the geographic ones.

Precisely because the facts and procedures of social research are social productions, they can be contested and transformed. With an eye to the politics of knowledge production, this chapter provides a broad overview of the philosophical premises that have underpinned the development of qualitative social research. The chapter explores a number of challenges to standards of qualitative research that have attempted to address particular analytical problems in Western social science. Subsequently, it provides a foundation for understanding ontology, epistemology, agency, subjectivity, and experience in relation to social science.

THE CHANGING DISCOURSES OF SOCIAL SCIENCE

Social science research faces two overarching tasks: formalization and interpretation. Formalization refers to the processes for systematizing knowledge production—processes that provide protocols for recognizing relevant phenomenon and transforming them into data. Processes of formalization generate what can be understood as "valid evidence." Indeed, a primary boundary between sciences and other disciplines has been formed by the demand that all scientific knowledge claims be authenticated by specific processes of formalization. Procedures for formalization enable researchers to make credible *scientific* claims about groups of people. Historically only specific processes of formalization (i.e., systematic elaboration) have been certified as generating "scientific" findings. Over time, these procedures have been naturalized—as a matter of common sense for "good" research. For example, most fundamentally, formalization requires empirical evidence—something to which one can point in a local context. Researchers examine local contexts as if they are unproblematic and naturally occurring. It would be more transparent to speak of *localized* contexts—emphasizing the construction of research contexts. However, this level of transparency is generally not regarded as necessary in mainstream social sciences. Indeed, it might even be construed as problematic since it refers to subjective processes involved in creating both contexts and data.

Within the past decade, emergent research methods have challenged processes of formalization. For example, scholars have challenged the processes of formalization through performance scholarship and autoethnography (cf. Ellis & Bochner, 1996; Richardson, 2004). These strategies are very useful, yet they have a fairly limited impact on social science precisely because they challenge the need for the broad coherence that continues to define social science. In very different ways, the earlier institutional ethnographies developed by Dorothy Smith also could be said to challenge processes of formalization. By examining the social organization of knowledge in institutional settings, Smith (1990a, 1990b, 1999) developed a cultural framing of knowledge production within the thick description of ethnography. Emergent methods such as these express a paradigm shift in what constitutes a social science—but one that remains highly marginalized by mainstream social research.

Perhaps some of the more substantial challenges to processes of formalization have come from scholars in education who more commonly broaden notions of empirical evidence by turning to the humanities (cf. Hendry, 2007; Kincheloe & McLaren, 1998; Korth, 2002; Lather 1991, 2001). Similarly, some scholars working in the social sciences also have turned to the humanities to more fully and effectively analyze social life (cf. Clarke, 2005; Clough, 1992, 2000; Denzin, 2003a, 2003b; Holstein & Gubrium, 2000; Saukko, 2003). This book owes a debt to all such scholarship as it attempts to take such efforts a bit farther.

The second task of social science research is interpretation—explaining the significance of evidence. Clearly, processes of formalization and interpretation are intimately linked. To a significant extent the ontological and epistemological frameworks used to interpret data are not separable from those that determine the systematic collection of evidence and its transformation into data to be analyzed. The two cannot operate independently—although they serve slightly different ends.[2]

The number of possible interpretations for any given pattern or theme is fairly large—at least in principle. A significant aspect of scientific activity is rendering some interpretations more plausible than others (Latour & Woolgar, 1986, p. 36). The numbers of interpretations that will be accepted as plausible by an informed audience are constrained by the forms of knowledge the audience holds and the particular context that is brought to bear on the reading. Yet rendering some explanations of evidence more, or less, plausible than others is always a political project—although it is a political project that is often masked by scientific discourse.

Historically, scientific discourse has been more invested in limiting processes of formalization than processes of interpretation. As a result, social scientists have elaborated on a variety of processes of interpretation, while processes of formalization remain largely unchanged. The subsequent sections examine key challenges and transformations to processes of interpretation in qualitative social research: feminist, critical race, and interpretive. The usual caveat applies: These challenges are neither as distinct, as limited, nor as linear as their presentation here may make them appear.

Feminist and Critical Race Challenges to Qualitative Research

Feminist scholarship began with a three-part challenge that confronted androcentric bias in research, in social theory, and in research methods. At the heart of feminist methodology is a critique of knowledge production as a site that has constructed and sustained women's oppression (DeVault, 1999; Hartsock, 1987). Feminist critiques of research methods (cf. Behar & Gordon, 1995; Haraway, 1991; Harding, 1991; Hartsock, 1987; Naples, 2003; Reinharz, 1992) transformed what is considered to be the production of valid

---

[2]The relationship between ontology and epistemology will be explored in depth throughout subsequent chapters.

knowledge by exposing the ways that traditional epistemology supported male dominance. In varying ways, "feminist empiricism, standpoint theories, postmodernism and transnational perspectives all recognize the importance of women's lived experiences with the goal of unearthing subjugated knowledge" (Hesse-Biber, 2007, p. 3).[3]

A central point of feminist critique has been the concept of objectivity. Ramazanoğlu and Holland (2002) wrote,

> Objectivity implies that the researcher can control the research process so as to produce neutral knowledge of social reality that is external to the researcher and independent of the observer's observations—just as the world turns whether we know it or not. (p. 48)

Donna Haraway (1991, p. 189) famously called the scientific emphasis on (and claim to) objective knowledge the "god trick" because it is predicated on a "view from nowhere." Sandra Harding (2007) also has leveled incisive critiques of the notion of objectivity. She wrote,

> Objectivity has not been [understood] in such a way that scientific method can detect sexist and androcentric assumptions that are "the dominant beliefs of an age"—that is, [it cannot confront beliefs] that are collectively (versus only individually) held. As far as scientific method goes (and feminist empiricist defenses of it), it is entirely serendipitous when cultural beliefs that are assumed by most members of a scientific community are challenged by a piece of scientific research. (p. 52)

Objectivity constructs usable, but not innocent knowledge.[4] Some feminists have argued that the goals of objectivity are better fulfilled by taking subjectivity into account (Code, 1993, p. 32). Acknowledging that all knowledge and all attempts to produce knowledge are socially situated, feminist scholars

---

[3]Referring to feminists working in Derridean grammatology and Foucauldian disciplinary genealogy, Clough (2008) wrote, "While these feminists questioned the politics of identity as well as experience as a ground of knowledge of reality, they nonetheless were concerned with experience and identity, reality and knowing. They meant to emphasize speech and voice, even while engaging these as nonintentional expressions of subjectivity shaped by unconscious desire" (p. 39).

[4]Patricia Clough (1992) cogently argued that social science research creates an authorized, factual representation of empirical reality that is the effect of an unconscious narrative process that prevents the narrative construction of factuality from becoming apparent (pp. 12–13).

(cf. Collins, 2000; Hartsock, 1987; Smith, 1990a) countered the emphasis on objectivism with standpoint theory—what might be called a view "from somewhere." Standpoint begins with the understanding that in stratified societies the activities of those at the top both organize, and set limits on, what they can understand about themselves and the world around them (Harding, 2007, p. 54).[5]

Within the framework of standpoint, researchers begin with the experiences and knowledge that are central to marginalized lives, and from there, problematize everyday practices.[6] In this sense, standpoint attempts to account for the contingency of both knowledge claims and knowing subjects. A primary goal of standpoint is to enable scholars to account for multiple perspectives while also maintaining a commitment to faithful accounts of a "real" world. Standpoint does not do away with the concept of objectivity but attempts to strengthen it by demanding strong reflexivity.

Some scholars have claimed that feminism's greatest strength is its ability to address the production of sexist results "with only a minimal challenge to the fundamental logic of research as this is understood in scientific fields and to the logic of explanation as this is understood in the dominant philosophies of science" (Harding, 2007, p. 53). If this conservatism has been useful in the physical sciences, it is not necessarily widely embraced by feminist scholars in the social sciences.

While there is enormous overlap among feminist and critical race challenges that have been leveled at traditional social sciences, some scholars have directed their primary critiques toward social science's ability to fully apprehend racial inequalities (cf. Cannella & Lincoln, 2004; Collins, 1993; Denzin, 1978; Glenn, 2002; Osha, 2005; Twine & Warren, 2000; Zuberi, 2001; Zuberi & Bonilla-Silva, 2008). Some critical race scholars have conceptualized "Blackness both as an epistemological standpoint and as a methodological one" (Dillard & Dixson, 2006, p. 244). Others argue that standpoint research is problematic; not all standpoints are critical ones. "Racial subordination does not mechanistically generate a critical stance vis-à-vis racism any more than colonialism created anticolonial subjectivities (Fanon 1967; Memmi 1991)" (Twine & Warren, 2000, p. 15). Standpoint research is necessary for

---

[5]Notably, the line between the positionality of standpoint and essentialism is thin: Standpoint research must be intensely and strategically qualified to avoid becoming bluntly universalizing.

[6]Importantly, within a standpoint framework, some social locations are better starting points than others for challenging the fundamental assumptions of hegemonic science and Western thought (Harding, 2007, p. 56).

confronting racism but not sufficient—the same must be said for confronting other forms of systematized subordination as well. Cultural discourses on race and racialization make all researchers vulnerable in different ways to reproducing knowledge that reinforces hegemonic conceptions of social life.

Some critical race critiques of social research have challenged both processes of formalization and processes of interpretation. For example, Stanfield (1993), Zuberi (2001), and Zuberi and Bonilla-Silva (2008) have leveled incisive critiques of "white research methods" generally, and more specifically regarding statistical analyses of race. In the 21st century, the emphasis on quantitative research methods continues to be endorsed as the gold standard of social research because of a belief that "numbers don't lie." However, there are many contemporary examples to the contrary—*The Bell Curve* (Hernstein & Murray, 1994) quickly comes to mind. Numbers are meaningless without narratives.

Assumptions and theories about social life guide how we collect and interpret data; this has particular implications for studying race, racism, and racialization. Given that social research methods were developed during periods of devastating racial oppression, researchers must consistently ask how white racial ideologies are embedded in existing research paradigms. The systematic and cumulative nature of racism requires that all practices need to be understood, and studied, as part of an overarching system, rather than isolated in localized contexts (Essed & Goldberg, 2002). Yet if scholars focus only on the overarching system of racism, we miss the particularities of time and place that give racism specific form and meaning. Social research needs to be able to do both.

Many feminist and critical race researchers have sought to develop a better grasp of the mechanisms and practices of social inequality by deepening understandings of the reflexive repertoires used both by researchers and the people we study (cf. Cannella & Lincoln, 2004; Hesse-Biber & Leavy, 2006; Holstein & Gubrium, 2000, 2005; Ladson-Billings, 2003a, 2003b; Prasad & Prasad, 2002). Yet it is also possible to use reflexivity in instrumental or utilitarian ways that do not challenge underlying assumptions about processes of formalization or interpretation in social research. There is no simple or formulaic way to create useful knowledge in the service of social justice.

Interpretive Challenges to Social Research

Many researchers have pointedly argued that the methodologies and methods of the natural sciences, which were used to study objects and organisms, are inappropriate and ineffective for studying the complexities of social life. Winch (1958) argued that causal explanations were too simplistic to capture social life and actually interfered with the ability to conduct valid social research. For example, we can see that cars stop at red traffic lights but if we formulate a simple causal relationship between red traffic lights and cars stopping we will never understand *why* cars stop (Winch, 1958).

Winch (1958, p. 95) asserted that the concepts that we use "for thinking about social events are logically incompatible with the concepts belonging to scientific explanation." For example, if we formulate a causal explanation of behavior, computers and robots responding to commands would appear to understand language; however, their responses are based on formulaic computations, not semantic content. Social behavior is not governed by fixed natural laws; there are no social equivalents of scientific laws such as gravity.

Many scholars have attempted to address the limitations of the natural science model of research by developing competing analytic frameworks for interpreting evidence. Such efforts have resulted in the fields of symbolic interaction, dramaturgy, and ethnomethodology. Each follows a distinct logic, yet taken together, they are broadly understood as styles of *interpretivism*. Most broadly, interpretive research is committed to the philosophy of social construction that posits a social world produced through meaningful interpretations. Social constructionism emphasizes the importance of contextual understanding, the subjective nature of research, and the importance of reflexivity (Willis, 2007). Chapter 3 elaborates on social constructionism. For now, suffice it to say that, at its most conservative, social constructionist ontology holds that the world exists objectively but the terms we use to define and describe it are socially produced.

Interpretive analyses begin with the belief that meaning is socially constructed through shared, rather than individual interpretations of reality—that is to say, it is constructed intersubjectively (Holstein & Miller, 1993). Rather than approaching research with predefined concepts, interpretivists use sensitizing concepts to help them better understand the social relationships being studied. For example, an interpretivist would want to discover how people in a particular community understand the meaning of "class," rather than approaching the community with a predetermined definition of "class."

Interpretive research seeks to broaden the possibilities of social research by directly challenging the limitations of the positivist and postpositivist foundations, which have been recognized historically as the primary (and often the only) valid model of social science research.[7] In order to understand a situation, interpretivists argue that researchers must understand the *meanings* the situation holds for the participants, not just their behaviors. For interpretivists, meaning and identity are ontological conventions, not absolute facts. For example, what makes a set of activities "work"? Is it the specific tasks one undertakes? The responsibilities one assumes? The remuneration one receives? Interpretive analyses attempt to pursue understanding, while necessarily allowing for degrees of indeterminacy (Charmaz, 2006). In social sciences, interpretive frameworks rely on the logic of analytic induction and have been used with feminist and critical race theories, as well as with a range of qualitative methods for data collection (including case studies, ethnography, interviews, and textual analysis).

Significant research demonstrates the importance, value, and necessity of feminist, critical race, and interpretive research frameworks. All scholars working to shift the discourse of social science have faced the overarching task of needing to pursue two directions simultaneously in order to challenge dominant research paradigms. On one hand, they must develop critiques of existing paradigms and on the other they must develop research that demonstrates the strength of the new frameworks. These two tasks often overlap in research that pushes the boundaries of existing analytical frameworks. The social sciences have changed in dramatic and useful ways. Feminist, critical race, and interpretive frameworks have changed the way social researchers think about epistemology and practices of interpretation. However, practices of formalization have been harder to challenge—precisely because they are fundamentally linked to issues of ontology and therefore more intrinsic to the discursive construction of science itself.

While processes of formalization constitute defining features of a science, it is critically important to consider that these processes were developed in an era that did not imagine the need to study routine social privilege and could not have anticipated the development and proliferation of 21st-century media. Consequently, it is important to broaden the discourse of social sciences to address these phenomena—both by problematizing the concept of formalization

---

[7]Postpositivism emerged as consonant with some of the main principles of positivism. It is premised on the belief that a single reality exists; however, unlike positivism, it is also premised on the belief that there is no way to know this reality in its totality. In postpositivism, knowledge about the objective world is filled with uncertainties that lead to somewhat imperfect and/or incomplete knowledge. Whereas positivism is often referred to as naive realism, postpositivism is often characterized as critical realism. Critical realist epistemology, often practiced by second-wave feminists and critical race scholars, posits an object social world but asserts that knowledge is socially conditioned and subject to challenge and reinterpretation (della Porta & Keating, 2008).

and by connecting philosophical concerns with practical ones. Qualitative research has made substantial contributions to culturally relevant and socially progressive research. Critically examining the philosophical foundations of qualitative research in relationship to the practice of qualitative methods promises to contribute to debates among interpretivist scholars, to feminist and critical race methodological critiques, to social science media research, and to the ongoing discussions regarding the emergence and evolution of new qualitative research strategies.

PHILOSOPHY AND PRACTICE

In order to examine how processes of formalization in social research paradigms are themselves implicated in sustaining hegemonic social orders, it is necessary to explore the philosophical foundations that shape process of formalization. To make that exploration possible in subsequent chapters, in this section, I consider the politics of social research practices in relationship to assumptions about the nature of existence (ontology) and in relationship to beliefs and assumptions about *how* the world can be known (epistemology). I then elaborate on the concepts of ontology and epistemology and finally consider how each is rudimentary to conceptions of subjectivity, agency, and experience.

In the social sciences, many scholars increasingly are turning toward critiques of *methodology* to take up foundational issues of ontology and epistemology in social research (cf. Clough, 1992; Denzin, 2003b; Flyvbjerg, 2001; Harding, 1987, 1991, 2007; Lal, 2008; Latour, 1993; Ramazanoğlu & Holland, 2002; Sandoval, 2000; Smith, 2004; Zuberi, 2001; Zuberi & Bonilla-Silva, 2008). Yet the most profound challenges to ontology tend to be theoretical discussions of methodology that stand apart from pragmatic concerns of implementation. Consequently, there is a significant gap between critical methodologies and the *practice* of social research—which should not be too surprising since the literatures seldom overlap. The gap between theory and practice is reinforced by funding agencies and publishers, who regularly accept research designs that include well-detailed characterizations of methods (i.e., data collection and analysis) but lack any consideration of ontology and epistemology.

Importantly, it is not only funding agencies and publishers that nurture the gap between critical methodology and critical research. Academic institutions tend to offer research courses that are focused on techniques for data collection—often without significant philosophical consideration. Yet, research paradigms offer scholars and students more than simple orientations for data collection and analysis. They provide frameworks for recognizing what we see, as well as for understanding the relevance and importance of what we see. Without understanding the theoretical underpinnings of social research methods, we are reduced to taking what is often referred to as a "cookbook approach" (Hesse-Biber & Leavy, 2006) to research that inevitably precludes a deeply critical stance.

By and large, empirical research is understood as having practical policy and community-based implications, whereas scholarship on methodology and the philosophy of science tend to be framed as "ivory-tower" issues. This binary juxtaposition between the philosophical and the practical has led generations of researchers to follow techniques for producing credible research without seriously examining ideologies sequestered in what appear to be commonsense assumptions about the nature of empirical research. It is a disempowering binary framework that encourages a lack of awareness, accountability, and agency.

Recall, for example, the earlier discussion of localized contexts. For centuries, empirical evidence has been limited to that to which we can point in a localized context. For those immersed in hegemonic scientific discourse, it is difficult to imagine why this could possibly be problematic—or how it might be otherwise. To the extent that the social sciences remain exclusively bound to empirical evidence in localized contexts, we will fail in our abilities to analyze particular aspects of power, privilege, culture, and knowledge—which always and inevitably exceed any local context. The epistemic foundations of social research prevent researchers from addressing the broader cultural conditions that shape the localized contexts.[8] For example, within the cognitive space of social science, it is impossible to critique social processes such as racialization, reification, and hegemony. If we don't see "the big picture, narrow empiricism provide[s] an ingenious smoke screen. It is a method perfectly tailored to an epistemology of ignorance. As the adage goes, we 'look' but never 'see'" (Steinberg, 2007, p. 11).

Generally ignorance is understood as a result of a bad or neglectful epistemic practice—not as a substantive epistemic practice in itself (Alcoff, 2007,

---

[8]Gramsci (1995) leveled this critique of the social sciences with regard specifically to the ability of social science to apprehend Italian politics.

p. 39). An epistemology of ignorance may sound oxymoronic: How can we have a theory of knowing and ignorance? Ignorance is not simply "not knowing" but an active misapprehension that systematically produces inaccurate information—*ignorance is an active social production*. An epistemology of ignorance exists when one uses socially acceptable but faulty systems of justification (Alcoff, 2007; Sullivan & Tuana, 2007).

Eugenics can be understood as an epistemology of ignorance (Zuberi, 2001; Zuberi & Bonilla-Silva, 2008). The intrinsically scholarly framing of race discourse was not, in itself, enough to establish the scientific legitimacy of race research in general or eugenics in particular. Such studies gain prominence in particular times and places because they also have practical applications that resonate with commonsense perceptions held by dominant groups in society. In this sense, academic research has applied what might be called "facticity" to racism—its appeal is not to greed nor to spiritual passion, but to reason.

Similarly, much of Freud's work was based on an epistemology of ignorance (Hoagland, 2007). Consider that although Freud initially believed the stories of women reporting rape, he subsequently chose to discredit their testimony in favor of a theory in which women and children fantasized about being raped—a theory that helped to silence women's voices and deny their experiences for decades. Misrepresentations of race and gender such as these found widespread scientific acceptance because they supported hegemonic worldviews in Europe and North America. Science validates itself; however, hegemonic culture provides structural validation—most particularly for epistemologies of ignorance that reproduce existing social hierarchies.

If we accept that all knowledge is socially constructed, and historically situated, we must understand social research methodologies as historically produced social formations articulated through particular discourses and systems of signification. The epistemological ground of social research developed, in part, as a legitimated form of knowledge about "the Other" produced by and for those in power. Social research is itself a relation of power that produces (and is produced by) "domains of objects and rituals of truth" (Foucault, 1977, p. 194). Science itself is a cultural activity—a kind of performance that enacts itself.

The most basic (and perhaps most powerful) level of critique recognizes that in all research methods, phenomena count as "evidence" only if they are recognized in relation to a potential analysis (Gordon, 1997; Scott, 1991). Evidence is always the political effect of decisions regarding what constitutes valid and relevant knowledge as well as decisions that regard the conditions a researcher must fulfill to give her or his work value as science. Consequently, critical empirical research must begin not with a theory/evidence dichotomy but rather with a theory/evidence *convergence* that recognizes the theoretical foundations that shape what constitutes valid knowledge.[9]

At the start of the 21st century, one of the characteristics of research methodologies must be the capacity to excavate the full range of social life, including the ways that it is mediated by technologies. In order to continue to develop a vision for social research that is capable of being fully compatible with a vision of a socially just world, scholars need to consistently explore, not only our own locations as researchers but also, the philosophical foundations and working assumptions of social research paradigms. Charting the terrain of commonsense assumptions about the nature of evidence disturbs some of the most enshrined principles of social science. It is a mapping that not only displaces old geographies but one that also contributes to new epistemic ground. It is a remapping that seeks to replace the dogmatism of historical assumptions with questions that raise doubts about the certainties and assumptions of social research.

As an inquiry into ontology, the analyses that follow in subsequent chapters will undermine notions of essentialism and call into question the assumptions and limitations of all forms of Cartesian dualism—even those related to critical realism and feminism.[10] This position might be interpreted incorrectly as being antipositivist; it is *intended* as an effort to call social research to account for how ontological commitments operate in social research. Gramsci (1995, p. 282) argued that every process of inquiry needs to be congruent with its own particular purpose. There is no definitive place from which to locate the necessary and sufficient conditions for establishing empirical knowledge once and for all. Hence the path forward is not proposing a single framework

---

[9] "It was not until forty years after Aston that Thomas Kuhn demonstrated in *The Structure of Scientific Revolutions*, a cornerstone of modern realist philosophy of science, that scientific facts and data are not separable from theory (or systems of hypotheses) but are 'theory-laden'; two of the main examples he cites are mass in the Einsteinian and Newtonian frameworks and the atom pre- and post-Dalton. He leaves no room for doubt that after such changes in scientific paradigm 'the data themselves had changed' and quoting 'force, mass, element, compound, cell' as examples, 'the ways in which some [of these terms—or signs. . . .] attach to nature has somehow changed,' i.e., 'the datum is such in light of theoretical interpretations and the reconstruction of facts is guided by theoretical hypotheses'" (Boothman, 1995, p. vii).

[10] Essentialism is the belief that there is a fundamental essence or unchanging core that characterizes all members of a group.

to replace another, but understanding the philosophical and political foundations of research well enough to recognize the potential and possibilities of additional frameworks.

Ontology and Epistemology

Although *discussions* of ontology and epistemology have been made, by and large, to fall outside standard social scientific discourse, all social research presumes and reproduces both an ontology and an epistemology—each of which has a system of internal logic and external validation. Ontologies are "theories of being" that map the kinds of things that can exist. Ontological questions regard the form and nature of reality—what can be known. Consider this, for example: To what extent does an objective, social world exist apart from human interpretation? Is gender socially constructed or biologically determined? These are ontological questions and the answers to them (consciously made or not) will profoundly shape the processes of social research. Ontological beliefs do not necessarily precede epistemological ones—they are not causal. Epistemological commitments can shape what we believe about the world. Consider, for example, the common expression: "I only believe what I can see." Ontological and epistemological beliefs are entwined in each other.

Every ontological premise implies certain epistemological commitments, that is to say certain possibilities for producing valid knowledge.[11] Should researchers treat interview data as neutral (i.e., transparent) descriptions of experience, as symbolic interpretations of experience, or as strategic meaning-making practices? This is an epistemological question that can be sensibly answered only in relation to a set of commitments about the nature of social life—which is an ontological premise.

In philosophy, the study of epistemology focuses on two questions: one regarding the *individuals* who know and the other regarding the *process* of knowing how anything can be regarded as true. Historically, the scientific emphasis on universal knowledge necessarily de-emphasized epistemology in

---

[11]The ontological premise about the nature of reality shapes not only what can be known and how it can be known (epistemology) but also the nature of what counts as a social problem, the nature of research ethics, practices of representation, as well as subsequent research and pedagogy that reproduces the field (Dillard & Dixson, 2006). Epistemological concerns in social research are central to the functions of hegemonic domination in knowledge production and dissemination (Stanfield, 1993, as cited in Dillard & Dixson, 2006, p. 236).

Table 2.1   Philosophical Foundations of Social Research

Ontologies are theories, beliefs, and assumptions about the nature and relations of existence. They are commonly referred to as "theories of being."

Sample ontological questions: To what extent is there an objective social world? What does it mean to say something exists objectively?

Epistemologies are theories, beliefs, and assumptions about the ways we can learn about the world. They consider the relationship between the knower and the known and how valid knowledge is created.

Sample epistemological questions: What issues or events constitute important points of social inquiry? How should such inquiry proceed?

---

this first sense—the nature of "knowers." The production of so-called universal knowledge demanded universal experiences shared by universal people. This emphasis on universal knowledge reinforced hegemonic social hierarchies by naturalizing and systematizing various forms of bias.

Feminist epistemological critiques beginning in the 1960s, with few exceptions (cf. Millman & Kanter, 1975), took up epistemological critiques regarding the nature of knowers. Feminists challenged existing scientific beliefs regarding who could produce valid knowledge about whom, and on what terms (cf. Harding, 1987; Hartsock, 1987). Standpoint epistemology became the center of feminist and critical race critiques of social science. Subsequently, the cultural turn heralded by poststructuralism and postmodernism ushered in a set of crises in social sciences regarding the second epistemological question regarding *how* we can know—how we can find or create "truth." Methodological critiques informed by the cultural turn concern the nature of existence, the politics of truth, and the production of knowledge. Pragmatically this is reflected in scholarship that centers questions regarding the nature of evidence, subjectivity, and meaning. These challenges to scientific ontology and epistemology have made inroads in the social sciences despite fierce resistance. Many researchers working in interpretive frameworks have turned to the humanities, particularly postmodern and poststructural thought, in order to explore key philosophical issues central to social research. This has, to varying degrees, destabilized traditional social science by challenging both epistemological and ontological foundations.

It is important to underscore once again that epistemologies and ontologies are *not* motives or points of origin for behavior; rather, they are integral (and often assumed) conceptual parameters that render particular courses of action more plausible, or implausible, than others. The epistemic foundation of social research directs our attention to certain "realities" and not to others and thereby determines the horizon of possibilities for any research project—what can and cannot be seen as well as what can and cannot legitimately be argued. As noted earlier, ontological and epistemological foundations establish strategies for recognizing, collecting, and analyzing data. They also provide conceptual commitments that include the nature and possibilities of subjectivity, agency, and experience.

Subjectivity

Theories of subjectivity stand at the intersection of ontology and epistemology (Hall, 2004, p. 4). An ontological investment inheres in every conception of subjectivity—and every qualitative framework articulates this investment in different ways. Overall, theories of subjectivity fall into two broad categories. The earliest of these defines a subject as a *person* with his or her own truth; the subject is synonymous with the self. From Plato through Popper, all phenomena (animate and inanimate) were thought to have fixed, essential natures—which made understanding both possible and, in some respects, finite. The self might be understood as divine or biological (or some combination of these) but it was not understood as a social product. The concept of "truth-as-essence" originated in the Enlightenment construction of science and objectivity. The conceptual separation of the self from social life makes it possible to think of research as mirroring what exists in nature, as producing a reflection of other fixed essential essences that exist around us.

Both Plato and Descartes allowed for a rational subject that stands apart from the world of objects. However, the struggle for epistemic autonomy was even starker for Descartes than for Plato. Descartes "suspended belief in all but his own existence in order to recreate a body of knowledge cleansed of faults, impurities, and uncertainties" (Longino, 2007, p. 104). In *Metaphysical Meditations* (1641), Descartes proposed what has come to be known as the modern, rational subject. For Descartes, subjective identity is the mind's awareness of its own representations—in this sense, it results from a rational process of reflection that bridges inner and outer worlds. Individual consciousness is transparent to itself and operates according to principles that are independent of embodied experience (Longino, 2007, p. 105).

Descartes used the term *subject* in opposition to the term *object* to indicate an individual fully endowed with consciousness and agency—hence the concepts of agent and agency collapse into each other. This subject/object dichotomy, known as Cartesian dualism, became the foundation of scientific research in which researchers (subjects) study and measure objects. Within the *social* sciences, this has particular consequences since the "objects" of social research are generally other people. Despite the logical problems created by subject/object distinctions, Descartes' radically isolated individual became the ideal knower. Cartesian presuppositions enable us to experience objects and facts as being in the world. Empirical claims are those that can be verified by sensory inspection— hence the conception of "evidence" as something one can point to in a localized context. However, despite this emphasis on sensory inspection, Descartes held that reason was always the ultimate tool of knowledge that validated the senses. Without reason, one could be mistaken about, or deceived by, sensory perception. In asserting the primacy of the mind, Descartes reduced bodies to vehicles for the mind.[12] The Cartesian self is by its very nature disembodied.

Cartesian dualism asserts an ontological premise in which there is radical separation between subject and object and between people and the external world; consequently, it advances an epistemology (a theory of how the world can be known) of objectivism, which as noted earlier, continues to be effectively challenged. Early Western science embraced Cartesian dualism, and despite hundreds of years and multiple challenges, it continues to define the heart of mainstream social science research.

The most recent theories of subjectivity regard subjects not as persons but as discursive categories that articulate collective social relations. Poststructuralists and postmodernists draw from Althusser to conceptualize subjects as the expression of social processes—the embodiment and reification of social structures. For example, terms such as "black" or "heterosexual" are understood as subject locations that are the products of culture and power. Subject positions, in this sense, are historical and discursive *categories of identification*. Individuals come to occupy subject locations through a process Althusser identified as interpolation, which might be understood as a dual process of ideological coercion and personal identification. For example, no one is born with a racial identification; culture "hails" individuals as belonging to a particular racial category or subject location that becomes part of a personal identity. Subjectivities are dominant cultural markers of "difference"

---

[12]Artifical intelligence literature rests largely in this kind of dualism. However, Cartesian dualism is effectively challenged by theories that posit the mind is both caused by and realized through the body (Searle, 2003).

that shape individual identity through the tension and interplay between the symbolic and the imaginary.

Subjects are produced through repetition but the process of repetition does not produce identical iterations—neither does the process of repetition produce subjects anew over and over again (Butler, 1993). Each iteration is an expression of others but also open to variation and change. Because subjects are created repeatedly, differently, and in different circumstances, the possibilities of resistance, nonconformity, and variation become possible. The process of repetition itself can undermine the normalizing force of interpellation (Butler, 1997a).

Our interior lives inevitably involve both other people generally and society more broadly (Mansfield, 2000) and this has particular consequences for marginalized subjectivities, which are always produced through, or in opposition to, dominant ones. For example, it is possible to understand selected attributes as "a disability," only in relation to attributes understood as "ability." If scholars no longer accept a simple or fixed notion of ability, it becomes incumbent upon researchers to understand the social conditions through which people come to occupy the subject position of "disabled."

Subject positions are never individual formulations; they are always linked to something beyond personal experience. Subjectivity "is a constant work of daily construction that involves both receiving representations made to us by culture—of gender, class, age, race, identity and so forth—and processing these significations so that we are at once produced and (re)producing" (Pollock, 2008, p. 252). Foucault (1972, p. 115) argued that a subject is "not the speaking consciousness, not the author of a formulation, but a position that may be filled in certain conditions by various individuals."

Theories of subjectivity have "unparalleled and enduring importance" for understanding the possibilities for social change (Hall, 2004, p. 5). In the 21st century, problems of subjectivity, agency, and experience are at the heart of questions about human existence. Subsequent chapters pose and answer three key questions with respect to issues of subjectivity. First, how do analytic induction, symbolic interaction, and ethnomethodology constitute their objects/subjects of knowledge? Second, what epistemological and ontological assumptions are implicit in the ways that objects/subjects of knowledge are constituted? And, third, what are the political effects? These questions are critical to understanding how each framework conceptualizes the ways that people are bound together and set apart in society. Consequently, they hold special importance to social science researchers in general and more specifically to those researchers who are invested in scholarship aimed at issues of social justice.

Agency

Every theory of subjectivity is tethered to a corresponding conception of agency. What does it mean to speak of agency? To a commonsense attitude, agency might be as simple as the ability to affect some aspect of our environment. The question becomes more complex if we ask, "Where is the locus of the action that affects our environment?" In order to understand "agency," we must first lay claim to an ontological narrative. For example, notions of agency derived from Cartesian (body/mind) dualism are associated with consciousness and the mind—agency begins with a thought or intention that directs action. In Cartesian dualism, bodies emerge either as the *conditions* of social action or as objects that are acted upon. Commonsense attitudes, and much of social research, reflect this orientation to agency.

Second-wave feminism, by challenging the notion of gender and sex as natural essences, complicated a commonsense understanding of agency. If we consider bodies not as natural but as socially constructed—that is, as the results of the processes of embodiment—we must reconsider *both* the meanings of bodies and the locus of agency. To the extent that feminist analyses are rooted in Cartesian ontologies, however, this tension is left unexplored. By contrast feminisms rooted in poststructural ontologies have placed issues of agency at the center of social analysis. If gender is socially constructed, rather than biologically inherent, people must learn to "construct" gender and by implication, put some measure of effort into making ourselves recognizable as gendered beings. This is not only a matter of hairstyle and clothing but also includes body language, demeanor, and interactional styles. From this perspective, how do we locate the source of agency behind the accomplishment of gender? If gender is not an individual choice, to what extent is gendered demeanor a matter of individual agency?

At the heart of issues of agency are ontological narratives regarding the nature of the world and epistemological narratives about how that world can be apprehended or known. Ontological narratives are central to agency. However, when faced with expressions of agency that cannot be said to be entirely individual, scholars initially turned to the constraining forces of social institutions to explain human behavior. Tradition, norms, and roles, along with other constraining forces such as false consciousness and formal social institutions (including legal and educational systems), emerged as key focal points. The tension between notions of free will, and the forces of social control that constrain free will, is directly related to the macro/micro divide in social research. Empirical analyses typically regard either macro analyses of constraining structures or micro analyses that foreground the agency of personal action. The binary distinction between micro and macro echoes the effects of Cartesian dualism. Again, at the heart of questions of agency is an ontological narrative about the nature of the world and an epistemological narrative about how that world can be apprehended or known.

Both radical and liberal feminisms rely on a humanist conception of subjectivity that conflates subjects with autonomous, rational individuals who exist separate from and outside of language. In contrast to a humanist subject that is essential and more or less fixed, poststructural scholarship posits subjectivity as constantly in process; it is both precarious and contradictory. The constituted character of subjectivity forms the precondition of agency (Butler, 1993). Indeed, the possibility of change exists precisely because there is not essential nature that binds us irrevocably. From this perspective, agency is always possible and always political. Agency is always situated in, and to some extent determined by, specific historical, political, and social factors—it is never entirely free, nor entirely constrained. Subsequent chapters take up this lingering tension regarding the nature of agency and attempt to demonstrate the importance of transcending the impulse to understand constraint as structural and agency as personal.

Experience

The Cartesian framework that underlies positivist research presumes a subject who has experiences, which can then be objectively measured. But do people simply have experiences that researchers can then study? Do we simply recognize objects and events that appear before us? Is language a neutral tool for describing reality? Does reality "speak for itself"? Interpretivists would answer "no" to these questions. Experience is always an interpretation of events, not a mere encounter with them (Scott, 1991, p. 777), and language is always implicated in constructing social meanings. Interpretivists argue that all meaning is situated in localized contexts; all efforts to understand social interaction must be located and described in a localized context. For interpretivists, decontextualized data are oxymoronic (Northcutt & McCoy, 2004). However, just how much context is necessary? What constitutes a context?

What is the social context of media? How does a researcher draw logical boundaries around the social contexts of a research design? How does the notion of context affect conceptions of subjectivity, agency, and constraint? What can a narrow sense of context offer to our research? What can it cost our research? As we shall see in subsequent chapters, analytic induction, symbolic interaction, and ethnomethodology each take a different position in response to questions of context. Questions about context are, of course, related to questions about the constructed nature of experience, about the constitution of subjects, and about whether or not experience can in itself serve as a kind of evidence. By engaging both the philosophy of science and the practice of science, subsequent chapters ground critiques of methodology in pragmatic concerns and practical applications of research.

IMPLICATIONS FOR SOCIAL RESEARCH

To varying degrees, all social research paradigms are implicated in sustaining hegemonic social orders. Understanding the philosophical/theoretical foundations of social research contributes to more effective social research. It also enables scholars to critique the reification of analytical constructs used in social research and thereby more broadly transform what counts as valid knowledge. In this sense, inquiries into the foundations of social research get at the root of how discourses of science can reproduce existing relations of power—even as they are used to reveal inequalities and advance remedies for social problems. Historically, qualitative researchers have been at the center of challenges to hegemonic conceptions of science. These challenges continue today as scholars attempt to make the methods most widely used by qualitative researchers both more effective and more accountable for their own processes of knowledge production.

In much of the social sciences, researchers tend to focus on *techniques* for creating valid knowledge and to treat theory as something that one brings to social research, rather than as something already embedded in the research process. This has had particular consequences for how students learn social research methodologies generally—and particularly dramatic consequences for training in interpretive research strategies. For example, symbolic interaction and ethnomethodology each have histories as somewhat amphibious frameworks; at times they are understood as research methodologies and at times as social theories. Textbooks typically introduce students to symbolic interaction and ethnomethodology as social *theories*, yet students learn to engage symbolic interaction and ethnomethodology as *methodologies*. Even within a single text it is possible to find ethnomethodology and symbolic interaction referred to as theories in one chapter and methodologies in another. Both symbolic interaction and ethnomethodology are engaged as part of the infrastructure of social research, but they are not research methodologies. Broadly speaking, research methodologies provide analytic frameworks that enable social researchers to design well-constructed research. Yet symbolic interaction and ethnomethodology are not social theories insofar as social theories provide (or are intended to provide) a significant level of predictive power and ably stand apart from empirical analyses as coherent explanations of social life. Typically, social theories serve to make social life intelligible by organizing phenomena into systems—feminism, world systems theory, and Marxism come quickly to mind.[13]

Some scholars refer to symbolic interaction and ethnomethodology as "soft theory" (Iser, 2006), some refer to them as "micro level theory" (Wodak & Meyer, 2009), others refer to them as "approaches" or "perspectives" (Blumer, 1986; Gusfield, 2003), and still others regard them as methodological frameworks (Prasad, 1993). I begin with the premise that symbolic interaction and ethnomethodology are more theoretically elaborate than research methodologies and yet less analytically developed than social theory—hence, I refer to them as *interpretive frameworks* for research that shift the foundations of empirical work.

By contrast, analytic induction is recognized as a research methodology and rarely discussed in theoretical terms not because it is theoretically barren but because the theoretical commitments of analytic induction generally function at the level of common sense for social researchers—that is to say they

---

[13]Socrates argued that theory rests on three critieria: (1) it must be explicit in its details, (2) it must also be conceptually abstract enough that it does not require reference to concrete examples, and (3) finally, theory must be understood as universal, applying to all times and places. Descartes elaborated on these three elements to create a list of six qualities that constitute an ideal-type for scientific theory. Descartes insisted that theory must also be formulated with elements that are independent of any specific context, action or interpretation; it must be systematic—that is to say the context–independent elements must be related to each other by rules or laws; and, it must be complete and predictive (Flyvbjerg, 2001, pp. 38–39). Critical theory, as a formal mode of research, first emerged in the Frankfurt School of Social Research, most particularly through the work of Adorno, Horkheimer, Marcuse, and to some extent Habermas. Critical theorists developed a reflexive style of inquiry that saw social science as implicated in the complex production of regimes of truth (Gannon & Davies, 2007, p. 76). Critical theory continues to be commonly used by qualitative researchers—however, the use of critical theory does not alter the premise of analytic induction in empirical research.

seem to require no elaboration. In standard analytic induction, often both researchers and research participants hold a belief that they are describing the social world as it exists. This has particular value for describing wage gaps and investigating discriminatory practices. However, when qualitative researchers and those they study both rely on realism, we enter the logical equivalent of a Möbius strip that offers two alternatives. Researchers must either adopt a consensus theory of truth and reiterate the most dominant view(s) expressed among research participants or researchers must presume to know more about what is going on than do the participants. As a consequence, realism limits insight into social processes and tends to reify social identities and structures. The problem is not with realism as an analytic strategy but with a discursive construction of social science that naturalizes some forms of knowledge production as "the gold standard" for *all* research questions. At the same time, by limiting both the discussion of ontological and epistemological concerns embedded within social research, this narrow range of analytic strategies prevents social research from fully accounting for human experience. That is a fundamental problem. While a range of interpretive practices have emerged in the past 50 years, it has been quite difficult to diversify processes of formalization, since these are what give social science its scientific credibility. Yet this is essential if social research is to move ably forward in the 21st century.

CONCLUDING THOUGHTS

Social scientific knowledge has accrued over the years not only by amassing studies but also by marginalizing research that did not adhere to the Cartesian foundations of the natural sciences. "Science" has produced subjugated knowledge by devaluing or disqualifying some forms of social research. Within this particular framework of rationality, controversies are seen as extraneous to scientific research; they arise because of errors, because decisions are made with insufficient evidence, or because researchers fail to act as they "should" (Barrotta & Dascal, 2005). This leaves little room for broadening conceptions of social research since all concepts and phenomenon can be explained only by appealing to the reasons already firmly lodged within the premises of "science" (Barrotta & Dascal, 2005).

All researchers inherit cartographies of knowledge, maps that throw into relief a research imaginary from within which social researchers begin to work.

This book works at deconstructing those maps in order to demonstrate how qualitative frameworks are situated within discourses of power/knowledge and to examine some of the ideological investments that both enable and constrain social research. Contemporary researchers cannot trust that research frameworks created by the most privileged, during eras of great oppression, will serve as the basis of socially just research. It is not a matter of good methods applied to bad uses but rather academia's lack of awareness regarding its own processes of reproduction. With that said, I also acknowledge that the idealized quest for knowledge can make it difficult to admit that knowledge leads as often to closures as to openings (Minh-ha, 1989, p. 40). I understand this work to be not a process of perfecting but of honing. To be fully compatible with a vision of a socially just world, we need to consistently explore not only our own locations as researchers but also the foundations and assumptions of the social research paradigms that we have inherited. This book is intended as a step in that direction. I hope that readers will test this book against their own experience, knowledge, and logic; argue when what is written here does not seem to fit; and more generally engage in public discussion by offering more and different interpretations.

FURTHER READING

Atkins, K. (2005). *Self and subjectivity*. New York: Blackwell.

Baert, P. (2005). *Philosophy of the social sciences*. Cambridge, UK: Polity Press.

Denzin, N. K., Lincoln, Y. S., & Smith, L. T. (Eds.). (2008). *Handbook of critical and indigenous methodologies*. Thousand Oaks, CA: Sage.

DeVault, M. (1999). *Liberating method: Feminism and social research*. Philadelphia: Temple University Press.

Hall, D. E. (2004). *Subjectivity*. New York: Routledge.

Jackson, P. T. (2010). *The conduct of inquiry in international relations*. New York: Routledge.

Mansfield, N. (2000). *Subjectivity: Theories of the self from Freud to Haraway*. New York: New York University Press.

Naples, N. (2003). *Feminism and method*. New York: Routledge.

Ramazanoğlu, C., & Holland, J. (2002). *Feminist methodology: Challenges and choices*. Thousand Oaks, CA: Sage.

Scott, J. W. (1991). The evidence of experience. *Critical Inquiry, 17*(4), 773–797.

Tolman, D. L., & Miller, M. B. (2001). *From subjects to subjectivities: A handbook of interpretive and participatory methods*. New York: New York University Press.

Winch, P. (1958). *The idea of a social science and its relationship to philosophy*. London: Routledge & Kegan Paul.

CHAPTER THREE

ANALYTIC INDUCTION

INTRODUCTION

Today researchers commonly use analytic induction as a qualitative method of inquiry—arguably it is the most common form of qualitative inquiry. All forms of research rely upon the logics of induction, deduction, and abduction to varying degree. However, as a *method*, analytic induction requires that researchers begin with numerous observations of a particular phenomenon; then, through processes of coding, researchers establish patterns (and their exceptions) in order to draw general conclusions. "In its most simple terms, induction is the scientific process of building theoretical explanations on the basis of repeated observation of particular circumstances" (Daly, 2007, p. 45). However, this was not the original intent or design of analytic induction.

Analytic induction as a method of inquiry actually began with a concern for causal explanations and universal generalizations (Glaser & Strauss, 1967; Husband & Foster, 1987; Rettig, Tam, & Magistad, 1996; Robinson, 1951; Smelser & Baltes, 2001; Znaniecki, 1934). While a quantitatively inflected style of analytic induction continues in some disciplines, contemporary qualitative researchers more commonly consider the strength of analytic induction to be its ability to provide a rich understanding of complex social contexts—not its ability to provide a causal explanation of events. This more common use of analytic induction is properly known as *modified* analytic induction; however, in practice, qualitative researchers seldom describe their work as such.

Beginning with a short history, this chapter will examine the ontological and epistemological foundations of analytic induction and then explore analytic induction in relation to grounded theory, postpositivism, and social constructionism. It offers a general summary of analytic induction before moving into analyses of data and corresponding critiques of these analyses. A discussion regarding the implications for social research and social justice follows, and the chapter ends with concluding remarks. Overall, the chapter attempts to provide a context for understanding the conceptions of agency, experience, and subjectivity that are embedded in analytic induction, as it is widely practiced today. By applying analytic induction to exemplars drawn from the *New York Times*, the television drama *Brothers and Sisters*, and a research interview with Tony Romero, I hope to demonstrate both the potentials and problems of analytic induction.

ANALYTIC INDUCTION: A BRIEF HISTORY

The move toward analytic induction emerged (at least conceptually) around 1930, and was elaborated upon in the 1950s and 1960s. A variety of scholars made significant contributions to the development of analytic induction. For example, in 1929 Dorothy Thomas developed techniques for describing small units of behavior that could be categorized and then quantified; and, in 1936, Robert Angell pioneered work in analytic induction in principle, if not in name (Platt, 1996, pp. 18–19). Today, however, the development of analytic induction is attributed to Florian Znaniecki, who sought to articulate the causal laws and universal patterns, which he believed escaped the grasp of quantitative methods as they were practiced (Ragin, 1994).

Early social researchers commonly pursued correlations through *enumerative induction*—a form of analysis that only could *confirm* instances of statistical correlations. Znaniecki believed that these correlations would always be troubled by exceptions; consequently, he developed analytic induction to build upon the strengths, and overcome the shortcomings, of enumerative induction. Znaniecki's analytic induction pursued correlations but emphasized the importance of examining negative, or deviant, cases (cases where there was no correlation) in order to develop a more comprehensive explanation (Robinson, 1951, p. 813). Znaniecki believed that by studying the essential features of a social phenomenon, researchers would be able to create comprehensive lists of characteristics that would always be associated with the occurrence of the phenomenon being studied—thus enabling researchers to generate exhaustive knowledge in the form of universal statements. He reasoned that by isolating the essential characteristics of a phenomenon, researchers could provide not only exhaustive knowledge and universal statements but also genuinely causal laws—even though case selections were not drawn from statistically representative samples.[1] Znaniecki's focus on characteristics that were both essential and typical led many researchers to refer to analytic induction as the *type* method.

Although Znaniecki claimed that analytic induction was the "true" method of the natural sciences (and ought to be that of the social sciences), he was criticized for not providing accessible examples of its methodological procedures (Robinson, 1951). Indeed, much of his efforts toward analytic induction can best be understood as describing a *logic* of analysis, as opposed to a *method* of inquiry. Perhaps among Znaniecki's most lasting contribution to qualitative research was his emphasis on personal experience and personal documents that ultimately expanded what researchers recognized as credible data (Platt, 1996).

The Polish Peasant in Europe and America by William Isaac Thomas and Florian Znaniecki gained early acclaim as one of the most important contributions to sociology (Young, 1941) and became a landmark study both in the development of analytic induction and in the use of life histories in social research (Platt, 1996; Reynolds & Herman-Kinney, 2003). Although the analysis was crafted in the causal language of physical sciences, the study broke new ground by examining life histories and by demonstrating that aspects of culture are dependent on the practices of individuals (Musolf, 2003; Young, 1941). *The Polish Peasant in Europe and America* caught the interest of early symbolic interactionists at the University of Chicago—in particular Edwin Sutherland, Donald Cressey, Alfred Lindesmith, and Herbert Blumer.

---

[1]In this usage, "essential" refers not to an ontological status but to a logical one of "necessary and sufficient" as operationally defined.

Yet many scholars, including Herbert Blumer (1941), were highly critical of the study and argued that it had no clear methodology.[2]

Most broadly, Znaniecki's contemporaries understood the particular brilliance of analytic induction as its capacity for knowledge-building and its self-corrective procedure of analyzing deviant cases (Robinson, 1951, p. 814). In the 1950s, W. S. Robinson began to formalize and systematize analytic induction. Robinson modified analytic induction by developing a clear method of causal analysis, which included calculations for standard deviation (Miller, 1982). In addition, Robinson argued that the process of analytic induction begins with a provisional definition of something to be explained and a corresponding explanatory hypothesis. As data were collected, they were to be compared with the hypothesis. If the hypothesis did not fit "the facts," either the hypothesis would be reformulated or the phenomenon to be explained would be redefined so to exclude the nonconforming case(s). The procedure would be continued exhaustively with the intent of establishing a universal relationship among observed facts. The final methodological step provided a distinctive element in early analytic induction: because conditions, which are always present when the phenomenon is present, should not be present when the phenomenon is absent. Consequently, the researcher was required to look for cases that fall outside of the area circumscribed by the definition of the phenomenon in order to determine whether or not the final hypothesis might apply to them.[3] This requirement—to account for every possible case (all positive and negative instances)—posed obvious practical problems and made analytic induction a daunting endeavor (Johnson, 1998, pp. 29–30).[4]

In the 1960s, major transformations occurred in the development of social research that moved analytic induction away from the quantitative model of

---

[2]In critiquing *The Polish Peasant in Europe and America*, Blumer argued that human documents lend themselves to a wide range of interpretations, depending on the experience, interests, competence, and theoretical framework one brings to it. Given the impossibility of truly exhaustive accounts, and the nature of documents as open to interpretation and abstraction, Blumer exhorted scholars to seek validation for their interpretations through statistical analyses in which findings can be compared with those of a control group rather than to specific experience (Blumer, 1986, pp. 123–126). Blumer argued that accounts can only make clear the *nature* of the interpretation, not its validity.

[3]The insistence on generating lawlike claims from empirical evidence created conceptual tensions. "Karl Popper's solution to these logical problems involved an inversion of the basic stance of the logical positivists: since lawlike claims could never be verified, and since scientific claims were phrased in lawlike—often universal terms—perhaps it made sense to stop asking whether a claim could be proven true and instead ask whether a claim could be proven false (1992, 92)" (Jackson, 2010, p. 21). This move toward falsification is reflected in early analytic induction.

[4]Robinson (1951, p. 814) imagined that analytic induction would not stand alone and argued that in order to "study cases in which the phenomenon does not occur would involve us in enumerative induction."

the physical sciences.[5] At a minimum, many qualitative researchers began to doubt the ontological premise that human behavior was governed by absolute laws such as those that Znaniecki and Robinson had pursued (cf. Ratcliff, 2006). Barry Glaser and Anselm Strauss (1967) flatly rejected the methods of analytic induction and initiated a move away from hypothesis testing and toward theory creation.[6] They argued that researchers were imposing theories on empirical settings and hence were using data to test theory—rather than actually investigating social life. Glaser and Strauss (1967) created what is known as grounded theory by inverting the typical paradigm that brought theory to the data. By observing social life without preconceptions, Glaser and Strauss asserted that researchers would be able to develop theory from categories and concepts that emerged organically from data.

Developed as comparative case analysis, scholars conduct grounded theory research by constantly comparing data in order to observe their analytically relevant properties (ten Have, 2004). In a very loose sense, one might say the researcher develops a hypothesis about what is going on and searches to see if an observation/case is typical. However, grounded theory was juxtaposed *against* the hypothesis testing and the causal proofs developed by Znaniecki (1934) and Robinson (1951). The language of grounded theory replaced the positivist notion of hypothesis testing with that of theory development.

In grounded theory, the researcher develops and tests any number of emerging theoretical explanations of the data against the increasing numbers of observations or cases and then revises her or his theoretical explanation in light of accumulating information.[7] Analytically, the process of grounded theory is characterized by a search for exceptions; pragmatically, it is characterized by several stages of coding.[8] Further, unlike the analytic induction of their predecessors, Glaser and Strauss (1967, p. 104) argued that the method does not require

---

[5]The pragmatist philosophy of James, Peirce, and Dilthey as well as phenomenological foundations provided by Husserl, Schutz, Berger, and Luckmann broadly influenced both the future direction of social research and analytic induction.

[6]Herbert Blumer was Strauss's advisor at the University of Chicago. Glaser had studied with Paul Lazerfield and Robert Merton at Columbia.

[7]"Theory produced by analytic induction is universal, precise, and limited" (Ratcliff, 2006, p. 2).

[8]"All variants of grounded theory include the following strategies: (a) simultaneous data collection and analysis, (b) pursuit of emergent themes through early data analysis, (c) discovery of basic social processes within the data, (d) inductive construction of abstract categories that explain and synthesize these processes, (e) sampling to refine the categories through comparative processes, and (f) integration of categories into a theoretical framework that specifies causes, conditions, and consequences of the studied processes (see Charmaz 1990, 1995b, 2000; Glaser 1978, 1992; Glaser and Strauss 1967; Strauss 1987, 1995)" (Charmaz, 2001, p. 677).

consideration of all possible data, but rather consideration of data until new information no longer contributes to the development of the theory or explanation—referred to as the point of saturation.

The influence of grounded theory moved the practice of analytic induction away from hypothesis testing, statistical calculations, causal analyses, and falsification and toward rich analyses of a complex social phenomenon through the process of examining, comparing, and coding/organizing data. Many researchers consider analytic induction today to be a variety of the constant comparative method associated with grounded theory in which there is a systematic search for negative cases (variations or exceptions) and the modification of one's analysis/theory until no disconfirming evidence can be found (Hammersley, 1981, p. 216).[9]

There are multiple variations of grounded theory today. The variations in grounded theory, like those included in the rubric of analytic induction, range from postpositivist to constructivist. However, it is safe to say that both grounded theory and analytic induction refer to an ongoing inductive process of identifying emergent patterns, both are recursive processes, and both build theory from the raw materials of data. In each, scholars are faced with the task of producing an ordered explanation of observations and interpretations.

In order to make sense of observations, the researcher tests out themes (potential explanations) in hopes of constructing a pattern. "If he [*sic*] can successfully use a theme to convince others of the existence of a pattern, he can be said, at least according to relatively weak criteria, to have 'explained' his observations" (Latour & Woolgar, 1986, p. 37). Well-written grounded theory and analytic induction make the processes of analysis and the logical warrants of interpretation available to readers for consideration and evaluation. These are rigorous ventures that provide accountability of methodology, methods, and interpretation.

For some researchers, a primary distinction between analytic induction and grounded theory is that analytic induction compares cases only *within* the specific sample being studied, while grounded theory relies on a constant search for cases that are external to the sample under investigation (Husband & Foster, 1987, p. 57). Grounded theory is an iterative process that requires one to remain in the field, analyzing data and using abduction to search for new cases to test emerging theory against, until the full analysis is

---

[9]As noted earlier, some disciplines continue to use the language of hypothesis testing in association with analytic induction, although contemporary practices are generally less formal processes of constant verification (Morse & Mitcham, 2002).

complete. However, the nature of research funding and academic life makes this approach to fieldwork largely untenable today. Scholars doing grounded theory, like those using analytic induction, are more likely to return home after initial data collection and return to the field if initial analyses require it.

At least initially, the relationship of theory to data was an obvious and primary distinction between grounded theory and other forms of analytic induction (Glaser & Strauss, 1967, p. 101). Analytic induction "begins with a pre-existing theoretical viewpoint or premise that guides the investigator's approach to the cases that are examined (Gilgun, 1995; Miller, 1982)" (Rettig et al., 1996, p. 208). By contrast, grounded theorists attempt to approach data with a theoretical tabula rasa—with the intent of generating theory from the data. Yet again, this is no longer necessarily the case today. For example, Strauss and Corbin (1998, p. 12) wrote, "A researcher does not begin a project with a preconceived theory in mind (unless his or her purpose is to elaborate and extend existing theory)." In this sense, the original goal of developing theory is retained, but it is no longer necessarily a development drawn from a tabula rasa.

While researchers using inductive analysis may not use the *language* of grounded theory (e.g., memoing or open, axial, and selective coding) the process of induction itself leads them to proceed through comparative analyses and multiple layers of coding that can be quite similar. In practice, both grounded theory and analytic induction use an ongoing inductive process to identify emergent patterns (and variations or exceptions) in order to build explanations in the form of concepts and/or theory. Finally, researchers using analytic induction, like those using grounded theory, work until they reach saturation—not until they have examined all possible cases as Znaniecki and Robinson had envisioned. For good reason, scholars today debate the extent to which the procedures of grounded theory are indeed *distinctive* of it (Pidgeon & Henwood, 2004, p. 625).

As practiced today, few qualitative researchers would describe analytic induction as an *interpretive* framework because it does not explicitly regard the interpretive practices of social life. Yet most social researchers accept that interpretation plays a central role in all human interaction and social processes. Qualitative research that does not account for the importance of human interpretation in interaction would seem to implicitly rely upon the behaviorist framework of stimulus–response. What other alternative is there for understanding interaction? Some researchers sidestep this question by claiming to focus only on interaction without consideration of meaning-making practices or motivation. However, when analyses that rely on analytic induction do not account for the gap between behaviorism and interpretation, they *assume* a realist ontology—as a matter of common sense.

From a realist perspective, a researcher faces limited options for understanding the complexities of social life: She or he can advance the most dominant views that emerge in the accounts being examined, or she or he can adopt a "god's eye view" by asserting that she or he "knows better" than those being studied. The first approach, advancing dominant views, is vulnerable to reproducing hegemonic relationships—it gives us truth by consensus. The second option is seldom tenable by contemporary standards of good research. This tension persists, in part, because discussions of analytic induction generally are limited to technical descriptions of procedures—as if these stand apart from interpretive practices. Further, ontological realism leads the categories of analysis created through induction to be presented as if they were derived intact—rather than as if they represent conceptual ideas about social life.

By and large, researchers are not expected to identify, much less analyze, the ontological and epistemological moorings of the research methodologies and methods that we use. Consequently, much of what we know about epistemology and ontology operates at the level of commonsense assumptions, making us vulnerable to replicating a Cartesian paradigm without necessarily recognizing it as such. Even analytic induction used in conjunction with social constructionism can reproduce ontological realism. The same can be said for Action Research, which includes both quantitative and qualitative methods in the service of developing social equality.[10]

The principles of Action Research mark a substantial departure from traditional academic research. Indeed, politically guided research projects that account for their investments in research can produce less partial and therefore less distorted results than those purportedly guided by value neutrality (Harding, 2007). However, Action Research, as a field, does not take up the more rudimentary critical analysis of the philosophical foundations of social research that would enable scholars to get at the politics of knowledge production embedded in conceptions of agency, subjectivity, experience, and the nature of evidence—as well as in a host of other assumptions regarding the nature of theory and method. Like all research that relies upon deductive or inductive processes of formalization, Action Research remains

---

[10]Action Research "is not so much a *methodology* as an *orientation to inquiry* that seeks to create participative communities of inquiry in which qualities of engagement, curiosity and question posing are brought to bear on significant practical issues" (Reason & Bradbury, 2008, p. 1).

tethered to traditional practices of *formalization* and consequently to the assumptions of a Cartesian paradigm.

It is important to note that I am not suggesting that researchers should *never* choose ontological realism; rather I am arguing that the ontological premise of social research should be a *conscious* choice that is both articulated and justified in the research design. I am asserting that responsible social research begins with an understanding of the philosophical and political commitments that underlie methods of data collection and analysis. Since analytic induction is frequently used with postpositivism and social constructionism, I take up each in the next section.

Analytic Induction, Postpositivism, and Social Constructionism

Postpositivism

As the previous section demonstrated, the historical roots of analytic induction are positivist. Positivism and grand theory emerged as dichotomous yet complementary ways of understanding the social world—both were in search of lawlike regularities to explain social life. Where grand theory was broadly explanatory but unverifiable, positivism offered undertheorized techniques for generating universal empirical proofs. Most broadly, positivism can be characterized by three core beliefs: (1) the world exists as an objective entity and is (at least in principle) knowable in its entirety; (2) science can study *only* phenomena that can be directly observed (empiricism); and (3) the work of science is to construct general laws that express relationships between observed phenomena.

Postpositivism—also referred to as naturalism (Gubrium & Holstein, 1997)—assumes there is an objective social world that researchers can describe (or quantify) more or less accurately and more or less objectively. However, in this paradigm, knowledge about the world will always be imperfect and incomplete. Postpositivism emphasizes an empiricist philosophy in which social relationships and processes exist thoroughly independently of human interpretation (Lincoln & Guba, 1985; Prasad & Prasad, 2002). But it rejects the pursuit of universal laws.

Positivism is often referred to as naive realism, whereas postpositivism often is characterized simply as realism (cf. Travers, 2001). Some postpositivist scholars adopt a position referred to as *critical* realism that goes one step further in recognizing that knowledge is socially conditioned and subject to reinterpretation. Second-wave feminists and critical race scholars often use postpositivist paradigms to analyze systems of oppression. Qualitative research conducted in this way can easily be combined with statistical analyses, since both methods rely on the same ontological premise. Critical realism shares some overlap with social constructionist frameworks, which will be explored in the next section. Suffice it to say for now that a naturalist ontology in qualitative research replicates conventionally positivist assumptions about the nature of social reality and the production of knowledge (Prasad, 2005, p. 4).

Table 3.1 Postpositivist Methodology and Method		
	Postpositivist Realism	**Postpositivist Critical Realism**
Ontology	An objective social world exists.	An objective social world exists.
Epistemology	Objective knowledge is possible but often incomplete.	Knowledge is incomplete and socially conditioned.
Methodology	Seeks objective knowledge regarding the social world	Seeks to reveal oppression and inequality
Methods	Surveys, quantitative content analysis, mixed methods, and interviews	Interviews, ethnography, mixed methods, surveys, and quantitative content analysis

In all postpositivist frameworks, the goal of qualitative research is to accurately capture and reflect an objectively existent, ongoing social world. This goal is possible only in Cartesian ontology, which presumes the separation of object and subject that is necessary to give rise to the possibility of objective social worlds. Epistemologically, postpositivism is concerned with maximizing the accuracy of scientific representations (measures or descriptions) of that external reality. Although the method of data collection may be qualitative, rather than quantitative, the epistemological emphasis is quite similar. "Realist epistemology assumes an equation of truth (albeit, partial truths) with the faithful reproduction of the object as factual knowledge. Language is understood as a purely referential medium" (Clough, 1989, p. 162). Much of qualitative research is conducted this way in the social sciences. Social research is valued for its accuracy in mirroring real-world events; hence even media studies tend to focus on critiques of the reality (or lack of reality) in media representations.

Scholars working in *interpretive* frameworks that emerged from this history critique methodological realism—both naive and critical realism—by arguing that a realist ontology is particularly problematic for apprehending how social life operates. For example, people's interactions are based on their interpretation of events—and in life, events seldom have a single, unchanging meaning for all people. In addition, to the extent that social research treats categories such as race, gender, and ability as natural, it necessarily reifies these categories as it attempts to mirror them. Further, a commitment to realism obscures the many layers of interpretation that occur at every level of the research process. For example, the assumption that the world exists in such a way that *can* be mirrored by research constitutes an *interpretation* about the nature of social life. Deciding what to study is a process of interpretation—one that is positioned/shaped by social and discursive relations. The ability to "recognize" evidence is an interpretive process made possible by commitments to paradigms that enable phenomena to be defined as such. The process of moving from cases to categories is an interpretive process that constructs "findings" from "evidence." Then, of

Table 3.2 Postpositivist and Interpretivist Frameworks

	Postpositivist Realism	Postpositivist Critical Realism	Interpretivist
Ontology	An objective social world exists.	An objective social world exists.	Social life is always intersubjective.
Epistemology	Objective knowledge is possible but often incomplete.	Knowledge is incomplete and socially conditioned.	Objective and subjective meanings are inseparable and always open to reinterpretation.
Methodology	Seeks objective knowledge regarding the social world	Seeks to reveal oppression and inequality	Seeks to understand the reflexive production of meaning
Methods	Surveys, quantitative content analysis, mixed methods, and interviews	Interviews, ethnography, mixed methods, surveys, and quantitative content analysis	Interviews, critical ethnography, discourse analyses, qualitative textual analyses, and media analysis

course, data analysis and representations of that analysis are both processes of interpretation. All epistemological pathways (that enable us to know about the world) are interpretations—at a minimum they are interpretations of what exists, how things that exist are related to each other, and what is relevant.

The discursive construction of science as "objective" through reliance on a Cartesian ontology does not remove the processes of interpretation involved in research; rather, it renders them less visible and therefore less accountable. By contrast, interpretive research rejects (to varying degrees and with varying success) the Cartesian subject/object dualism and attempts to draw meaning-making processes to the surface of analyses. To understand the various forms of interpretive research, it is helpful to turn to a brief history of social constructionism.

Social Constructionism

In the mid-1960s, social constructionism challenged the essentialist paradigms of methodological realism. The term *social construction* is credited to Berger and Luckmann (1966), who used it to describe the process by which people assign (or socially construct) meaning. Unlike a Cartesian commitment to an objectively distinct social world, social constructionism approaches social worlds *as social products*. Social constructionism posits that knowledge and meaning are always partial, conditional, and perspectival—therefore there is no possibility of timeless or universal knowledge. However, social constructionism generally does not challenge the processes of systemization/formalization that give science its credibility—in this sense it transforms processes of interpretation to generate new forms of knowledge without addressing processes of formalization. (The exception to this is radical constructionism, which will be discussed shortly.)

Multiple variations of social constructionism exist today, and the degree to which social constructionists view meaning as socially constructed varies dramatically within and across disciplines. Each variation of social constructionism implies different ontological commitments. So it may not be surprising that among constructionists, the concept of reality, as socially constructed, is itself a point of controversy and debate (Ibarra, 2008, p. 355). For example, some social constructionist research is completely consistent with critical realism. Ontologically, it is grounded in the belief in an objective social world but holds that meaning is socially/historically constructed. "One can reasonably hold that concepts and ideas are invented (rather than discovered) yet maintain that these inventions correspond to something in the real world" (Schwandt, 1994, p. 126). In this sense, even socially constructed identities can be understood, or treated, as intractable—thus perpetuating a kind of determinism, despite antiessentialist claims. For example, gender can be understood as socially constructed but *treated* as real.

By contrast, other social constructionists account for the world in much the same way that poststructural analysts do: Absolutely nothing stands outside of, or apart from, meaning-making processes. There is no objectively existent social world that can serve as a reference point for knowledge—all knowledge is intersubjectively produced.

Table 3.3 Philosophical Extremes Used With Analytic Induction

Postpositivist Social Constructionism	Radical Social Constructionism
Realism	No meaning exists beyond what we create
Subject = Person	Subject = Discursive category
Subject/object dualism	Intersubjective
Objective truths exist	Truth is always problematized
Subjects have experiences	Subjects are constituted through experience
Language is neutral (transparent) bearer of information	Language is productive

Broadly speaking, social constructionism takes three different directions today, although the distinctions are not always as firm as they might appear. *Strict constructionism* emerged in relation to studies of deviance and directed analyses toward claims-making activities (Ibarra, 2008; Ibarra & Kitsuse, 1993). Strict constructionists examine how people define activities— for example, how behaviors come to be labeled as deviant. Although it might *loosely* be understood to concern meaning-making practices (e.g., how some behaviors come to be labeled deviant), it is premised on a postpositivist ontology of critical realism. *Social constructionism* (sometimes called *contextual constructionism*) is concerned with the collective generation of meaning shaped by social processes, rather than with the claims-making activities of concern to strict constructionists (Schwandt, 1994). Social constructionism examines how social processes in local contexts generate particular meanings (Best, 1993; Ibarra, 2008); it is also premised on a post-positivist ontology of critical realism.

The third form of constructionism is known as *radical constructionism*. It is based on the premise that it is impossible to know an independent, objective world that stands apart from our experience of it (Schwandt, 1994, p. 127). These constructionists are concerned with the *production* and *organization* of social differences (Fuss, 1989, pp. 2–3) and evaluate their research with concepts such as credibility, transferability, dependability, and confirmability, rather than with positivist criteria such as internal and external validity, reliability, and objectivity used in critical realism. Philosophically, radical constructionism is more closely aligned with poststructuralism. Given the ontological premise that objective experience is impossible, radical constructionism interrogates how ideology functions to naturalize and privilege some forms of knowledge over others.

Each form of constructionism is rooted in a slightly different epistemology. For example, in studying poverty, strict constructionists would look at claims that people make about poverty. By contrast, social (or contextual) constructionists would examine how the meanings of poverty are collectively generated in a specific setting. And, alternatively, radical constructionists might examine the cultural discourses through which wealth and poverty gain meaning.

Importantly, some social science disciplines that are *not* rooted in the Berger and Luckmann (1966) concept of social constructionism refer to social *constructivism*. If social constructionism can be understood to refer to sociological processes of knowledge production that are external to the individual (socialization), constructivism can be understood as being directed at processes of knowledge production that are more internal (Hruby, 2001). Social constructionism enables scholars to pursue empirical data to uncover the meanings of gender produced through symbolic, structural, and interactional process. By contrast, constructivism enables scholars to consider the discursive production of gender as collectively produced and achieved—in this sense, it is more consistent with postmodern/poststructural approaches to social life.

Within the framework of constructivism, scholars distinguish broadly between weak and strong *constructivism*.[11]

> Weak social constructivism is the view that representations—either linguistic representations or mental representations—are social constructs. When it is said that "gender" is constructed, a weak interpretation of this is merely that people's *representations* or *conceptions* of gender are socially constructed. (Goldman, 2002, p. 196)

Weak constructivism does not pose a challenge to objectivism, since facts exist independently of their representations. By contrast, strong social constructivism claims not only that *representations* of gender are constructed but that gender itself is socially constructed. This extends to all "social facts" and is consequently more controversial.[12]

It is important to keep in mind that all forms of social constructionism in social research rely on analytic induction. Berger and Luckmann's (1966) social constructionism may be the most widely practiced in the social sciences today. Consequently, I will use their variation of social constructionism with analytic induction to analyze three forms of empirical data. I intend these analyses to explicitly illustrate the respective philosophical commitments of social constructionism and analytic induction as well as their political effects. First, however, I review the basic premise of analytic induction.

THE BASIC PREMISE OF CONTEMPORARY ANALYTIC INDUCTION

Most broadly, analytic induction *today* refers to the systematic examination of similarities within and across cases to develop concepts, ideas, or theories. Analytic induction is a " 'double fitting' of ideas and evidence that focuses on similarities across a limited number of case studies studied in depth"

---

[11]Some scholars distinguish among social, literary–rhetorical, and ideological constructivism. For a further discussion of these, see Hruby (2001).

[12]Strong constructivism is divided into two schools: causal constructivism and constitutive constructivism. Causal constructivism claims that human activity sustains social facts. By contrast, constitutive constructivism claims that human activity constitutes, or makes up, the entities we call social facts—the latter is ontologically consistent with poststructuralism.

(Ragin, 1994, p. 183). Researchers use inductive *reasoning* to code data and, based on these codes, identify patterns and construct potential explanations.[13] As she or he locates exceptions in existing data, or in new cases, the researcher either refines the emerging theme or pattern, and its explanation, to include the exceptions, or explains the presence of the exceptions.

Exceptions are an integral part of developing a thorough analysis because they provide clues for how to alter concepts, shift categories, and modify developing explanations or theories (Ragin, 1994). The concern here is for developing comprehensive accounts. The ability to conclude that one's theory or explanation is accurate depends upon the search for exceptions to the pattern being as thorough and complete as possible. Consequently, researchers focus their data collection to maximize the possibility of encountering data that does not fit with the developing pattern(s).[14]

Researchers using analytic induction pursue three fundamental questions: Under what contexts do patterns arise? Under what contexts do the exceptions to the patterns arise? What significance do these patterns and exceptions hold? It is important to note that there is no single correct answer to questions of meaning. Like all research, analytic induction is a subjective process. However, researchers build their analyses carefully and provide enough information for readers to evaluate the credibility of their argument. "The strategy of *analytic induction* involves a rather strict way of steering the fit between ideas and evidence, through adapting any generally formulated conclusion to what can be said about all cases in a relevant population of cases" (ten Have, 2004, p. 147).

A major strength of analytic induction is that it avoids weak and abstract conclusions by taking exceptions to patterns seriously (ten Have, 2004). In analytic induction, exceptions to an emerging pattern often are referred to as *negative cases*—a term that comes from quantitative research and is related to the concept of falsifying a hypothesis. However, among contemporary

---

[13]For example, in a previous study (Pascale, 2007), I asked interviewees if they had a racial identity. I noticed that some people responded to my question with the question of "Who, me?" I coded these instances as answering a question with a question. As I analyzed my data by this category (answering the question with a question), I realized that the only people who responded to my question about racial identity this way were people who later identified as white or Caucasian. Based on the pattern and the exceptions to the pattern, I then interpreted the significance of this finding within the broader context of the interviews.

[14]Exceptions, or negative cases, "are especially important because they are either excluded when the relevant category is narrowed or they are the main focus when the investigator attempts to reconceptualize commonalities and thereby reconcile contradictory evidence" (Ragin, 1994, p. 94).

researchers, there is an increasing effort to move away from language rooted to quantitative research—in particular, the term *negative case*. Since researchers build a theory or explanation that accounts for the pattern and all exceptions to the pattern, across all of the cases, many scholars simply say that they seek to explain 100% of the *variation* (cf. Clarke, 2005). In developing an explanation or theory, the researcher tries to locate as many cases as possible, in as many circumstances as possible.

Analytic induction works best when there are multiple instances of the phenomenon—a diversity of contexts and empirical evidence (Ragin, 1994, p. 101). Eventually, this produces a point of saturation—a point in the research process when new instances do not contribute new information, either to the existing explanation or theory regarding the pattern or its exceptions. Data collection concludes when saturation is reached or when all cases in a small, self-limiting sample have been examined. The strength of analytic induction is its capacity to generate complex, theoretically rich understandings of social life. To some extent, analytic induction does enable researchers to theorize and anticipate contexts in which a phenomenon might arise, yet this is quite different from the generalizability of quantitative research.

The following section presents exemplars from three forms of empirical data (*newspaper, television*, and *interview*). Each of the exemplars is relevant to issues of social justice: The newspaper article is about access/ability; the television drama centers gender/sexuality; and an interview focuses on matters of race/racialization. After analyzing each exemplar, I then reflect on how the various philosophical commitments of analytic induction and social constructionism shaped my data analysis. I conclude the chapter by considering the relevance of ontology and epistemology to social justice.

ANALYSIS OF NEWSPAPER, TELEVISION, AND INTERVIEW EXEMPLARS

In an effort to replicate the presentation of research findings as if they came from a larger study, in each of the subsequent sections I introduce empirical data as an exemplar of an overarching pattern inductively derived from a broader collection of articles. This practice is consistent with the presentation of qualitative research and provides important context for the ensuing analysis. In every analytical chapter, I present the same excerpts and the same framing of the excerpts in order to highlight the various features of analysis that analytic induction, symbolic interaction, and ethnomethodology bring into relief.

Newspaper Analysis

One can say that, at a minimum, newspapers contribute to public discourse about current events. Yet *how* social researchers understand the nature and means of newspaper contributions depends upon the research paradigms that we use. This exercise is an attempt to demonstrate analytic possibilities using analytic induction and social constructionism to develop a reflexive critique of the ontological and epistemological commitments that shape both the promise and limits of analysis.

Newspaper Exemplar

Being a double amputee is not often described as an unfair advantage, but that is the argument made by the governing body of world athletics, the International Association of Athletics Federation (IAAF) in newspaper articles about Oscar Pistorius, a 20-year-old South African runner. Pistorius was born without fibulae in his legs; his parents, on the advice of multiple medical experts, had their son's legs amputated just beneath the knee when he was 11 months old (Philip, 2005). Pistorius has run for many years in the para-Olympics with record performances in this and other events at 100 meters (10.91 seconds), 200 meters (21.58 seconds), and 400 meters (46.34 seconds) (Longman, 2007). While those times do not meet Olympic qualifying standards for men, Pistorius is fast enough that his marks "would have won gold medals in equivalent women's races at the 2004 Athens Olympics" (Longman, 2007).

When the Beijing Games were still 15 months away, Pistorius petitioned the IAAF to run in the 2008 Olympics. I examined newspaper articles about Pistorius's petition and the IAAF administrative response and found that administrators, athletes, and ethicists argued that Pistorius's prosthetic legs create a potentially unfair advantage for him over runners with biological legs. The following newspaper excerpt is an exemplar of coverage on the issue:

"The rule book says a foot has to be in contact with the starting block," Leon Fleiser, a general manager of the South African Olympic Committee, said. "What is the definition of a foot? Is a prosthetic device a foot, or is it an actual foot?"

I.A.A.F. officials have also expressed concern that Pistorius could topple over, obstructing others or injuring himself and fellow competitors. Some also fear that, without limits on technological aids, able-bodied runners could begin wearing carbon-fiber plates or other unsuitably springy devices in their shoes.

Among ethicists, Pistorius's success has spurred talk of "transhumans" and "cyborgs." Some note that athletes already modify themselves in a number of ways, including baseball sluggers who undergo laser eye surgery to enhance their vision and pitchers who have elbow reconstruction using sturdier ligaments from elsewhere in the body. At least three disabled athletes have competed in the Summer Olympics: George Eyser, an American, won a gold medal in gymnastics while competing on a wooden leg at the 1904 Games in St. Louis; Neroli Fairhall, a paraplegic from New Zealand, competed in archery in the 1984 Olympics in Los Angeles; and Marla Runyan, a legally blind runner from the United States, competed in the 1,500 meters at the 2000 Olympics in Sydney. But Pistorius would be the first amputee to compete in a track event, international officials said.

A sobering question was posed recently on the Web site of the Connecticut-based Institute for Ethics and Emerging Technologies. "Given the arms race nature of competition," will technological advantages cause "athletes to do something as seemingly radical as having their healthy natural limbs replaced by artificial ones?" wrote George Dvorsky, a member of the institute's board of directors. "Is it self-mutilation when you're getting a better limb?" (Longman, 2007).

The excerpt reveals core arguments by officials against allowing Oscar Pistorius to compete in the 2008 Olympics in Beijing alongside able-bodied athletes. In the process, the officials construct the meaning of being disabled. The IAAF officials challenge Pistorius's ability to participate in the upcoming Olympic Games through their interpretation of Olympic guidelines regarding the status of an athlete as someone who has feet—or at least a foot. The officials also challenge Pistorius's identity as an athlete (as opposed to being seen as a "special" athlete) by constructing Pistorius's presence on the track as a potential hazard for other athletes. Consequently, the meaning of being *disabled* is constructed as being potentially problematic for able-bodied others.

The IAAF is responsible both for matters of fairness and safety at the Olympics, and Pistorius's unusual circumstances cause administrators to rethink both. In addition to raising concerns about the potential safety of other athletes, the officials describe concerns that success of Pistorius's carbon prosthetics might lead other athletes to cheat by inserting carbon devices in their shoes—or worse, to amputate their biological legs to gain a technological advantage. In this sense, the article illustrates how the IAAF constructs Pistorius's bid to compete through a series of potentially wide-ranging moral dilemmas.

Notably, *ethicists* are called upon to comment on Pistorius's potential Olympic participation—further contributing to the construction of disability as a moral status. Yet at the heart of the ethical issues is an expression of concern for fairness with regard to his competitors—not fairness to Pistorius. Indeed the moral construction of Pistorius slides from "disabled" to "transhuman," which marginalizes Pistorius further.

Analyzing the Analysis

As noted earlier, social constructionism is the process of interpretation, and analytic induction is the process of formalization in this analysis. While analytic induction shapes what can be understood as an exemplar, indeed what is understood as evidence, in the analysis itself, the process of analytic induction through which the patterns and exemplars were created is not visible. The power and influence of analytic induction as a methodological framework is never at the surface of analyses—it is never accountable as a productive force in this analysis. However, in this instance, social constructionism is visible as the interpretive process. Much of qualitative research lays claim only to analytic induction and not explicitly to a realist, constructionist, or interpretive framework. Consequently, the evidence appears to simply unfold on the page, and research that is least accountable for its assumptions comes to be seen as most objective.

On the surface, the use of social constructionism would seem to mitigate a realist ontology while producing some potentially useful insights regarding the construction of ability/disability. However, it is possible to observe a realist ontology at work on two levels: First, the article is not analyzed for how it constructs what counts as news—the news story is treated as an objectively real event. Second, as the analysis pursues a social constructionist analysis, it also relies upon a realist ontology, which is evident in the way that contemporary debates serve as unproblematic *referent* for the analysis.

The ontological realism of the analysis implies a Cartesian notion of subjectivity, agency, and experience. The ontological realism of the analysis is supported by, if not derived from, the use of analytic induction to select data, identify patterns, and generate the analysis—processes that are referred to in the introduction but are not actually part of reporting the analysis. This gives rise to several practical implications regarding subjectivity that are embedded here and worth some elaboration.

First, the analysis brings the social construction of disability as a moral enterprise to the surface. However, disability is never really interrogated as a *subject position*—it presents subjects as being synonymous with persons. In addition, the analysis does not address the underlying assumption that there are two different kinds of people: those with ability and those with disability. The analysis relies on an implicitly Cartesian concept of persons as having a more or less fixed and essential nature—even as disability is analyzed for being socially constructed. In this sense, ability seems to be a natural phenomenon that rests within the individual rather than within material or social aspects of culture. This conception of ability is reinforced by the fact that the analysis never explicitly names ability but allows it to function as the unmarked center of the analysis. Disability is named and emerges implicitly as a less "natural" state of being—a socially constructed state of being that is used to reify the apparent naturalness of ability.

Within a Cartesian framework, agency resides within the individual and is evidenced in the ability to affect (or failure to affect) the surrounding world. Agency is never explicitly analyzed because it is implicitly assumed as a property of a Cartesian subject. The ability of "disabled" athletes to participate in the Olympics is constrained, in this article, by the external force of the Olympic vetting process—through the exercise of its own agency. Congruently, the nature of experience, in this analysis, is unproblematized—actors within the news article are treated as simply responding to the environment around them.

Television Analysis

Any analysis of a television series provides several important analytical challenges. Minimally, it raises analytical tensions between content and form, between cultural representation and daily life, and between production and consumption. These tensions speak to a historical cleavage between the humanities, which approach television as collaboratively produced systems of symbolic meaning, and the social sciences, which have tended to approach television either as mirrors of daily life or as having a causal relationship to social life.

Importantly, television is not always or only a mirror of daily life; and causal relationships are nearly impossible to study, even if scholars feel they are worth proving. Perhaps, as a consequence, television studies have accounted for a very small proportion of social science research. Yet at the start of the 21st century, social life involves media, in general, and television, in particular, in important and unprecedented ways. One might argue that it is impossible to understand industrial and postindustrial societies without understanding their media. For this reason alone, it is important that social researchers understand the potential and the limits of existing research paradigms.

Television Exemplar

The ABC drama *Brothers and Sisters* features a white, upper-class family in Southern California involved in the daily dramas of a family-run business—complicated (of course) by interpersonal relationships and family intrigues. The series is unusual in that one of the adult siblings in the Walker family is gay, which makes it a potentially interesting site for examining talk about sexuality. I examined shows from the first season and found two relevant patterns.

First, scenes consistently allowed for multiple and contradictory audience engagements with politically controversial issues related to sexuality. *Brothers and Sisters* commonly dramatizes political issues that affect many families in the United States—particularly with regard to same-sex marriage and the Republican/Democrat partisan divides that characterized the George W. Bush administration.

Second, scenes consistently left disagreements about sexuality unresolved. The show framed these disagreements within the contexts of family intimacy, human frailty, and political aspirations—and typically used humor to drain or divert dramatic tension when very harsh or divisive conflict threatened to break out.

The following excerpt features a scene between siblings Kitty Walker, played by Calista Flockhart, and Kevin Walker, played by Matthew Rhys. Kitty enters this scene having just come from a meeting with Republican Senator Robert McCallister (played by Rob Lowe), who offered her a position as head of communications for his presidential campaign. Their meeting holds particular significance to the following scene for two reasons: Kitty and her deceased father have been the only Republicans in a family with strong Democrat affiliations, and it exposed romantic tension between Kitty and the senator, who is a father of two young children and is in the process of a divorce.

Kitty has just mentioned the job offer to her brother, Kevin, who is an attorney and the only gay primary character in the show in the first season.[15] As the scene opens, Kevin is upset with Kitty because Robert McCallister has voted in favor of a constitutional ban on same-sex marriage. Throughout this scene, Kitty is preoccupied with the mail while Kevin is consumed by the conversation; the camera alternates with the speaker, taking the view of the listener.

Kevin: Well, why *you*?

Kitty: Well, what the hell does that mean?

Kevin: [*stuttering*] Well, c-cause it's completely absurd. You can't work for this guy!

Kitty: Why? [*Kitty laughs.*] Why, Kevin? Because he's a Republican?

Kevin: No, because he's against gay marriage!

Kitty: There are lots of people in the world, Kevin, for instance *me*, who have no problem with gay people but still believe that marriage is fundamentally a religious institution that has nothing to do with the [*camera turns to Kevin who is visibly upset*] state and that does not discount civil unions or domestic partnerships or anything you . . . .

Kevin: [*Voice escalates*] Oh come on! That's just a cover that people like you provide for people like him who hate people like me.

[*Kitty shakes her head.*]

(Continued)

---

[15]Subsequent seasons have included several other white gay men.

(Continued)

Kitty: Oh, Kevin! Please, let's not make it personal.

Kevin: Ah, ah . . . [*Raises eyebrows*] Personal? Kitty, in 10 years . . . in
        20 years, when I am finally . . . m-mature enough to sustain a
        committed relationship I would like to settle down and get
        married. That's personal.

        [*Kitty stops glancing through mail and looks up to speak.*]

Kitty: That's improbable.

Kevin: Don't take this job, Kitty. I'm warning you it will cause a great deal
        of . . . .

Kitty: Wait a minute. Wait, wait, wait, wait, wait a minute. You're
        warning me?

        [*Brothers and Sisters,* Episode 11: "Family Day" 1/7/07]

The scene opens with Kevin attempting to control Kitty's behavior—the
motivation for his behavior is not immediately clear to Kitty, who initially
attributes it to Kevin's dislike for Republican politics. Kitty is aware that
Robert McCallister is against same-sex marriage so she might reasonably anticipate this to upset Kevin. Yet Kitty constructs "the problem" between herself
and Kevin as Republican politics more broadly. However, if it seems possible
that she completely failed to anticipate Kevin's investment in his own ability to
marry, consider that Kitty shares McCallister's views on same-sex marriage.
Kitty explains this as she invokes a "separate but equal" paradigm and develops a distinction between marriage as a religious issue and civil unions as a
state matter—even as she seems to support amending the Constitution of the
United States to protect what she claims to see as a solely religious practice.
This distinction between religious and state institutions enables her to frame
same-sex marriage as a matter of social institutions and to refuse to recognize
same-sex marriage as a matter of personal relationships, civil rights, and
homophobia—a common alternative, which appears to be Kevin's position.

The dual constructions of the problem are driven home in the conversation when Kevin challenges the equity of the framework. Kitty responds, "Oh,
Kevin! Please, let's not make it personal." At this moment in the exchange,
when Kevin could pursue same-sex marriage as a civil rights issue, he avoids

the confrontation and uses humor to drain the dramatic tension. Significantly, the humor is itself a homophobic stereotype ("Kitty, in 10 years . . . in 20 years, when I am finally . . . m-mature enough to sustain a committed relationship I would like to settle down and get married. That's personal."). The humor dissipates some of the tension and maintains the conflict as familial rather than political. Yet in this shifting context, Kitty's response of "That's improbable" appears to support the homophobic stereotype and/or be a comment about the personality of her younger brother. The ambiguity continues as the conflict escalates again.

Analyzing the Analysis

This analysis of an episode from *Brothers and Sisters* examines the social construction of the argument about same-sex marriage. The influence of analytic induction again is not at the surface of the analysis; although it is evident in the style of analysis. The analysis makes no contribution to understanding media or society and very little contribution toward understanding processes of representation. Analytic induction tethers the analysis to evidence in a localized context. Consequently the analysis proceeds as if the transcript was an interaction between two people. The analysis does not substantially address the excerpt as a media representation and consistently refers to "Kevin" and "Kitty" rather than to characters or writers. Consequently, the analysis itself lends a sense of reality to a carefully constructed fiction. In this sense, the segment is analyzed as the reality it purportedly represents. With that said, the analysis does not analyze the segment in terms of its accuracy in mirroring contemporary political debates as some postpositivist analyses would do.

Consistent with a realist ontology, the analysis does not address issues of agency explicitly—recall that in realist ontology agency is implicitly understood as a quality possessed (or not) by people. Consequently, issues of agency appear to be irrelevant to this excerpt; "Kitty" and "Kevin" both possess an implied agency. Actors seem to "stand in" for real people—either as a mirror of reality or as a simulacrum—a representation or copy of "the real" for which there is no original. Notably, agency is not attributed to writers, editors, producers, or advertisers. In addition, the analysis lacks any consideration of agency on the part of the viewer/researcher, in constructing meaning. One could argue that I allude to audience participation at both the beginning and end of the analysis when I allow for the possibility of more than one interpretation of the dialogue. However, that is a long way from an analysis of active audience participation.

Just as an implicit sense of agency haunts this analysis—it is present but out of view—the same can be said for conceptions of subjectivity and experience. Although not addressed explicitly, those conceptions linger implicitly as part of a realist ontology that conflates agency with individuals and subjectivity with identity, while rendering the nature of experience as self-evident—all of which is ironic, to say the least, for an analysis of a television drama.

The analytical conflation of subjectivity and identity erases the sociohistorical processes that create and reproduce subject locations (such as sexuality or gender). Hence those locations become reified even as they are acknowledged as socially constructed. The social constructionist framework does not substantially mitigate the ontological and epistemological investments of analytic induction that control what counts as evidence. In this sense, one might say the effects of analytic induction are profoundly present but unnoticed in the analysis.

While the analysis uses a social constructionist framework, it advances, and is constrained by, a realist ontology. It is this commitment to realism and a Cartesian paradigm that underpins a seemingly self-evident epistemology in which the researcher needs to focus only upon apparently objective "evidence" in the localized context—in this case the scene excerpted as an exemplar. Of course, the same can be said of the earlier newspaper analysis.

Interview Analysis

Interviews may be the most common form of empirical data in the social sciences. As such, analytic approaches to interviews can vary a great deal, depending on the ontological and epistemological foundations of research—most particularly, how one conceptualizes the nature of "truth." As in the previous sections, I introduce this exemplar as part of a larger research project. The introductions to each of these exemplars could be quite different, depending on the analytic framework being used. I sought to create a rhetorical/analytical middle ground in an effort to develop one introduction that could work across social constructionism/analytic induction, symbolic interaction, and ethnomethodology.

Interview Exemplar

While dominant public discourses in the United States construct race as natural, and apparently self-evident, in interviews with Native American Indians, I found that talk about race consistently exposed the social, historical, and legal processes of racialization. The exemplar that follows is from my interview with Tony Romero an Esselen Indian. It is important to note that in the early 1900s, Esselen Indians (indigenous to the land that came to be called California) were declared "extinct" by the U.S. government. The federal government's policy of recognition for Native Americans requires genealogical evidence of unbroken ancestry over hundreds of years. Indigenous nations unable to provide that evidence were "terminated" by the government—that is to say denied federal recognition that would have entitled them to land and other settlement claims, as well as university scholarships and other forms of affirmative action candidacy. The Esselens, however, were never officially terminated but rather declared "extinct."

The federal declaration of their "extinction" has become part of a dominant cultural discourse. For example, the *Economist* featured an article on the Esalen [*sic*] Institute, and described it as "named after the Esselen, a now-extinct Indian tribe that used the place as their burial ground. In 1910 the Murphy family bought the land from homesteaders" (*The Economist*, 2007). The Esalen Institute is a spa/retreat center that has drawn renowned authors including John Steinbeck, Aldous Huxley, and Henry Miller. In the 1950s, the beat poets visited Esalen, and it later became a home to Alan Watts (*The Economist*, 2007).

In the following excerpt from my interview with Tony Romero in 2000, he talks about growing up in California as an Esselen Indian.

Celine-Marie: I wonder if you could tell me what it was like for you growing up and crossing worlds between your family and your home and the rest of the culture you experienced around you.

(Continued)

(Continued)

Tony: Well grownin' up, uh, growin' up, I remember my mom and dad always told me, "Don't tell anybody you're Indian." Uh, they were scared because I had uncles that were either drug behind horses or hung just 'cause they said they were Native American Indians. I have documentation of that. I had a couple of my relatives that were hung in a barn in Carmel Valley 'cause they wouldn't sell their property.

Celine-Marie: I'm so sorry.

Tony: It's things like that that happened in those days, and you know were talkin' like the '50s—1950s—and things like that were still goin' on like I remember when I was in high school I used to go down Monterey, I used to go to Louis' Bar on Alvarado Street. My uncle used to hang out, and there were two Obispo used to hang out in front of Louis' all the time and sit, they used to have these benches in front of all the pool halls. They were like, I guess there were like 10 or 12 pool halls you know on Alvarado Street and all these bars. So the Indians always used to carry these little pints of whiskey. I'll never forget the whiskey bottles cause they're, they're made in a shape where you can put 'em in your back pocket and they just fit perfect cause they had a little concave, concave shape to 'em.

Celine-Marie: Mmm.

Tony: And, uh, I remember 'em always sippin' out them damn whiskey bottles and, uh, but I remember one time I was comin' out of Louis' pool hall and my uncle was fightin' with these two white guys. He was tellin' how they were on his land, he didn't like it you know, he was feelin' a little tipsy there. So then I just ignored him, went across the street with some friends of mine to another place. And about a half an hour later I came back out and my uncle was sittin' on the same bench but he had a bloody nose, his eye was all black and blue, what they did was, they drug him in the back alley, beat the shit out of him to teach him a lesson, you know, that it wasn't his land anymore, it was theirs. And, uh, it was things like that that happened in Monterey where my mother was scared. She said well don't tell anybody you're Indian, tell 'em you're Spanish. So then when I *did* tell people I was Spanish and Indian, the first thing that came into mind was you're *Mexican*. I said no, no. I said bein' a Spanish Indian didn't make you Mexican. It wasn't the idea that I was ashamed of bein' a Mexican, it was the idea of wanting to be called what I really *was*. And I wasn't a Mexican. And I *knew* that and my parents knew that and, uh, so anyway, I went through that through my whole school years. You know OK, Tony, you're Spanish and Indian but you're Mexican. I says no. So anyway I had to go through this whole thing when I was a kid. I was always, I was always, when I was a kid I was always fightin' to protect my heritage.

Celine-Marie: Mmm.

Tony: Always fightin' you know to show people I was Native American Indian and I was proud of it. But then, uh, after a while I just, I just ignored the whole thing. But then after my mom passed away, I will never forget my mom passed away in 1970, she, uh, she looked at me and says you're Native American Indian. She said be proud of it. I'll never forget that. She says you're Esselen Indian. She said be proud of it. And, uh, so ever since then I've been fightin' for my recognition as a Native American Indian. I'm doin' it not only for her, but for my family, you know my existing family I have now, which isn't much.

In this excerpt, Tony constructs the meaning of being a Native American through four central "fights"—all of which regard various levels of systematic violence directed by whites toward Indians/Native Americans. His narrative began with his parent's injunction of "don't tell anybody you're Indian." Tony seems to have reconciled this injunction by describing himself as Spanish and Indian. This identity shift seems to protect him by leaving him with no apparent claim to land in the United States—as opposed to revealing himself to be an Esselen Indian (with a long historical claim to the land). However, this protection from physical violence came with enormous personal cost. The relationship between land and identity shapes Tony's narrative and all four "fights" that define his experience. Tony begins with family stories of loved ones being hung in a barn and/or dragged behind horses because they would not sell their land. Notably the people who murdered his family are not named as white—perhaps because they don't need to be.

Tony went on to describe a second fight that occurred when he was in high school. He was hanging out on Alvarado Street when he saw his "tipsy" uncle get into a fight "with two white guys" who beat him "to teach him a lesson." The violence is humiliating and painful—not intended to take land—but made possible because the land had already been taken. In his telling of the story, Tony did not represent himself as attempting to diffuse the conflict or to intervene to protect his uncle at any level. Neither did he offer an explanation, or a sense of regret, about having ignored the fight. So when Tony described himself as always fighting ("I was always, I was always, when I was a kid I was always fightin' to protect my heritage."), I understand this to refer not to physical altercations but to verbal fights and to a deep internal struggle about his inability to name himself as an Esselen Indian. This is evidenced also in his description toward the end of his third remark when he described the verbal conflicts that characterized his youth.

What began as a story about growing up jumps ahead to a time when Tony was about 40 years old, and his mother, on her deathbed, liberated him from the secrecy that opened the excerpt, the secrecy that she had hoped would protect him from violence. Tony twice repeated her encouragement to be proud of being an Esselen Indian. And it is this moment that resolves one conflict and inaugurates another—the fight for recognition as a living people, the remaining Esselen Nation. If the fight for survival of the Esselen people once depended on the ability to hide, it now depends on their ability to become visible in the struggle for federal recognition of the Esselen Nation's existence.

Analyzing the Analysis

Researchers employ social constructionist analyses in a variety of ways, according to their skill and interest. Many social constructionist analyses would have used Tony's narrative as evidence that reflected, or failed to accurately reflect, an objective world—the veracity of his claims would be determined by how broadly they are shared among interviewees or validated by other sources. This would be consistent with the analytical lens brought to the television excerpt. By creating a different inflection of a social constructionist analysis, I hope to demonstrate a more nuanced critique of how analytic induction operates beneath the surface of analyses. Again, analytic induction brings this exemplar to the printed page in this form. The process of analytic induction shapes both what counts as evidence (in this case an interview) and what can be said about it (the evidence for all claims must physically exist in this excerpt).

The analysis of my interview with Tony Romero focused on the social construction of Native American identity through four conflicts, yet it does so without abandoning a Cartesian ontology. For example, the analysis replicates a commonsense view (ontological realism) regarding the way the world exists. It examines the social construction of identity in Tony's narrative but does not take up the social construction of social worlds or social experience. However, to the extent that the analysis does not use the same *logic* that Tony used to describe his experience, it steps away from ontological realism. In this sense, it is quite unlike the earlier analyses. In addition, by using "I" in relationship to the construction of the analysis, there is a very slight acknowledgment of the subjective process of creating an analysis. In this sense, the use of this particular style of social constructionism brings some weight to bear against the ontological investments of realism embedded in analytic induction. Given the style of the analysis, the commitment to ontological realism is less obvious and more conflicted.

Epistemologically, I have treated the interview data as a way of gaining access to the "real" world. The analysis does not consider the accomplishment of the interview itself or the construction of interviews as a research genre. The interview process is not problematized at all but treated as a transparent window into the lives of others. This commitment to ontological realism is deeply embedded in the assumptions of research.

Agency, subjectivity and experience remain sequestered as the *presuppositions* of social research. The locus of agency appears to reside within individuals who have experiences that could be more or less accurately and objectively described. There is no consideration of subjectivity or its cultural production. As a consequence, identity and subjectivity appear to be conflated—as in a Cartesian realist ontology. The same can be said regarding the nature of experience, which appears to be self-evident—experiences are simply what people have, even if we interpret them differently.

The commitment to a Cartesian ontology is anchored in the use of analytic induction that defines both context and evidence—the foundation of any science. The transparent structure of analytic induction controls the deeper levels of analysis while allowing for variation in focus and interpretation. Analytic induction is a process of systemization (i.e., formalization) that gives research its "scientific" credibility whereas social constructionism is a process of interpretation that offers some analytical range for making sense of social life without challenging the foundation of what counts as science.

IMPLICATIONS FOR SOCIAL RESEARCH

Scholars working in analytic induction and social constructionism have produced many fine contributions to scholarship—contributions that often critique inequalities. The general strength of this combination for getting at the active production of social meaning is evident in the previous analyses. However, as noted earlier, these are not the only social constructionist analyses that are possible for these exemplars. Certainly they could have been enriched by recourse to feminist, critical race, or poststructural theories. Yet as a bare-bones approach, these exercises provide useful insights into the philosophical underpinnings of both analytic induction and social constructionism.

While social constructionism provided an analytic focus on social life as the product of socially produced meanings, it did not liberate the analyses from the philosophical foundations of ontological realism at the heart of analytic induction. Analytic induction is the process of formalization that gives most of qualitative research claim to "scientific validity." It is arguably the primary technique of data collection/analysis used by qualitative researchers, yet research is written in such a way that makes it difficult to apprehend how analytic induction shapes what can be known and on what terms. Researchers tend to consider the implications of social constructionism but not the analytic induction that underlies it. So on one hand there is a commitment to social life as constructed, and on the other, the social world is reified as inherently, objectively real. Commonsense assumptions among researchers can lead to disjointed and contradictory analytical claims.

Most obviously, analytic induction provides methodological tools for apprehending patterned occurrences in localized contexts. Researchers often refer to "finding patterns in data" or examining "patterns that emerge in data";

this is the language of scientific discovery, the language of Cartesian dualism. This discourse has two immediate effects. First, Cartesian dualism privileges the mind over the body and presupposes a correlative emphasis on visuality.

Within a Cartesian framework correlation of vision and mind is evident in the use of the verb "to see" as a metaphor for "to know" or "to understand." Concomitantly, the metaphor of blindness came to stand for ignorance—for example, "double-blind experiments" and "blind to her own process of interpretation." To the extent that we rely upon Cartesian dualism, we talk as if data analysis is a matter of *recognizing* what we see before us. The ontological realism of Cartesian dualism emphasizes the power of vision—not only must evidence be located in a local context (it must be something "seen") but it also dominates the intellectual landscape, since to see is to know. In this sense, the distant perspective of a social researcher both clarifies some forms of knowledge and subjugates others.

Second, the language of analytic induction minimizes, if not obscures, the need for reflexivity at every stage of the research process: from the formulation of the research problem through research design, data collection, data analysis, and writing. Its roots in the ontological and epistemological realism of Cartesian dualism make it possible to believe that one only needs consistently systematic techniques for accurately apprehending social life in local contexts. Typically, the practice of analytic induction obscures even the construction of what counts as a localized context.

An emphasis on reflexivity would create different demands on researchers using analytic induction. On one hand, reflexivity is the recognition of the ways that the self always mediates the social world: Researchers know only about the world through our own experience of it. On the other hand, reflexivity is also a constant awareness of how the social conditions of research affect the production of knowledge. Historically, analytic induction has rendered both forms of reflexivity external to analytic induction—although contemporary researchers often bring principles of reflexivity, as they bring other theoretical frameworks, to the practice of analytic induction.

Despite the sequestered realist ontological and epistemological commitments of analytic induction, as social researchers, our work begins not with objective observation of social life but with logical processes of interpretation. We begin with key questions: What counts as a viable topic of research? What establishes viable data? What constitutes the presence of patterns? What is the meaning or significance of those patterns? The answers to all of these questions are matters of interpretation—although they often are taught as matters of fact. Importantly, interpretation is itself always a matter of positionality—how one is situated within networks of power, geographies of privilege, and the histories of experience. It might seem that standards of good research would require scholars to be accountable for the many processes of interpretation involved in knowledge production—certainly feminist standpoint and critical race scholarship succeeded in making research more accountable for these processes of knowledge production. However, there is more work to do.

Even while pursuing a social constructionist analysis, the technical procedures of social research pull us back into the mythical vision of Descartes. Analytic induction combined with social constructionism created a modified version of Cartesian dualism—not a radically different ontology as one might have expected. Ontological commitments form the horizons of possibility for social research. Analytic induction limits the scope of study to that which we can point to in a localized context—indeed, the commitment to empirical evidence may seem like a matter of common sense. What else should researchers be looking for if not empirical evidence? Where else might we find "evidence" but in a localized context? And yet, in each of the exemplars, the commitment to empiricism left me unable to even pose (much less answer) questions about ability, whiteness, wealth, and masculinity in relation to Oscar Pistorius's success as an athlete.

Newspaper articles about Pistorius do not discuss whiteness, wealth, or masculinity, so there is no evidence in a localized context that would enable me to examine the routine relations of privilege that provided him with access to the material and emotional resources that made his success possible. In addition, although Pistorius had experienced (and indeed was fighting) "separate but equal" segregation as an athlete, news articles did not mention this. Consequently, there were no data, no means for considering segregation based on ability even though this bears distinctly on his petition to compete. And there is no way to demonstrate how such segregation is related to the belief that there are two distinct kinds of people (able and disabled) rather than a continuum of abilities for every person that change over the life course. The emphasis on empirical evidence from a local context also makes it impossible to consider the social production of news—the fact that "news" in and of itself does not exist; events are assembled into news for popular consumption.

Some researchers may understand these problems as related to the data—not to analytic induction. Social researchers draw evidence from a local context; if you want a different kind of analysis, you need a different kind of context. Perhaps I should interview athletes about segregation, talk to reporters about the construction of news, or perhaps engage audiences through focus groups. Yet here again, whole sets of questions would still need to be bracketed as falling outside of the local context. Analytic induction, and social research more broadly, requires that researchers learn to see "local contexts" as naturally occurring—as a matter of common sense. However, there are no local contexts that exist in and of themselves; there are only localized contexts that have been produced and reified through scientific discourses and that now appear to be self-evident and objectively existent. The localization of contexts has profoundly political consequences since routine relations of power are effective precisely because they exceed immediate contexts.

Using analytic induction and social constructionism, I was able to examine talk about sexuality in the *Brothers and Sisters* excerpt; however, I was unable to explore whiteness, wealth, and gender because these aspects of the production were reduced to matters that one can see—in the dialogue and interaction, they appeared to have no meaning. The ontological realism of Descarte privileges the senses, in particular vision, as a way of knowing, when combined with reason. Yet visuality itself proves not to be very useful without access to the discourses that give images meaning. White skin color—devoid of historical discourses of power that give it meaning—appears as just that: white skin color. Yet in film and in daily life, skin color rarely functions at such a simplistic level. Similarly, wealth seems to form only the details of the background of this interaction—there is no way to even transcribe it. And gender, like race, is reduced to what we see on the screen or read in the transcript. Race, class, and gender are social relationships whose meanings exceed this localized moment. If they truly were as irrelevant as analytic induction makes them appear, they would not be recognizable as such.

Despite the contributions of social constructionism, analytic induction produces an analysis in which whiteness, wealth, and gender seem to have no relevant bearing on the media construction of sexualities. As in the analysis of the news article, analytic induction does not give me access to processes of media production or audience consumption. Given these limitations, perhaps it is not surprising there are so few qualitative studies of media. If this construction of localized contexts made sense in the 19th century, it certainly does not in the 21st century. Social sciences are being left behind in one of the most important developments of this century: media, both "old" forms such as newspapers, television, and film as well as new forms including wikis, blogs, vlogs, texting, and Twitter.

If the constraints of analytic induction seem particularly significant only when analyzing forms of media, the excerpt from my interview with Tony Romero demonstrates otherwise. For example, although this interview exposed racial violence that has been central to historical processes of racialization, I was unable to analyze the process of racialization—again that would have required my ability to move from the evidence of a localized context. Although I examined the social construction of racialized conflicts in the interview, to the extent that I wrote about race as though it simply existed as a material reality, I reified race—despite my claim in setting up the exemplar that processes of racialization were evident in my interviews with Native American Indians. Gender and class were left outside of the analysis completely—though one could make the argument for "fighting" itself as a class-based, masculine metaphor or practice and one that in this case presumes the unmarked category of physical "ability."

Analytic induction is based upon the presuppositions of a realist ontology and epistemology that requires researchers to show the relevance of whiteness, racialization, wealth, gender, ability, and so forth in the empirical evidence of a localized context—this is, the discursive production of "data." Empirical analyses are limited literally to what one can point to in the data, as if data themselves were not constructed. The logic behind this mandate is that if researchers were not constrained in this way, we would be vulnerable to imposing our own assumptions and drifting away from science. Yet science secures its own discourse by reifying its own practices and obscuring its processes of production.

While analytic induction has much to offer social sciences—indeed there have been many excellent studies of oppression—it is unable to apprehend routine relations of privilege. This is particularly significant since privilege does not operate independently from mechanisms of oppression—oppression always, simultaneously, produces privilege. The ontology of analytic realism can produce good analyses of marginalization, while allowing routine privilege to pass without comment—precisely because it is so rarely commented upon.

Social research that is confined to a localized context will always be significantly rooted in ontological realism. That is because localized contexts (in and of themselves) cannot provide the range of analytical resources necessary for examining the cultural and historical aspects of social processes or for examining the social construction of localized contexts. By limiting analyses to localized contexts, researchers cannot examine the cultural forces that give rise to the embodiment and reification of historical relations of power, privilege, and inequality.

CONCLUDING THOUGHTS

The relative importance of race, class, gender, sexuality, and ability never depends on a localized context—or even on multiple localized contexts—but rather on their repetition in multiple contexts over time. For example, if race can be analyzed in a local context, *racialization* must be understood as a process over time in multiple contexts. The categories of social difference upon which inequalities are built, consistently exceed the frame of inductive analysis.

Analytic induction was designed to "study down" to point toward the disadvantaged and make visible marginalized social locations. It can do this quite well—as fields such as social problems demonstrate. However, analytic induction was never intended to study how the machinery of marginalization produced viable subjects for exploitation. Nor was analytic induction intended as a method for examining routine relations of power and privilege. The epistemological foundations on which it is moored render it ineffective for such analysis today.

If analytic induction were an objective way of producing knowledge about the world, it would seem logical to believe that analytic induction could get at power and privilege as effectively as it gets at exploitation and domination. It does not. Common sense leads us to understand evidence as something that appears in a "local context." However, this belief is both a political and historical construction. This leaves researchers with the conundrum of imagining other ways that evidence could be logically constructed to enable systematized analyses. If the task seems impossible at this point, perhaps the next chapters will be helpful in imagining it as both possible and necessary.

FURTHER READING

Berger, P., & Luckmann, T. (1966). *The social construction of reality: A treatise in the sociology of knowledge.* Garden City, NY: Doubleday.

Charmaz, K. (2006). *Constructing grounded theory: A practical guide through qualitative analysis.* Thousand Oaks, CA: Sage.

Clough, P. T. (1992). *End(s) of ethnography.* Thousand Oaks, CA: Sage.

Glaser, B., & Strauss, A. (1967). *The discovery of grounded theory: Strategies for qualitative research.* New York: Aldine.

Holstein, J., & Gubrium, J. (Eds.). (2008). *Handbook of constructionist research.* New York: Guilford Press.

Ladson-Billings, G. (2003). Racialized discourses and ethnic epistemologies. In N. Denzin & Y. Lincoln (Eds.), *The landscape of qualitative research* (pp. 398–432). Thousand Oaks, CA: Sage.

Latour, B., & Woolgar, S. (1986). *Laboratory life: The construction of scientific facts* (2nd ed.). Princeton, NJ: Princeton University Press.

Ragin, C. (1994). *Constructing social research.* Thousand Oaks, CA: Pine Forge Press.

Robinson, W. S. (1951). The logical structure of analytic induction. *American Sociological Review, 16*(6), 812–818.

CHAPTER FOUR

SYMBOLIC INTERACTION

INTRODUCTION

Max Weber's work was particularly influential among early social scientists who wanted to break away from using the physical science model in the social sciences. Weber had argued that it is meaningless to attempt to reduce empirical findings to social laws. According to Weber, laws are only conceptual aids for understanding reality—knowledge of social laws cannot constitute an understanding of reality. Weber (1978) argued that knowledge of cultural processes is possible only by understanding the meanings that the specific and shared reality holds for those involved. He used the term *verstehen* to characterize the deep level of understanding that is necessary in order to *interpretatively re-create* (not just to follow) cultural processes. These two aspects of Weber's work were particularly influential among the early efforts of social researchers to examine social interaction.

In addition to Weber, the philosophical school of American Pragmatism profoundly influenced the development of symbolic interaction.[1] Inspired by Charles Darwin, the work of American pragmatists contrasted sharply with that of Descartes. Pragmatists argued that reality is *not* ready-made and waiting to be discovered. Rather, knowledge acquisition is the active process of coping with life's demands and therefore always "in the making" (Baert, 2005, p. 129).[2]

From these philosophical roots, symbolic interaction began with the premise that the individual and society are interdependent and inseparable—both are constituted through shared meanings. Symbolic interaction emerged as an effort to understand social life through something other than laboratory research and behaviorist conceptions of stimulus–response. Consequently, it shifted the goal of social research from an objective study of an empirical reality to a deep understanding of the symbolic practices that make a shared reality possible.

This chapter begins by offering some key linkages between pragmatist philosophy and contributions to social research by Charles Horton Cooley, George Herbert Mead, and Herbert Blumer. It then offers a brief glance at the varied landscape of symbolic interaction today and offers a general summary of the framework. From this foundation, it moves into analyses of data and corresponding analyses of symbolic interaction before concluding with discussion about the implications for social research and relevance for social justice.

SYMBOLIC INTERACTION: A BRIEF HISTORY

American pragmatists John Dewey and William James were particularly influential among scholars who were thinking about symbolic processes and social interaction (Reynolds, 2003b). Dewey distrusted the theoretical premise of what

---

[1]The philosophical school of pragmatism originated in the late 19th century. William James (1902) attributed the term *pragmatism* to Charles Sanders Peirce; however, Peirce never claimed to be the founder of modern pragmatism (Helle, 2005).

[2]"Darwinism taught pragmatists that it is perfectly possible to explain how the human species developed language as one among many sophisticated methods of survival, but it is difficult to see how human beings would have acquired the capacity to represent the universe as it actually is" (Baert, 2005, p. 129).

he called "spectator knowledge"—the idea that knowledge is based on the accurate observation and representation of existing realities. He, like other pragmatists, conceptualized knowledge production as an active process. Pragmatists argued that truth is not the property of an idea or thing; rather, truth is a process of becoming: truth is *made* true. "Truth lives, in fact, for the most part on a credit system. Our thoughts and beliefs 'pass,' so long as nothing challenges them, just as bank-notes pass so long as nobody refuses them" (James, 1948, pp. 163–164). Pragmatism shifted notions of truth from the academic to the everyday—from what scholars think about the world to the "everyday truths" that everyone encounters and uses as the basis of decisions and actions (Helle, 2005, pp. 35–36). Both pragmatism and symbolic interaction are defined in some measure in relation to these two key points regarding truth and knowledge: Truth is not the property of things, and truth is made true through everyday interactions.

William James's philosophy of instinct, habit, and self were also of key importance both to pragmatists and to the development of symbolic interaction. James was a Cartesian materialist—that is to say he believed that the self was identical with the brain. Like Descartes, he believed that bodily states follow from perception. He famously argued that people do not run from a bear because we are frightened; rather, we are frightened because we are running from a bear. James argued that given the human capacity for memory, repeated patterns of behavior must be understood as reflecting socially learned habits—not as basic instinct as had been thought previously.

For James (1902, 1948, 1971), the self was not an expression of some unitary inner being, but rather, it was the *effect* of caring about the opinions of distinct groups of people. This is particularly significant for two reasons. First, it means that the self is a social product—not a divine creation or a biologically determined one. Second, to the extent that individuals care about the opinions of many groups of people, each person could be said to have multiple selves. It is important to note this is not a postmodern notion of multiple selves but closer to a conflation of roles (e.g., parent, student, or athlete) and identity. Pragmatists believed that the potential of human nature could only be actualized in interaction with others; therefore, they were concerned with identifying the conditions that would most effectively develop that potential. Early scholars working in (what was to become) symbolic interaction drew strongly from these concepts in pragmatist philosophy to develop theories of self and interaction.

Table 4.1 Cartesian and Pragmatist Ontologies

Cartesian Dualism	Pragmatism
Ontological realism	Modified ontological realism
Subject = Person	Subject = Person
Subject/object dualism	Intersubjective
Objective truth	Truth is made true
Subjects have experiences	Subjects interpret experience
Language is neutral (transparent)	Language as symbolic communication

The influence of William James and John Dewey can be found in the ideas of Charles Horton Cooley, George Herbert Mead, and Herbert Blumer as well as in the most defining features of symbolic interaction: the looking-glass self, significant symbols, and lines of action. For example, Cooley's concept of a "looking-glass self" synthesized William James's philosophy of self and J. M. Baldwin's earlier theory of a looking-glass self. Cooley argued that a sense of self develops along two parallel lines: one in which the child develops a sense of power (agency) through her/his ability to manipulate the social and physical environment and one in which the child becomes aware of the fact that his or her own self-image reflects the imaginations of others concerning him/her. In this later sense, the self exists as an imaginative fact: People imagine how they are viewed by others and act accordingly.

Cooley, like James, believed that society does not restrict human behavior and creativity but rather, nurtures these and other qualities in social settings—social experience provides the conditions under which individuals develop. Cooley is linked to George Herbert Mead by a continuous analytic thread: the attempt to find a methodically satisfactory solution to the problem of the separation of subject and object (Helle, 2005, p. 53). Taking up this problem, George Herbert Mead extended what previously had been the province of psychology into sociology.

Mead belonged to an early tradition of scholars who viewed themselves as both philosophers and scientists: As a philosopher, Mead was a pragmatist, and as a scientist, he was a social behaviorist (Mead, 1962). Both fields mark his contributions to symbolic interaction. Mead (1962) drew from William James's concept of multiple selves to argue that institutional order is real only insofar as it is *realized* in performed roles (such as manager, parent, scholar); however, roles are *defined and rendered apparently objective* by institutions (Rousseau, 2002, pp. 238–239).

In order to develop a framework for understanding interaction, Mead drew from John Dewey. Like Dewey, Mead argued that in order to effectively understand social interaction, researchers need to examine how "lines of interaction" are fitted together in what he called flexible, ongoing, and spontaneous ways (Blumer, 2004). Mead contended that interactions are an ever-evolving series of gestures that can spontaneously change directions. For example, Mead wrote

> Much subtlety has been wasted on the problem of the meaning of meaning. It is not necessary, in attempting to solve this problem, to have recourse to psychical states, for the nature of meaning, as we have seen, is found to be implicit in the structure of the social act, implicit in the relations among its three basic individual components: namely the triadic relation of a gesture of one individual. A response to that gesture by a second individual, and a completion of the given social act initiated by the gesture of the first individual. (Mead, 1962, p. 81)

Mead's understanding of interaction is related to the pragmatist notion of truth. For Mead, as for the pragmatists, *truth* and *meaning* must be understood relative to purposeful action, rather than as expressions of relationships of correspondence to reality.

In addition, this excerpt makes clear Mead's social behaviorist perspective—both through his conceptualization of interaction as a linear trajectory as well as in his focus on social behavior—phenomenological processes of interaction, not interior processes of understanding. Further, as a social behaviorist, Mead theorized how individuals fit lines of interaction together by distinguishing between what he called gestures and significant gestures or significant symbols.

According to Mead, a gesture foreshadows action; gestures also presuppose a response on the part of the other. Mead offered dogfights as a classic example of gestures. Dogs signal a potential fight through their behavior, and this stimulates a response in another (Mead, 1962, p. 43). Gestures do not represent ideas nor do they stimulate ideas in response. People respond to gestures without thought or conscious awareness—much like a boxer responds to a punch.

Mead argued that in interaction people more often respond to a considered *interpretation* of gestures—what he called significant gestures or significant symbols. Significant gestures entail the use of symbols for specific meaning and hence become "language" (Mead, 1962). For example, one must interpret whether the person shaking her or his fists is expressing anger or playfulness. Any gesture will become a significant symbol if it is interpreted as indicating forthcoming lines of action—an anticipated future (Blumer, 2004, pp. 18–20).

According to Mead, interaction pivots on three key points. First, since the interpreted meaning of an action depends upon what the action appears to portend for the future, interaction is always conducted with regard to *anticipated* behavior. Second, in role-taking, one imaginatively rehearses the prospective action of the other person; hence, the social ceases to be a purely external event and assumes an interiorized relation. Third, activity is self-directed, not evoked; prospective actions are not simply reactions, rather they are intentionally chosen actions (Blumer 2004, pp. 30–31).

Mead's theorization of self and of lines of action influenced Herbert Blumer (1986, pp. 70–77), who drew from Mead to develop a distinction between a personal "I" (how one sees oneself) and a social "me" (how one imagines that one is seen by others). Blumer referred to the ongoing process of "conversation" between the "I" and the "me" as "self-indication." This process entails internal conversations, which include questions such as Should I say this? Will this joke be funny? Will I look foolish if I do this? To answer questions that we pose to ourselves, we must take the position of another person looking back at us. We then shape our behavior in response to her or his imagined perspective.

For Blumer (1986), the foundation of all social interaction rests in the process of representing ourselves to ourselves—of thinking about ourselves as we think about other objects of consciousness.[3] Joint action requires the ability to think about ourselves as we do others. Individuals fit lines of action together by first imagining how those with whom we are interacting might perceive us and then adjusting our behavior accordingly.[4] Thus people communicate

---

[3]Blumer (1986) delineates three types of objects: (1) social objects (such as children, professors, or painters), (2) abstract objects (concepts such as loyalty or compassion), and (3) physical objects (such as buildings, parks, open spaces, and desks). Physical environments are never "just" backdrops for social interaction; they are an important part of interaction because people assign both symbolic value and forms of agency to them (Smith & Bugni, 2006).

[4]While joint lines of action are generally orderly, they are necessarily open to uncertainties. Joint actions must be initiated; can be interrupted, abandoned, or transformed; and may be oriented to different premises. Even while definition of a joint action is shared, participants may take quite different lines of action: New situations may arise that call for new lines of joint action and participants may rely on considerations outside of the immediate context to interpret each other's lines of action (Blumer, 1986, pp. 71–72).

symbolically and imaginatively with others, and also with ourselves, as we experiment with potential lines of action in our minds.[5] In short, self-indications enable individuals to create meaningful, purposive action; to adjust to circumstances that emerge; and to imagine how others might react. In addition, the process of self-indication involves the concept of multiple selves. For example, a person will shape joint lines of action on campus (when thinking of one's self as a scholar) differently than she or he would at home around a dinner table (when thinking of one's self as a lover, spouse, or parent). Blumer believed that the salience of any identity is context dependent and therefore should be thought of as identity-in-use.[6] Since identities change over time—both in terms of substance and meaning—they are far from being fixed or permanent.

According to Blumer, the empirical world is always interpreted through a human imaginary (Blumer, 1986, p. 22). Therefore, all objects are social products that emerge out of social interaction; the meaning of an object exists in terms of how people make it meaningful. Yet Blumer was not a radical constructionist; he did not believe the world existed only in terms of the conceptions and images that people hold of it—Blumer argued that the world can and does "talk back." Blumer (1986) argued that reality does not necessarily bend to our conceptions of it; the task of a social science is to test the images and concepts that people use by scrutinizing the empirical world.

Although Blumer was concerned with the symbolic and interpretive processes of social life, he worked within a model of science that was derived from the physical sciences. Consequently, Blumer argued that human documents, such as life histories, can only make clear the *nature* of the interpretation, not its validity. Given the impossibility of providing truly exhaustive accounts of human behavior, Blumer sought *validation* for interpretations in statistical analyses that compared research findings with a control group (Blumer, 1986, pp. 123–126).

In 1937, Herbert Blumer characterized ongoing research regarding the use of significant symbols at the University of Chicago as "symbolic interaction"

---

[5]Social control is understood fundamentally as self-control (Blumer, 1986). Social disorganization is understood as the inability to mobilize action effectively, not as the failure of social structures.

[6]"The fluidity and multivocality of these identities also implies that socially constructed realities are likely to be characterized by multiple and changing meanings rather than fixed and shared ones. This is a point of departure for SI from the European phenomenological tradition, which tends to more strongly emphasize the intersubjective and shared aspects of reality construction. SI on the other hand, is definitely more concerned with the multiplicity of realities within any situation" (Prasad, 2005, p. 22).

(Platt, 1996, pp. 120–121). Today there is no single school of symbolic inter-action. Over the years, symbolic interaction has thrived in a variety of schools and genres, none of which represents a homogenous intellectual presence. At a minimum, some scholars have inflected symbolic interaction with feminist and critical race theories. Yet several distinctions have been institutionalized as par-ticular schools of symbolic interaction—although the number and significance of the schools continues to be strongly debated (cf. Denzin, 1992). With that caveat emptor, I want to note a few of the competing lines of thought that have emerged. These delineations are not intended to point to homogeneous schools that are absolutely distinct from each other but to provide a brief, descriptive overview that might be useful as a general heuristic for conceptualizing move-ments of thought.[7]

Roughly between the First and Second World Wars, social scientists work-ing at the University of Chicago began to move away from laboratory research and toward a more naturalistic mode of inquiry; their research is referred to as the first Chicago School (Travers, 2001, p. 18). This school includes scholars such as Robert Park, Herbert Blumer, Nels Anderson, W. I. Thomas, Louis Wirth, and Everett Hughes. Research from the first Chicago School is characterized by case studies and ethnographic fieldwork that tend to incorporate functionalist analyses and emphasize social competition for scarce resources. In addition, these studies draw particularly from the functionalist language of norms and values and rely on positivist standards of data analysis (Herman-Kinney & Verschaeve, 2003). Perhaps most notable among these ethnographies was *The Polish Peasant in Europe and America*, published in 1918 by Thomas and Znaniecki. As noted in Chapter 3, *The Polish Peasant in Europe and America*, although crafted in the causal language of physical sciences, broke new ground by examining life histo-ries (Musolf, 2003, pp. 92–93).[8] While *The Polish Peasant in Europe and America* broadened sociological notions of evidence in ways that were critically important to symbolic interactionists, it also drew strong criticism from Blumer (1941) and other symbolic interactionists for a lack of clear methodology.

The second Chicago School refers to research after the Second World War and today is commonly referred to simply as the Chicago School. The second

---

[7]It is beyond the scope of this book to provide analyses of the social, economic, and political contexts that gave rise to these schools. However, it is important to keep in mind that all research paradigms are products of such contexts.

[8]Thomas's axiom of "If men (sic) define situations as real, they are real in their consequences" has since become foundational in sociology (Musolf, 2003, p. 93).

Chicago School differs from the first in that it rejects generalizability as an analytic goal and focuses instead on internal validity and the production of theory. It includes the "new" ethnographies of Herbert Gans, Howard Becker, Elliot Liebow, Blanche Greer, and Elijah Anderson. These later ethnographies emphasize the unfolding and emergent nature of human interaction. In addition, the second Chicago School is characterized by sympathetic introspection, participant observation, and interviews—the hallmarks of contemporary ethnographic research.

By contrast, Manford Kuhn at the University of Iowa drew from the more behaviorist aspects of the first Chicago School, as well as from the physical sciences, to develop what came to be known as the Iowa School (Katovich, Miller, & Stewart, 2003). Kuhn emphasized the positivist features of Blumer's work—in particular standardization and hypothesis testing (Herman-Kinney & Verschaeve, 2003) and incorporated only those aspects of Blumer's and Mead's work that could be operationalized (Helle, 2005, p. 41). The result was quantitatively driven and expressed a more fundamentally deterministic view of human behavior. After Kuhn's death, Carl Couch continued a quantitative approach to symbolic interaction and created the New Iowa School (now referred to as the Iowa School). Couch incorporated a positivist approach with a pragmatist philosophical foundation; research in this school emphasizes the study of dyadic relationships over time.[9]

Yet Couch was not alone in developing a variation of Kuhn's first Iowa School. Jan Stets and Peter Burke also modified ideas from the original Iowa School to develop what is known as the Indiana School, which focuses on *structure*, both as the source of identity and action. In this framework, social roles are understood as expressions of social structures; the analytic emphasis concerns interactions between *roles* (parents, teacher, spouse, etc.) rather than between individuals (cf. Burke, 1980; Stryker, 1980). The Indiana School may be best known for its pioneering work in technology, particularly cybernetic models of mind and social interaction and artificial intelligence (Herman-Kinney & Verschaeve, 2003, p. 223).

At the University of Illinois, Norman Denzin cultivated what has come to be known as the Illinois School—a version of symbolic interactionism combined with postmodern and poststructural theories (Travers, 2001). The

---

[9]The Iowa School itself has been subdivided into four waves of research, each connected to Mead and Couch's empiricism but with distinctly different themes (Katovich, Miller, & Hintz, 2002).

Illinois School takes up the politics of representation by deconstructing symbolic practices, as well as by incorporating a psychoanalytic perspective. With a primary focus on cultural production and consumption, the Illinois School reorients symbolic interaction toward cultural studies. It also underscores the reflexive nature of interaction and extends the concept to researchers as well who must role-take (place themselves in the position of those they study) in order to make sense of interactions, objects, events, and contexts.

In this sense, symbolic interaction in the Illinois School involves a double hermeneutic: one involving the relationships and interpretations among participants, and another involving the researcher's relationship to, and interpretation of, the social context or interaction. The researcher is not just an observer but someone who is actively (re)constructing the process of meaning in order to be able to understand and interpret it (Helle, 2005, p. 19). In addition, researchers actively construct their findings for others—this could be said to constitute another double hermeneutic: one regarding the researcher's process of writing and one regarding the reader's interpretation of the text.

While the Chicago, Iowa, Indiana, and Illinois Schools constitute the *primary* variations of contemporary symbolic interaction, some scholars identify two subfields of symbolic interaction: dramaturgy and ethnomethodology. Erving Goffman (1959b, 1967) argued that the process of interpretively recreating social knowledge has an essentially dramatic structure that makes reality appear to simply unfold—hence Goffman developed what now is called dramaturgy. The influence of Cooley's looking-glass self is evident in Goffman's concept of dramaturgy. Goffman took the premise that, in interaction, each person behaves (consciously or not) in ways that attempt to manage the impressions that others might gain of them—in effect, individuals put on a "show," or performance, for others. Goffman's dramaturgical framework centers issues of role-taking, as well as front stage and backstage performances. Goffman also drew from Cooley's work on emotion, specifically regarding pride and shame (Scheff, 2005). In particular, Goffman (1963) famously examined shame in relation to stigmatized performances. In his later work, Goffman shifted his analytical emphasis from face-to-face interaction to frame analysis, which regards broader aspects of language. This shift remains controversial, with some scholars choosing to ignore frame analysis as a blemish on an otherwise brilliant career and others asserting that his research on frame analysis was the pinnacle of his intellectual achievement.

The second of these subfields is ethnomethodology, which was developed by Harold Garfinkel. Concerned with the production of apparently natural social worlds, Garfinkel (1967) pursued a distinctively different path in order to examine the *assumptions* underlying the meaning-making processes of ordinary activities in daily life. Ethnomethodology is discussed in detail in Chapter 5; for now, suffice it to say that ethnomethodological research is characterized by a primary concern: How is a particular social activity done and what must be assumed in doing it?

It is important to repeat that there are fundamental challenges to nearly all delineations of interactionist schools. For example, while some scholars (Boden, 1990; Denzin, 1970) consider the general project of ethnomethodology to be congruent with symbolic interaction, others (Maynard & Clayman, 2003) have argued that it is *fundamentally incompatible* with symbolic interaction. In addition, although both symbolic interaction and ethnomethodology claim Erving Goffman as part of their lineages, in his lifetime, he chose not to affiliate with either. More generally, scholars continue to debate whether researchers should refer to symbolic interaction or symbolic interactionism; the latter is contested as an inappropriate reification. While a rich debate continues, I will sketch the basic principles of symbolic interaction as an interpretive framework in the following section.

THE BASIC PREMISE OF SYMBOLIC INTERACTION

Today, symbolic interaction is most often practiced as a loose amalgam of Cooley's "looking-glass self" and Blumer's sociological interpretation of Mead's theories. Generally, symbolic interaction is associated with three basic tenets.[10] First, people act toward things based on the meanings that the things hold for them (Blumer, 1986). A tree might be a sacred object for one person, an example of a particular botanical species for another, and cubits of lumber

---

[10]Manis and Meltzer provide seven principles of symbolic interaction: (1) Distinctively human behavior and interaction are carried on through the medium of symbols and their meanings. (2) The individual becomes humanized through interaction with other persons. (3) Human society is most usefully conceived as consisting of people in interaction. (4) Human beings are active in shaping their own behavior. (5) Consciousness, or thinking, involves interaction with oneself. (6) Human beings construct their own behavior in the course of its execution. (7) An understanding of human conduct requires study of the actors' covert behavior (Manis & Meltzer, 1978, pp. 6–8 in Musolf, 2003, p. 104).

for another. Each person will act toward the tree on the basis of the meaning it holds for him or her. This first tenet is a critical but not a defining feature of symbolic interaction.

Second, the meanings of things are generated over time through human interaction (Blumer, 1986). The source of meaning for symbolic interaction is collective; it is not individually determined nor is it intrinsic to objects. This is a key point for symbolic interaction and one that distinguishes it from analytic realism in which a chair is seen as a chair in and of itself. In symbolic interaction, objects and events are never just backdrops for interaction. Mead (1962) argued that people imagine not only the likely positions of other people but also the objects and places with which we interact. Consequently, inanimate objects can be understood to have a kind of agency in that they have profound and integral effects on human responses and interactions. The field of material culture is socially alive.[11]

Third, meanings are modified during interaction through interpretive processes (Blumer, 1986). A sense of meaning involves an interpretive process during which an individual communicates with him/herself; in the process of self-indication, he or she may come to suspend, regroup, or transform meanings. For example, in the course of reflecting on cutting down trees, a logger may come to see trees not as lumber but as sacred objects to be protected.

As a qualitative interpretive framework, symbolic interaction is dependent on the procedural techniques of analytic induction or grounded theory. As described in Chapter 3, analytic induction and grounded theory both rely on inductive logic and empirical evidence in localized contexts. Common modes of study for symbolic interactionists include ethnography, participant observation, life history, unstructured interviews, focus groups, as well as textual and visual media (including photographs, film, and vlogs) analyses.

Significantly, Blumer (1933, 1986) believed that the task of media was to accurately reflect the empirical world; in this sense, Blumer treated film as an iconographic sign that represented the real world. Consequently, from this perspective, the primary task of media analyses necessarily regards the

---

[11]This perspective is distinctly different from ethnomethodology in which inanimate objects are generally not analyzed in the production of meaning.

success or failure (the relative accuracy) of the media's reflection of the world it claimed to represent. Blumer (1933, 1986) also asserted a causal relationship between film and the social behavior of audiences, although he never developed a method of analysis that could pursue the relationship. Contemporary scholars (cf. Clough, 1988, 2000; Denzin, 1992, 2002b) associated with the Illinois School have developed analyses of media analysis that go well beyond Blumer's realist conceptions—often by combining symbolic interaction with poststructuralist and/or psychoanalytical theory. I turn next to a practical application of symbolic interaction, followed by reflexive analyses.

ANALYSIS OF NEWSPAPER, TELEVISION, AND INTERVIEW EXEMPLARS

This section uses what might be called the tenets of mainstream symbolic interaction associated with the Chicago School highlighted in the previous overview. Subsequent sections present exemplars from three forms of empirical data (newspaper, television, and interview) as done in Chapter 3. They are the same exemplars with the same brief contextualizing overviews. After analyzing each exemplar, I then reflect on how the various philosophical commitments of symbolic interaction shaped my analysis. As in Chapter 3, I conclude the chapter by considering the relevance of ontology and epistemology to social justice.

Newspaper Analysis

The purportedly objective nature of news reporting makes it a particularly interesting site for analysis. News stories are carefully crafted narratives that select and assemble a narrow range of sources and events from a wide range of possibilities. Through multiple revisions and edits, a story is shaped into an apparently linear "news event." Despite this well-established process, the general public commonly reads a news story as a *description* of an event. This holds particular promise and pitfalls for social researchers. What is the most effective way of analyzing news articles? Symbolic interaction provides a distinctive framework.

Newspaper Exemplar

Being a double amputee is not often described as an unfair advantage, but that is the argument made by the governing body of world athletics, the International Association of Athletics Federation (IAAF) in newspaper articles about Oscar Pistorius, a 20-year-old South African runner. Pistorius was born without fibulae in his legs; his parents, on the advice of multiple medical experts, had their son's legs amputated just beneath the knee when he was 11 months old (Philip, 2005). Pistorius has run for many years in the para-Olympics with record performances in this and other events at 100 meters (10.91 seconds), 200 meters (21.58 seconds), and 400 meters (46.34 seconds) (Longman, 2007). While those times do not meet Olympic qualifying standards for men, Pistorius is fast enough that his marks "would have won gold medals in equivalent women's races at the 2004 Athens Olympics" (Longman, 2007).

When the Beijing Games were still 15 months away, Pistorius petitioned the IAAF to run in the 2008 Olympics. I examined newspaper articles about Pistorius's petition and the IAAF administrative response and found that administrators, athletes, and ethicists argued that Pistorius's prosthetic legs create a potentially unfair advantage for him over runners with biological legs. The following newspaper excerpt is an exemplar of coverage on the issue:

"The rule book says a foot has to be in contact with the starting block," Leon Fleiser, a general manager of the South African Olympic Committee, said. "What is the definition of a foot? Is a prosthetic device a foot, or is it an actual foot?"

I.A.A.F. officials have also expressed concern that Pistorius could topple over, obstructing others or injuring himself and fellow competitors. Some also fear that, without limits on technological aids, able-bodied runners could begin wearing carbon-fiber plates or other unsuitably springy devices in their shoes.

Among ethicists, Pistorius's success has spurred talk of "transhumans" and "cyborgs." Some note that athletes already modify themselves in a number of ways, including baseball sluggers who undergo laser eye surgery to enhance their vision and pitchers who have elbow reconstruction using sturdier ligaments from elsewhere in the body. At least three disabled athletes have competed in the Summer Olympics: George Eyser, an American, won a gold medal in gymnastics while competing on a wooden leg at the 1904 Games in St. Louis; Neroli Fairhall, a paraplegic from New Zealand, competed in archery in the 1984 Olympics in Los Angeles; and Marla Runyan, a legally blind runner from the United States, competed in the 1,500 meters at the 2000 Olympics in Sydney. But Pistorius would be the first amputee to compete in a track event, international officials said.

A sobering question was posed recently on the Web site of the Connecticut-based Institute for Ethics and Emerging Technologies. "Given the arms race nature of competition," will technological advantages cause "athletes to do something as seemingly radical as having their healthy natural limbs replaced by artificial ones?" wrote George Dvorsky, a member of the institute's board of directors. "Is it self-mutilation when you're getting a better limb?" (Longman, 2007).

This excerpt demonstrates how "disability" emerges as a product of inter-subjective social agreements about what constitutes ability/disability, rather than as the result of any particular physical, emotional, or mental characteristic. The excerpt illustrates that social agreements regarding the nature of disability are reached over time, in multiple contexts, and by multiple actors. In some respects, the excerpt also demonstrates how such social agreements can change; in the article, the meaning of being a double amputee shifts from a disadvantage to a potential advantage.

At issue for IAAF officials is the kind of body that Pistorius has—not his ability to meet required starting times or his ability to run the distance of the race. The article demonstrates how the meaning of disability is created not in relation to *ability* but in relation to a conventional body—not even necessarily an athletic body. Because disability gains meaning through the perception of bodies, rather than abilities, the article is able to characterize an Olympic gold medal winner, George Eyser, as disabled. To the extent that disability is framed in relation to an idealized human body, eye surgery and elbow reconstruction can be understood as *restoring* elements of a "natural" body rather than as *replacing* them—which begins the journey to becoming "transhuman."

Pistorius's Olympic bid is symbolically framed as a moral contest between humans and technology that threatens to redefine the ideal body—and indeed challenges the meaning of humanness. Further, by placing the human body, rather than athletic ability, at the center of the discussion about disability, the article constructs Pistorius as a potential threat to human bodies. Consider for instance Dvorsky's concern that Pistorius might inspire other athletes to willingly amputate their own legs.

Although people may have different limbs, sense faculties, and so forth, *disability* is the product of how the social environment and cultural institutions interpret and respond to those differences—becoming disabled is a symbolic and interactional process. Pistorius's bid for admission to the Olympics is a clear (if implicit) assertion that he rejects limitations associated with being labeled *disabled*—and consequently, rejects the cultural meanings of ability and disability produced through idealized bodies. This rejection seems to be at the core of the IAAF's apparent troubles. Embodiment that diverges from a hegemonic ideal remains deliberative grounds for disqualification as the meaning of disability slides from being a potential disadvantage to being a potential advantage.

Analyzing the Analysis

Symbolic interaction is not a form of textual analysis per se; it enables the researcher to bring broader concepts and theories to bear on the reading of the text.[12] For example, to analyze disability as a symbolic process, I made reference to "social agreements" about disability. At the most basic level, the preceding analysis illustrates the ways that various actors (Pistorius, the IAAF, and ethicists) respond to the range of meanings that ability/disability hold for each. Yet none is acting from an individual construction of meaning—the tenacity of the various meanings has been established over time and through multiple contexts. And they remain open to challenge—as is evident both in Pistorius's bid for Olympic competition and as the meaning of being a double amputee shifts from a disadvantage to a potential advantage.

However, as in Chapter 3, the analysis does not substantially address the symbolic construction of ability. Human bodies are treated as a *referent* rather than a symbolic construction in and of themselves. In this sense, ability is still the unmarked center from which difference is measured. Overall, the analysis demonstrates how the meaning of humanness is tethered to an idealized body as the article raises the question of cyborgs and transhumans. While the analysis is not tightly tied to the text, broader considerations, such as athletic segregation and the effects of race and gender, are inaccessible because they are not reflected in the text. Again this likely appears to be a matter of common sense—why should researchers analyze what is not in the text?

---

[12]This is why, in part, some ethnomethodologists seek to distance the two frameworks. In addition, in symbolic interaction, researchers often verify their emerging understandings of an ethnographic context through interviews with key informants. In ethnomethodology, this process of verification is problematic and will be discussed in Chapter 5.

Rooted to a pragmatist philosophy, the analysis does not rely upon, or offer, a fixed notion of reality but rather examines a series of negotiations through which Pistorius is symbolically constructed as "disabled," despite his ability to run competitively. However, the analysis also relies upon the procedural technique of analytic induction—the exemplar is brought to the page through analytic induction. What are the effects of combining a process of formalization/systemization that relies on a Cartesian ontology, with a process of interpretation, which relies on a pragmatist ontology?

First, the analysis treats the newspaper article as a transparent accounting of news; it does not examine how events are assembled to appear as news. However, this could simply be a shortcoming of the researcher's analysis. There is nothing in symbolic interaction that would preclude an analysis of the symbolic construction of news—although this omission is extremely common among symbolic interactionist analyses. So while it is possible to argue that the influence of a Cartesian ontology might foreclose or restrict the analytical impulse to study news as a cultural product, for now I want to simply acknowledge that the analysis (as done) examines the symbolic production of disability, and at another level, it also replicates the realist ontology that it resists. The competing theoretical foundations have perhaps clearer effects where the analysis encounters many of the same limitations as in Chapter 3 regarding the nature of evidence and the production of knowledge.

If people create the meaning of social realities through symbolic interactions, we must accept a limitless number of layers to the meaning-making process. Given that all meaning is a link in an infinite chain of meanings, at what point(s) can/should the researcher bracket the meaning-making processes? Symbolic interaction is rooted to a Cartesian ontology through the procedural techniques of analytic induction/grounded theory. The process of formalization determines, most broadly, what can count as potential evidence. Consequently, my examination of meaning-making processes is confined to localized contexts—even though epistemologically, I take up an interpretive analysis of meaning-making processes.

The resonance of a Cartesian ontology also is evidenced in the subject/object dualism that enables the analysis to appear to write itself. Because there is no consideration of how the researcher is constructing data, evidence, or meaning, the analysis creates the appearance of objective (if interpretive) knowledge. The analysis lacks reflexivity—both as a critical expression of self-awareness and more broadly as an acknowledgment of the symbolically mediated, intersubjective relational process of social research.

Although experience is understood as an interpretive process, the analytical process can obscure the locus of agency and the meaning of subjectivity. The early founders of symbolic interaction equated subjects with persons and hence directed their analyses to the production of identities-in-use. Today, mainstream symbolic interaction acknowledges the fluidity of identities but also conflates identities with roles (parent, scholar, banker). This is particularly problematic, not only because some identities are more fixed and permanent than others, but also because it reduces identity to roles. For example, many scholars today would assert that gender, sexuality, and race are *subject locations*, not roles, precisely because there is no place to stand outside of them.

An implicitly Cartesian concept of subjectivity is evidenced in the treatment of disability and ability as dichotomous and fixed positions—even as symbolic interaction demonstrates that the meaning of those positions is culturally created. There is no empirical evidence in the article that would support an analysis of the ways that segregation makes it possible for "able-bodied" athletes and audiences to ignore the ways in which all ability exists on a continuum—or that such segregation also encourages "able-bodied" athletes and audiences to ignore how their own behavior *produces* what they have come to perceive as "disability" in others.

Also, in the earlier analysis, the question of agency never explicitly arises because it is implicitly assumed as a property of a Cartesian subject. The ability of "disabled" athletes to participate in the Olympics is constrained in this article by the external force of the Olympic vetting process—through the exercise of its own agency. Congruently, the analysis does not problematize the nature of experience—it is simply something that individuals have. In this sense, experience seems to be constituted in an interactional environment.

Finally, because Pistorius's gender, race, and class are never mentioned in the article, they fall outside the context available for analysis and hence appear to be irrelevant. Yet as a South African who was born without fibulae, his race, class, and gender have much to contribute to his success as an Olympic athlete. Had they been mentioned in the article, I could have brought cultural knowledge and social theory regarding whiteness, wealth, and masculinity to bear on the analysis. Analyses of the symbolic construction of ability and disability (which are rooted to a pragmatist ontology) are dramatically shaped and constrained by the demands of Cartesian ontology, which forms the basis of analytic induction/grounded theory.

Television Analysis

Generally television dramas are premised on the commonsense attitude of ontological realism—viewers believe that the drama is a realistic portrayal, even if this requires temporarily suspending particular moments of disbelief. Audiences are invited to engage in a kind of voyeurism, in which the drama serves as a private window into events unfolding, apparently spontaneously, in the lives of others. For researchers, the pitfalls of approaching television shows with an analytic foundation premised on ontological realism are obvious. Yet it would seem from existing media studies in mainstream social sciences that such an approach is equally hard to avoid. To what extent does symbolic interaction offer promising insights?

Television Exemplar

The ABC drama *Brothers and Sisters* features a white, upper-class family in Southern California involved in the daily dramas of a family-run business—complicated (of course) by interpersonal relationships and family intrigues. The series is unusual in that one of the adult siblings in the Walker family is gay, which makes it a potentially interesting site for examining talk about sexuality. I examined shows from the first season and found two relevant patterns.

First, scenes consistently allowed for multiple and contradictory audience engagements with politically controversial issues related to sexuality. *Brothers and Sisters* commonly dramatizes political issues that affect many families in the United States—particularly with regard to same-sex marriage and the Republican/Democrat partisan divides that characterized the George W. Bush administration.

Second, scenes consistently left disagreements about sexuality unresolved. The show framed these disagreements within the contexts of family intimacy, human frailty, and political aspirations—and typically used humor to drain or divert dramatic tension when very harsh or divisive conflict threatened to break out.

The following excerpt features a scene between siblings Kitty Walker, played by Calista Flockhart, and Kevin Walker, played by Matthew Rhys. Kitty enters this scene having just come from a meeting with Republican Senator

(Continued)

(Continued)

Robert McCallister (played by Rob Lowe), who offered her a position as head of communications for his presidential campaign. Their meeting holds particular significance to the following scene for two reasons: Kitty and her deceased father have been the only Republicans in a family with strong Democrat affiliations, and it exposed romantic tension between Kitty and the senator, who is a father of two young children and is in the process of a divorce.

Kitty has just mentioned the job offer to her brother, Kevin, who is an attorney and the only gay primary character in the show in the first season.[13] As the scene opens, Kevin is upset with Kitty because Robert McCallister has voted in favor of a constitutional ban on same-sex marriage. Throughout this scene, Kitty is preoccupied with the mail while Kevin is consumed by the conversation; the camera alternates with the speaker, taking the view of the listener.

Kevin: Well, why *you?*

Kitty: Well, what the hell does that mean?

Kevin: [*stuttering*] Well, c-cause it's completely absurd. You can't work for this guy!

Kitty: Why? [*Kitty laughs.*] Why, Kevin? Because he's a Republican?

Kevin: No, because he's against gay marriage!

Kitty: There are lots of people in the world, Kevin, for instance *me*, who have no problem with gay people but still believe that marriage is fundamentally a religious institution that has nothing to do with the [*camera turns to Kevin who is visibly upset*] state and that does not discount civil unions or domestic partnerships or anything you . . . .

Kevin: [*Voice escalates*] Oh come on! That's just a cover that people like you provide for people like him who hate people like me.

[*Kitty shakes her head.*]

Kitty: Oh, Kevin! Please, let's not make it personal.

Kevin: Ah, ah . . . [*Raises eyebrows*] Personal? Kitty, in 10 years . . . in 20 years, when I am finally . . . m-mature enough to sustain a committed relationship I would like to settle down and get married. That's personal.

[*Kitty stops glancing through mail and looks up to speak.*]

---

[13]Subsequent seasons have included several other white gay men.

Kitty: That's improbable.

Kevin: Don't take this job, Kitty. I'm warning you it will cause a great deal of . . . .

Kitty: Wait a minute. Wait, wait, wait, wait, wait a minute. You're *warning* me?

[*Brothers and Sisters,* Episode 11: "Family Day" 1/7/07]

Brothers and Sisters, like all television shows, finds an audience by representing the social world in ways that resonate with large numbers of people. Viewers become part of a regular audience when they reliably find characters and situations with which they can identify in reality or in fantasy. In this sense, studies of popular media can offer important insights into contemporary social life. For example, the excerpt from *Brothers and Sisters* both draws upon and exposes the tensions that exist in many contemporary U.S. families around issues of same-sex marriage and politics. The excerpt highlights these tensions in the argument that arises between Kitty and Kevin in response to McCallister's job offer to Kitty.

Throughout the show, and in this scene, Kitty represents the current "moderate" Republican view that asserts marriage is a religious issue having nothing to do with the state or with quality of life issues. Her family more consistently represents positions associated with "liberal" Democrats. Yet with regard to this particular issue, only Kevin, who is gay, advances marriage as a civil rights issue that regards basic equality; other family members are silent on the issue. In this scene, Kevin advances an emotional response rather than an analysis of how the state is involved in allocating special rights to married people. The emotionality may bring to light that this is a personal issue for him as a gay man, or it may frame this as a sibling conflict; it also may raise some questions about his maturity and masculinity in ways that are consistent with dominant homophobic views.

Kevin's response and his difficulty in maintaining intimate relationships (again an element of a homophobic discourse) are parlayed into a sibling conflict between an older sister and younger brother—which enables both interpretations of the conflict to coexist. While sibling intimacy *enables* a conversation about personal and political differences that emerge in relationship to same-sex marriage, as a political argument begins to unfold, Kevin de-escalates the conflict from a political debate to a sibling spat through self-deprecating characterizations of his own marital aspirations. The show thus brings up political issues but reduces them to personal differences by stripping arguments of their political/social value.

Analyzing the Analysis

Consistent with the Chicago School, this analysis takes up media representations as being reflective of social life. It provides some insight into how political tensions in the show are introduced and averted as well as demonstrating how multiple interpretations of the scene would enable a broad range of viewers to find their own political values validated by the show. While the analysis takes up the issue of representation from the point of view of potential audiences, we lack the necessary audience for making arguments regarding the dialogic relationship between audiences and representations.

Similarly, the analysis does not take up the *construction* of television shows—the deliberate practices of writers, editors, producers, actors, and advertisers. Although the scene is acknowledged as a constructed representation, "mainstream" symbolic interaction does not provide the necessary tools for analyzing the processes of representation that would be relevant to this scene. As a consequence, even though the analysis critiques representational practices, agency seems to be limited to what one sees—the lines of action taken (or not taken). This is consistent with the realist ontology of a Cartesian framework and contributes to the somewhat transparent quality of representation: The show appears to be the equivalent of social life, which leaves the meaning of experience in a liminal state that is at best irrelevant and at worst the property of the television characters. The analysis carries an implicit Cartesian understanding of social subjects as equivalent to persons—even if those persons are fictional.

While the symbolic interactionist epistemology expresses the commitments of a pragmatist philosophy directed at processes of interpretation, the analytical focus expresses those of a Cartesian ontology embedded in analytic induction. This is evident by the notion of evidence that is bracketed in such a way as to focus only on what is on the screen, or in this case in the transcript. Clough (2000, p. 92) argued that television is not narrative media but rather is a ceaseless flow, an endless circulation of information and images. This flow cannot be accounted for in my analyses because it is rooted to the processes of analytic induction. In addition, because no one talks about race, gender, ability, or class, there is no evidence to analyze in this excerpt. Hence, these systematic forms of cultural privilege appear to be irrelevant to representations of and political debates about sexuality.

Interview Analysis

Historically, scholars working with symbolic interaction have tended to produce ethnographies; interviews are an important cornerstone of ethnographic study. However, the strong emphasis on behavioral observation in symbolic interaction leads researchers to use interviews to check the validity of the researcher's emerging interpretations of events and situations in the ethnographic context (Cahill, 1987). My analysis of my interview with Tony Romero attends only to symbolic elements rather than to processes of verification, which exceed the structure of the example.

Interview Exemplar

While dominant public discourses in the United States construct race as natural, and apparently self-evident, in interviews with Native American Indians, I found that talk about race consistently exposed the social, historical, and legal processes of racialization. The exemplar that follows is from my interview with Tony Romero an Esselen Indian. It is important to note that in the early 1900s, Esselen Indians (indigenous to the land that came to be called California) were declared "extinct" by the U.S. government. The federal government's policy of recognition for Native Americans requires genealogical evidence of unbroken ancestry over hundreds of years. Indigenous nations unable to provide that evidence were "terminated" by the government—that is to say denied federal recognition that would have entitled them to land and other settlement claims, as well as university scholarships and other forms of affirmative action candidacy. The Esselens, however, were never officially terminated but rather declared "extinct."

The federal declaration of their "extinction" has become part of a dominant cultural discourse. For example, the *Economist* featured an article on the Esalen [*sic*] Institute, and described it as "named after the Esselen, a now-extinct Indian tribe that used the place as their burial ground. In 1910 the Murphy family bought the land from homesteaders" (*The Economist*, 2007). The Esalen Institute is a spa/retreat center that has drawn renowned authors including John Steinbeck, Aldous Huxley, and Henry Miller. In the 1950s, the beat poets visited Esalen, and it later became a home to Alan Watts (*The Economist*, 2007).

In the following excerpt from my interview with Tony Romero in 2000, he talks about growing up in California as an Esselen Indian.

(Continued)

(Continued)

Celine-Marie: I wonder if you could tell me what it was like for you growing up and crossing worlds between your family and your home and the rest of the culture you experienced around you.

Tony: Well grownin' up, uh, growin' up, I remember my mom and dad always told me, "Don't tell anybody you're Indian." Uh, they were scared because I had uncles that were either drug behind horses or hung just 'cause they said they were Native American Indians. I have documentation of that. I had a couple of my relatives that were hung in a barn in Carmel Valley 'cause they wouldn't sell their property.

Celine-Marie: I'm so sorry.

Tony: It's things like that that happened in those days, and you know were talkin' like the '50s—1950s—and things like that were still goin' on like I remember when I was in high school I used to go down Monterey, I used to go to Louis' Bar on Alvarado Street. My uncle used to hang out, and there were two Obispo used to hang out in front of Louis' all the time and sit, they used to have these benches in front of all the pool halls. They were like, I guess there were like 10 or 12 pool halls you know on Alvarado Street and all these bars. So the Indians always used to carry these little pints of whiskey. I'll never forget the whiskey bottles cause they're, they're made in a shape where you can put 'em in your back pocket and they just fit perfect cause they had a little concave, concave shape to 'em.

Celine-Marie: Mmm.

Tony: And, uh, I remember 'em always sippin' out them damn whiskey bottles and, uh, but I remember one time I was comin' out of Louis' pool hall and my uncle was fightin' with these two white guys. He was tellin' how they were on his land, he didn't like it you know, he was feelin' a little tipsy there. So then I just ignored him, went across the street with some friends of mine to another place. And about a half an hour later I came back out and my uncle was sittin' on the same bench but he had a bloody nose, his eye was all black and blue, what they did was, they drug him in the back alley, beat the shit out of him to teach him a lesson, you know, that it wasn't his land anymore, it was theirs. And, uh, it was things like that that happened in Monterey where my mother was scared. She said well don't tell anybody you're Indian, tell 'em you're Spanish. So then when I *did* tell people I was Spanish and Indian, the first thing that came into mind was you're *Mexican.* I said no, no. I said bein' a Spanish Indian didn't make you Mexican. It wasn't the idea that I was ashamed of bein' a Mexican, it was the idea of wanting to be called what I really *was.* And I wasn't a Mexican. And I *knew* that and my parents knew that and, uh, so anyway, I went through that through my whole school years. You know OK, Tony, you're Spanish and Indian but you're Mexican. I says no. So anyway I had to go through this whole thing when I was a kid. I was always, I was always, when I was a kid I was always fightin' to protect my heritage.

Celine-Marie: Mmm.

Tony: Always fightin' you know to show people I was Native American Indian and I was proud of it. But then, uh, after a while I just, I just ignored the whole thing. But then after my mom passed away, I will never forget my mom passed away in 1970, she, uh, she looked at me and says you're Native American Indian. She said be proud of it. I'll never forget that. She says you're Esselen Indian. She said be proud of it. And, uh, so ever since then I've been fightin' for my recognition as a Native American Indian. I'm doin' it not only for her, but for my family, you know my existing family I have now, which isn't much.

Through a narrative defined by conflicts (internal and external) Tony represents himself as both a victim and a warrior. His identification as an Esselen Indian is anchored to a life history that seems to revolve around pool halls, whiskey pints, and various forms of social and cultural violence. Tony represents his survival as an Esselen Indian—perhaps economically as well as physically—as being dependent upon becoming culturally invisible. Yet if his parents' admonition to deny that he was Esselen Indian protected him from racist violence, it also enacted another form of violence characterized by continuing forms of conflict in Tony's life. Further, the cultural invisibility that saved the lives of Esselen Indians also advanced a quite lethal form of violence by enabling the U.S. government to declare them extinct. If the word *extinction* conjures species of plants, animals, and insects, it works here to mask the more appropriate word *genocide*. Metaphorically, Tony's mother gave birth to a "new" Tony on her deathbed when she told Tony to stop hiding his identity, to be proud, and to never forget that he is Esselen Indian. The excerpt ends with a claim to cultural citizenship as Tony pursues both personal and cultural visibility by launching a fight for the Federal recognition of the Esselen Nation.

Analyzing the Analysis

This analysis offers some broad and interesting insights into symbolic processes at work in this interview. It seems to articulate key concepts of pragmatist philosophy: Identities are negotiated and changeable, and social life is understood as an emerging process, rather than as a defined reality. In addition, my focus on symbolic processes moves the analysis away from ontological realism. Yet the philosophical commitments are not entirely clear. Notably, my analysis did not problematize subjectivity, agency, or experience; hence, they appear to be either irrelevant or self-evident—qualities of a Cartesian ontology in either case. Although symbolic interaction understands experience as an interpretive process, the analytical process obscures the locus of agency and the nature of experience.

The system of formalization (analytic induction) is evident through the implicit ontological realism that dominates the analysis. In addition, it is evident as well in the way the analysis is presented as transparent—written by no one in particular. To the extent that interviews appear to be less constructed (there are not hosts of writers, editors, and advertisers that escape the analytical frame), interviews can seem to be more objectively accessible and more effective forms of social research. Again, these are features of ontological realism. Although my analysis concerns symbolic processes of interpretation in the *narrative*, the analysis is not self-reflexive with respect to the production of knowledge. The researcher always frames the analysis—bringing some things to the fore and leaving others behind. This process alone must undermine the belief that interviews are not constructed events.

IMPLICATIONS FOR SOCIAL RESEARCH

Symbolic interaction is a process of interpretation that draws from American Pragmatism and which also relies on a Cartesian framework for the process of formalization that generates evidence. The double nature of symbolic interaction as rooted to *both* philosophical pragmatism and Cartesian dualism enables the proliferation of schools with apparently contradictory approaches to social life and social research. On the one hand, symbolic interaction is practiced as an interpretive framework—leading some to incorporate poststructuralism. On the other hand, its grounding in Cartesian dualism leads others to implement it as a quantitative strategy committed to models of scientific inquiry associated with physical sciences. To the extent that both pragmatist and Cartesian ontologies are present in symbolic interaction analyses, schools with completely oppositional ontological and epistemological frameworks share the same rubric of symbolic interaction.

The pragmatist and Cartesian cross-currents enable and disable quite a variety of potential analyses. This also produces a sizable dilemma in which human interactions (and representations of human interaction) are reduced to, or made equivalent to, free will. Symbolic interaction is not able to get at unconscious processes or the constraining effects of cultural forces. Further, Mead's notion of multiple selves, reduced to social roles, seems to mask an underlying commitment to a Cartesian self who enacts the various roles. This is presumably what Blumer called "the self that is known only to the self"—a purely transcendent self that is not shaped by, or known to, others.

Further, while symbolic interaction emphasizes the way definitions and shared meanings are worked out between people in a localized setting, it has some trouble getting at routine relations of power. As in Chapter 3, the commitment to a particular kind of empirical evidence left me unable to analyze race, class, gender, and ability as routine relations of power and privilege—both with respect to Oscar Pistorius and the representation of same-sex marriage in the *Brothers and Sisters* excerpt. In the transcript of my interview with Tony Romero, I was able to analyze the symbolic meanings of being an Esselen Indian but unable to analyze the processes of racialization or the production of whiteness that is critical to the meanings of being an Esselen Indian in his narrative. Further masculinity, heterosexuality, whiteness, and ability, as unmarked categories of privilege, appear to be irrelevant. Scientific reality creates a particular type of order by enclosing (i.e., ordering) phenomena that fit within that which has already been ordered; science is a way of creating order out of chaos, albeit "at a cost" (Latour & Woolgar, 1986, p. 246). Ultimately, even as I pursued processes of symbolic meaning, my analyses reified categories of race, gender, sexuality, class, and ability.

CONCLUDING THOUGHTS

While symbolic interaction can tell us a great deal about the processes of representation through which social life is constructed, it carries analytical constraints that prevent analyses of forms of power that produce and shape the localized context.[14] In localized contexts, a commonsense view necessarily reduces subjects to persons because there is no way to apprehend the processes of subjectification. If interpretive frameworks do not allow us to take up questions of subjectivity, how are we to understand social locations, such as race, gender, class, sexuality, and ability? They must be understood as real conditions that have symbolic meanings—they are features of a real world that in Blumer's words "talks back to us." This seems to imply that while we can (perhaps) change the associated symbolic meanings, these categories are vested with an inherent existence. The implications of this view raise serious concerns. For example, if the ability to recognize race is itself a product of racism (Memmi, 2000), scholars must ask what is the liberatory potential of analyzing the shifting symbolic meanings of race? While symbolic interaction is a very useful framework for social research, its promise for disrupting relations of power and generating insights into the creation of research useful to social justice seems to be more limited—despite the best intentions of researchers. The unresolved paradigmatic conflicts embedded in symbolic interaction create logical inconsistencies that are broadly relevant to social research.

FURTHER READING

Blumer, H. (1986). *Symbolic interaction: perspective and method.* Berkeley: University of California Press.

Blumer, H. (2004). *George Herbert Mead and human conduct.* Walnut Creek, CA: AltaMira Press.

Clough, P. T. (1989). Letters from Pamela: Reading Howard S. Becker's writing(s) for social scientists. *Symbolic Interaction, 12,* 159–170.

Denzin, N. K. (1992). *Symbolic interactionism and cultural studies.* New York: Blackwell.

Helle, H. J. (2005). *Symbolic interaction and verstehen* (Vol. 4). New York: Peter Lang.

Reynolds, L. T., & Herman-Kinney, N. J. (Eds.). (2003). *Handbook of symbolic interactionism.* Walnut Creek, CA: AltaMira Press.

---

[14]These are precisely the limitations that scholars in the Illinois School have attempted to address by incorporating poststructural and psychoanalytic frameworks into symbolic interaction.

CHAPTER FIVE

ETHNOMETHODOLOGY

INTRODUCTION

The emergence of ethnomethodology is often understood as a critical response to the structural–functionalism that once dominated both theory and methods in the social sciences. Harold Garfinkel developed ethnomethodology, in part, as a response to what was then mainstream sociology's tendency to treat people as "cultural dopes" who respond to external social forces and are motivated by internalized norms. As its name might suggest, ethnomethodology is a study of ethnomethods or "people's methods" (Garfinkel, 1967). Ethnomethodology begins with a twofold premise: Social life is a series of ongoing interactional accomplishments, and descriptions, conversations, and representations are not merely *about* the social world—they actively *constitute* it. Daily life is understood as an intersubjective process that becomes ordinary, or predictable, through systems of shared meaning. This ontological grounding means that the truth or accuracy of any statement is irrelevant—ethnomethodologists are interested in the meaning-making processes of interpretation that can be identified in interaction.

Unlike formal logic or structural linguistics, ethnomethodological analysis brings into view that which is seen but unnoticed in social interaction. Since people rarely say literally what they mean, listeners must constantly interpret what was *said*, in order to understand what was *meant*. For example, even the apparently simple question of "How are you?" demands that the listener interpret what the speaker means by this question in order to formulate an appropriate response.[1] Is the question a greeting or an inquiry? Is it an inquiry about one's physical health? Emotional well-being? How much detail is appropriate? Does the question deserve a simple nod of the head, an elaboration of ailments, or something in between? In all social interactions, *the person talking must trust the listener's ability to respond to what was* not *said*, in order to make sense of what *was* said. This trust is often, but not always, rewarded.

At one point or other in life, everyone seems to encounter the awkward moment of having responded to what was *said*, rather than to what was *meant*. For example, a very casual "How are you?" offered as a greeting can be met with a much more detailed response than expected—or desired. Given that people rarely say literally what they mean, it is remarkable that such confusion happens as rarely as it does. The analytic interest for ethnomethodological analyses regards the commonsense knowledge that people use every day as we rely upon each other's interpretive capacities. Consequently ethnomethodology provides tools for apprehending and analyzing the interpretive practices through which people assemble what then comes to be seen as objective features of social life—such as rationality, morality, and social order. In short, it provides tools for examining how people's daily actions and practical reasoning produce the appearance of a stable, objective social reality.[2]

---

[1] Here readers will recognize some common ground with symbolic interaction. Ethnomethodology is distinct from symbolic interaction in that it does not attend to symbolic processes but to assumptions that are evident in the exchange and required to make sense of interactions.

[2] Ethnomethodology and symbolic interaction are both "concerned with the methods and practices whereby participants in talk, action, and social interaction—who are 'communicating' with one another by the use of symbols and language—manage their joint affairs. . . . [However] symbolic interactionist empirical studies tend to focus on comparatively broad meanings and persistent definitions of the situation rather than singular actions and the sequences in which their meanings emerge" (Maynard & Clayman, 2003, p. 174).

Ethnomethodology and symbolic interaction share an analytical focus on interaction; consequently, their approaches to social life are often construed as being the same. While a meaningful comparison exceeds the limits of this book, most simply ethnomethodology and symbolic interaction can be differentiated by their orientations toward social structures as well as toward language and interaction. Symbolic interaction is rooted in an ontology that is consistent with Weber and Durkheim (Maines, 1977). Hence, symbolic interactionism addresses social structures as existing contexts for interaction. Further, it examines the relationships between people and structures through analyses of symbolic communication and action.

By contrast, for ethnomethodologists, social structures are processes to be understood through the social interactions that reflexively constitute them. The ethnomethodological concern with the production of meaning in interaction demands a narrowly focused analytical context, which does not regard social structures in the abstract, as either empowering or constraining forces. In addition, for ethnomethodological analyses, language and interaction are *constitutive* elements that produce an apparently objective social world; they are not *symbolic* practices of meaning-making. Further, the analytical point of interest is not language per se but the shared assumptions that are revealed through what is not said.

This chapter takes up key analytical tools used in ethnomethodology: accounts, documentary method, category analysis, and indexicality. It is especially important to note that Garfinkel (1967) intended ethnomethodology to be used to analyze naturally occurring events and interactions—not newspaper articles, television dramas, or interviews. With that said, many scholars (cf. Watson & Seiler, 1992) have found ethnomethdology to be a fruitful framework for analyzing a wide range of data including interviews, cultural texts, and ethnographies. At the very least, the empirical evidence used in this chapter will provide a basic understanding of core principles that will help to distinguish ethnomethodology from other interpretive frameworks and to provide a context for understanding conceptions of agency, experience, and subjectivity. As with previous chapters, this chapter is not intended to provide how-to instruction. It begins with a short history of the development of ethnomethodology and a general summary of the framework. It then turns to analyses of exemplars and then corresponding analysis of ethnomethodology.

ETHNOMETHODOLOGY: A BRIEF HISTORY

In developing ethnomethodology, Harold Garfinkel strategically drew from phenomenologists Edmund Husserl and Alfred Schutz.[3] A significant influence for Husserl was his own teacher Franz Brentano. Husserl drew from Brentano's intentional theory of mind to develop the concept of conscious as always intentional and always *about* something (Husserl, 1964). By asserting that the relationship between perception and its objects is not passive, Husserl distinguished himself from other phenomenologists including Hegel, Heidegger, Sartre, and de Beauvoir (Holstein & Gubrium, 1998).[4]

Husserl (1964) attempted to study the essence of consciousness by distinguishing between consciousness and the objects that consciousness apprehends. Husserl argued that one could know the essential essence of objects by bracketing all assumptions about the world. Consequently, he sought to develop knowledge that was free of presuppositions. In pursuit of this goal, Husserl (1960, 1964, 1970) examined first-person experiences with phenomena in order to discover, and then generalize, the *essential* features of experience through ideal types.[5]

Although Husserl believed that Descartes misconceived the problems of knowledge, he developed Cartesian motifs in his own work and even referred

---

[3]"Phenomenology is defined in Husserl's *Logical Investigations* (1901) as the study of the essence of human consciousness. Essence is not a question of empirical investigation but rather a matter of pure abstractions—the very foundation of logic and mathematics. A case is made by Husserl for 'an *a priori* necessity of essence' (1901:443); objects are seen to have 'pure essences' which are self-evidently true—'non-empirical, universal, and unconditionally valid' (1901:446). Husserl believed that by removing essence from the empirical realm of natural science and relocating it in the universal realm of pure logic he was achieving a radical break with metaphysics. Essence, in this early twentieth-century phenomenological view, is not something that lies behind a given thing, but rather essence is that which is most *self-evident* and *self-given* about that thing: a figure is, in essence, a triangle if the sum of its angles add up to 180 degrees. In Husserlian phenomenology, then, it is self-evidence which operates as the basis of epistemology, the validation of the truth of all knowledge" (Fuss, 1989, pp. 14–15).

[4]It is important to note that Husserl's emphasis on consciousness does not include any consideration of the unconscious; further, he was concerned only with inferred consciousness.

[5]Ideal types are generated from characteristics that are not exhaustive of all cases, but they point to elements common to most cases. Typification is a conceptual tool that stresses defining features of a phenomenon for purposes of comparison. The term is most often associated with Weber, who developed ideal types.

to phenomenology as "neo-Cartesianism" (Husserl, 1960, p. 43). The influence of Descartes is evident in Husserl's assertion that it is both possible, and necessary, to examine objects and behavior without presuppositions, indeed without regard to any internal psychic or psychological landscapes, or broader cultural structures and influences. Yet to the extent that Husserl asserted that consciousness was always "about something," he can be understood as challenging the rigidity of Cartesian subject/object dualism. Husserl (1964) argued that in daily life a "natural attitude" is held wherein people view objects as existing independently from their own consciousness of them. Notably Husserl used the term *natural attitude* to refer to what he considered to be a naive life—not completely devoid of practical, critical reflection but *pretheoretical* and therefore naturalistic.

Phenomenology requires the researcher to bracket his or her natural attitude in order to investigate how consciousness actively constitutes the objects of its experience (Husserl, 1964). However, Husserl worked from the ontological premise that real objects exist independently of human perception, so exactly what then does it mean to say, "consciousness constitutes the objects of experience"? Husserl argued that objects do not simply exist as external to human consciousness; they also are formed by shared meanings. In this sense, Husserl's thinking was aligned ontologically with Blumer's.

Husserl had considerable influence on his student Alfred Schutz, yet Schutz was much more critical of Descartes than was Husserl. Schutz began his critique of Descartes by challenging the logical foundation of Descartes' theory of pure reason. Descartes had established the primacy of pure reason through the concept of doubt; he argued that everything is open to doubt *except* the existence of a thinking subject who doubts. Schutz argued that doubting everything except our thoughts might be useful philosophically, but practically speaking, it is impossible. He contended that if people doubted the reality of everything around us, we would not be able to function. Consequently, daily life must be conducted on some other basis. Schutz inverted Descartes' work by pursuing not what people *doubted* but what they *assumed*. In the process, Schutz reoriented Husserl's philosophical project away from structures of consciousness and toward the assumptions that people make in daily life. This philosophical foundation remains at the core of ethnomethodology.

Table 5.1   Cartesian and Phenomenological Ontologies

Cartesian Dualism	Phenomenology
Ontological realism	Modified ontological realism
Objective truth	Emphasis on meaning, not truth
Subject = Person	Subject = Person
Subject/object dualism	Intersubjective
Subjects have experiences	Experience requires assumptions and interpretations
Language is neutral (transparent) bearer of information	Conversation/talk in localized contexts is productive

Drawing from Husserl, Schutz (1970) used the term *natural attitude* to refer to the daily assumptions that people bring to ordinary events—assumptions that enable us to take our daily social worlds for granted. A hallmark of Schutz's natural attitude is the belief that the world exists precisely as we see it: If someone could stand where I am, they would see things just as I do. "[W]e assume that others experience the world basically in the way we do, and that we can therefore understand one another in our dealings in and with the world" (Holstein & Gubrium, 1998, p. 263). Like Husserl, Schutz's concept of a natural attitude is intersubjective. That is to say it is collectively and interactively produced; it does not arise out of an individual's mind, nor is it isolated from history or culture (Cuff, Sharrock, & Francis, 2006). Of course, the practice of routinely counting on shared assumptions does not always work out—we all encounter a few people who behave in unexpected or unpredictable ways. Given the many differences among us, Schutz wanted to understand how people manage to succeed *so often* in maintaining a sense of a shared social world.

In a radically empirical turn, Schutz combined a phenomenological sensibility with an analytical concern for interaction (Gubrium & Holstein, 1997). Schutz (1970) reasoned that people approach interaction with shared stocks of knowledge—socially established structures of meaning. However, Schutz believed that meaning is never completely predetermined by these stocks of knowledge. Consequently, he argued that in order to understand social life, researchers must bracket the presence of their own shared stocks of knowledge and seek to understand interpretive practices solely by examining the processes of interaction. Further, he argued that researchers must be able to convincingly and accountably indicate which stocks of knowledge are relevant to the interaction by referring to the concrete details in interaction.[6] One must be able to point to the precise behaviors or exchanges in the interaction that indicate that the individuals are drawing from a particular stock of shared knowledge.

While Garfinkel acknowledged that people draw from broad stocks of knowledge to help them make sense of what they see and experience (ten Have, 2004), he bracketed this knowledge as being outside the field of analytic interest for ethnomethodology. Garfinkel rooted ethnomethodology to a radical, or fundamental, notion of personal sovereignty—ethnomethodological analyses examine people in interaction as sovereign actors. Yet ethnomethodology has no analytical interest in concepts such as intentionality, consciousness, or will with regard to human action.

Garfinkel developed ethnomethodology by drawing from two key phenomenological components: an emphasis on daily practices that constitute an apparently objective, social world and tacit, or commonsense, knowledge. In this framework, conduct is understood to be a product of commonsense rationalities of judgment that are *observable*, accountable, and orderly features of everyday reality (Garfinkel, 1967). As might be apparent, ethnomethodology is intended as a descriptive, not a critical, framework. Ethnomethodology's concern with the interactional accomplishment of a shared sense of reality forms its specific analytic contours: From this perspective, the truth, or accuracy, of any statement is irrelevant to the procedures people use to make sense of it.

Ethnomethodological analyses are premised on the belief that meaning is reflexively created, self-generating, and context dependent. Consequently, the analytical focus is always on *how* participants cooperatively create shared meanings. For example, consider the following statement: "I'd like you to meet my invisible friend." It might be easy to imagine how this interaction would unfold differently for a child talking with a parent, for a comedian talking with an audience, or for a client talking with a psychiatrist. An ethnomethodological analysis would examine the concrete details of the interaction to understand how the participants involved interpreted this statement.

To understand how (and why) a researcher might bracket her or his own stockpiles of knowledge in the process of examining an interaction, consider

---

[6]This is a key distinction between ethnomethodology and symbolic interaction.

Goffman's (1959a) research on psychiatric institutions and the residents' practice of collecting string and foil. If one understands this behavior through a common-sense understanding of a mental illness diagnosis, collecting string and foil appears to be evidence of mental illness. However, if one understands this behavior through an appreciation of the value of personal possessions in an institution that denies the right to all personal possessions, the same behavior can be understood as a way of preserving mental health. Researchers are asked to "bracket" or try to suspend their own knowledge, judgments, and expectations in order to understand meaning-making practices from the perspectives of those who are interacting.

In addition to phenomenology, ethnomethodology draws from several other intellectual resources, including Durkheim (Garfinkel, 2002). Yet it might be most useful to understand the development of ethnomethodology, in relation to Garfinkel's mentor, Talcott Parsons (Heritage, 1984). For Parsons (1970), social order was made possible through institutionalized systems of norms, rules, and values. Parsons argued that social actors are broadly unreflexive with respect to social norms; through socialization, people internalize norms as part of their personalities. Deviant behavior results from inadequate socialization and hence the failure to follow social rules. Garfinkel completely rejected the notion that people follow social rules (Boden & Zimmerman, 1991). Departing radically from Parsons, Garfinkel argued that the whole notion of following rules fails to capture the constantly shifting social contexts. In every context there would need to be a rule to follow, and there cannot be preexisting rules for contexts that have not yet emerged (Feldman, 1995, p. 10).

Further, Garfinkel argued that shared values could not be the answer to questions of social order because shared values *presuppose* the existence of a social order. Garfinkel also rejected the belief that social structures precede interaction and cause (or condition) social conduct. He contended that structures (be it capitalism, race, or the banking industry) exist only through the interactions that make them possible (West & Zimmerman, 1987).[7]

Garfinkel asserted that an orientation to normative conceptions underpins the interpretative nature of social interaction—these constitute the edges, the parameters, of recognizably appropriate behaviors. They are *not* standards that one must "live up to." Rather, normative conceptions are the materials that people employ

---

[7]"In maintaining, elaborating or transforming their circumstances by their actions, the actors are also simultaneously reproducing, developing, or modifying the institutional realities which envelop these actions" (Heritage, 1984, p. 180). Since institutional realities must be generated, maintained, and transformed at the level of human interaction, ethnomethodologists do not face a micro–macro binary (Watson & Goulet, 1998).

to make sense of their circumstances, to evaluate what is going on in an interaction, and to produce and to recognize a range of expectations for "appropriate" behavior. Behaviors are "unremarkable" to the extent that they are "seen to be in accord with culturally approved standards" (West & Zimmerman, 1987, p. 136). Social order, according to Garfinkel, is built through the contingent, embodied, and ongoing interpretive work of ordinary members of society. Through social interaction, people accomplish, manage, and reproduce social structures.

In order to understand how people maintain social structures, Garfinkel developed breaching experiments as an analytic framework that focused not only on conduct but also on apprehending the commonsense rationalities behind conduct. He believed that people rely on commonsense rationalities, *unless* there is a breakdown that prevents them from seeing "business as usual." Breaching experiments were designed to cause just such a breakdown and enable researchers to observe "repair work" that would reveal the shared assumptions that had been disrupted. Garfinkel asked his students to violate basic social expectations—the social trust on which collective assumptions rest. *Importantly, breaches are not violations of social norms wherein a person might be seen as deviant. Rather they violate the meaningful social order of daily activities and thereby cause varying levels of confusion.* For example, Garfinkel asked his students to take what people say literally. So when asked the question "How are you?" in passing, students provided long and detailed accountings of their physical and emotional well-being rather than the expected nod of the head. Garfinkel also had students pursue detailed clarification of quite ordinary events that "should have been" (and were assumed to be) familiar to them. He then examined how people attempted to address or repair the breaches made by the students in order to understand the assumptions that were involved in producing an apparently objective, shared social world.

As he developed ethnomethodology, Garfinkel leveled two fundamental challenges to social research methods. One challenge targeted the epistemological foundation of social research: Garfinkel (1967) argued that any notion of "objective science" is fundamentally flawed because researchers rely on their own commonsense assumptions in order to make sense of the world(s) they are researching and in order to make sense of their data. As a consequence

> what purport[s] to be objective and scientific descriptions can turn out to be partial and distorted, lacking a grasp upon the contextual conditions of activities concerned and the meaning of those circumstances and activities for those who are situated in them. (Cuff et al., 2006, pp. 121–122)

A methodology more appropriate to understanding social life, according to Garfinkel, must require that scholars analyze all of their own cultural resources and assumptions that are used for analyzing phenomena.

Garfinkel's second challenge to social research targeted the nature of data and data analysis. For example, an ethnomethodological critique of *Le Suicide: Étude de Sociologie* undermines Durkheim's notion of "social facts" by asserting that these are not facts at all but rather they are practical accomplishments.

> In other words, while classical sociology is in the business of explaining social facts, the effort of ethnomethodology is directed towards an explication of their constitution. In his *Le suicide: etude de sociologie*, Emile Durkheim tried to explain variations in suicide rates in terms of variation in kinds of social integration. An ethnomethodologist, however, might investigate the ways in which cases of sudden death get constituted as being suicide, or at a different level, how statistical information about various "rates" is used to construct a sociological explanation of suicide in terms of social "causes." (ten Have, 2004, pp. 14–15)

This analysis demonstrates a distinctive ethnomethodological focus on the meaning-making processes through which the world comes to appear objectively real.[8] The same logic applies as well to the notion of data. To the extent that the word *data* suggests social facts that need to be uncovered, it is a misleading term because it elides the processes through which "data," like "reality," are always being produced in one way or another.

Ethnomethodology requires the researcher to take up social interaction not as social facts or symbolic practices but rather as practical accomplishments that constitute meaning. Broadly speaking, the mandate of ethnomethodology is to produce specific, context-dependent analyses—which are not to be treated as general theories of human action. Given this focus on describing a narrow, localized context, it should not be surprising that ethnomethodology does not explicitly address issues of subjectivity but rather implicitly assumes that subjects and persons are synonymous. In addition, its phenomenological foundation limits conceptions of agency to human action in a local context—agency is a human property. And, as noted earlier, experience is a process of interpretation. Although the focus is on meaning-making practices, ethnomethodology is ontologically consistent with both phenomenology and symbolic interaction—and like them uses analytic induction as a method of formalization.

---

[8]See, for example, Dorothy Smith's analysis of suicide in *The Conceptual Practices of Power: A Feminist Sociology of Knowledge* (Smith, 1990b).

The fundamental usefulness of Garfinkel's framework inspired several variations of ethnomethodology. Aaron Cicourel developed a distinct variation that pursues issues of cognition and draws from Wittgenstein; Jeff Coulter further refined and developed this line of research. Following a different trajectory, Harvey Sacks (Garfinkel's student) along with Emanuel Schegloff and Gail Jefferson developed conversation analysis as a very specific and highly technical variation of ethnomethodology.[9] In addition, other scholars (cf. Hak, 1992; Holstein & Gubrium, 2005; Moerman, 1992; Pascale, 2007; Smith, 1999) have developed variously hybridized variations of ethnomethodology intended to apprehend not only localized practices but also to critically examine how those practices are situated within broader cultural structures.

There are many disagreements about the variations of ethnomethodology. While conversation analysis is frequently regarded as the most typical form of ethnomethodological research, some researchers (cf. Holstein & Gubrium, 1998, 2005; Lynch & Bogen, 1994) contend that despite sharing key concerns, the particular emphasis of conversational analysis on the sequential structuring and micro-features of talk-in-interaction makes its connection to ethnomethodology somewhat tenuous. In addition, attempts to modify or extend Garfinkel's original project are nearly always contentious among those attempting to preserve Garfinkel's original contributions.

The ethnomethodological concern with common sense leads researchers to regard extraordinary activities or events, which disrupt commonsense assumptions, as particularly rich sites for social research. There are four primary research strategies associated with ethnomethodology: (1) close study of meaning-making activities through breaching experiments, (2) analyzing extraordinary circumstances in which we can examine our own ability to make sense of events, (3) ethnographic fieldwork to study the routine competences involved

---

[9]Conversation analysis, developed by Harvey Sacks, seeks to identify and analyze structural components of conversational sequencing. John Heritage (1984) summarized the fundamentals of conversation analysis in three premises. First, interaction is structurally organized, and this may be observed in the regularities of ordinary conversation. All aspects of interaction can be found to exhibit organized patterns of stable, identifiable structural features. They stand independent of the psychological or other characteristics of particular speakers, representing ubiquitous features of talk-in-interaction itself to which participants orient. Second, all interaction is contextually oriented in that talk is both productive of and reflects the circumstances of its production. Third, these two properties characterize all interaction so that no order of detail can be dismissed as disorderly, accidental, or irrelevant to the ongoing interaction. This focus on the real-time, sequential details of ordinary conversation requires naturalistic methods of study. Naturally occurring talk is tape recorded (increasingly, videotaping is encouraged) and transcribed to reproduce the fine-grained detail of speech exchanges.

in performing daily activities, and (4) ordinary or natural practices (uncontrived by the researcher) that are recorded and then transcribed and analyzed, not for what is said, but *how* it is said (ten Have, 2004, pp. 32–34). These strategies are often combined. In all cases, ethnomethodologists begin with a focus on mundane interaction and use analytic induction to build analyses.

THE BASIC PREMISE OF ETHNOMETHODOLOGY

While there are many forms of ethnomethodological analysis, in order to demonstrate the distinctiveness of the basic premise of ethnomethodology, this section focuses on a nexus of Garfinkel's key concepts/tenets: indexicality, reflexivity, accounts, documentary method, and commonsense knowledge. Ethnomethodological analysis uses the techniques and standards of analytic induction: searching for patterns (themes) and negative cases as well as working toward saturation (cf. Maynard & Clayman, 2003) but the processes of interpretation are quite different. Ethnomethodology begins with the premise that all meaning is indexical—that is to say it depends on context (Heritage, 1984). It is easy to see how concepts such as short/tall, yesterday/tomorrow as well as pronouns (you, him, her) are always indexical—it is impossible to know to what (or whom) these words refer without some understanding of the context in which they are used.[10]

Fundamentally, all meaning is indexical, or context dependent. The simple declaration "It is raining" will mean different things depending on the context in which it is spoken. The statement will mean one thing in a place experiencing drought, another in a place experiencing flooding, and a third on the day of a wedding—"if you think of it, on all occasions, all expressions (and actions) are in fact indexical" (ten Have, 2004, p. 21). The meaning of any statement becomes evident by examining the various ways in which participants respond in the interaction. In this sense, interactions are also reflexive—they shape and are shaped by localized settings. Just as a reflexive verb is one whose subject and object is the same, in ethnomethodology reflexivity refers to the "self-explicating property of ordinary actions" (ten Have, 2004, p. 20). The reflexive nature of all interaction refers to the ability of practices to both describe and constitute a social framework (Coulon, 1995, p. 23). Reflexivity, in this sense,

---

[10]This is different from Volosinov's formulation of indexicality—as meaning embedded in orders of value.

is not a conscious process: Participants generate a constantly emerging social reality through the dialogic production of meaning in interaction.

The reflexive and indexical nature of interactions enables researchers to analyze them as *accounts* that organize and constitute that which they describe.[11] The difference between conversation and accounts is an important epistemological one. Researchers who analyze conversation through a postpositivist framework are concerned with what people say or don't say, how they describe events, and the relative truth of their statements. Researchers who analyze the same conversation as an account are concerned with responses that indicate how statements are interpreted, how claims are accepted or discredited, and the shared assumptions, or tacit knowledge, underlying the conversation. This last point may be regarded as a defining feature of ethnomethodological analyses.

Researchers analyze accounts not only for the particulars of what is said but also as pointing toward "a mass of unstated assumptions" (Heritage, 1984, p. 181). This analytical focus is referred to as a documentary method—that is to say, researchers treat appearances as a document pointing to, or standing on behalf of, a presupposed underlying pattern (Garfinkel, 1967, p. 78). "The appearances and the underlying patterns are reflexively related. The point of documentary analysis is to examine the tacit knowledge underlying what is said that enables 'what is said' to make sense" (Pascale, 2007, p. 11).

Consider, for example, the following statement: "Please have more." The meaning of the statement is produced through more than just these words. Is the person being sarcastic? Playful? Is the person merely being polite? Is she or he earnest? All participants in an exchange around this statement would necessarily rely upon tacit knowledge to make sense of the interaction. The way each person responds would point the researcher toward assumptions (shared or not) in the interaction. Someone who struggles with overeating might interpret "please have more" as a form of sarcastic ridicule—regardless of whether or not it was intended in this way. The details of the interaction would reveal various sets of interpretations at play. By treating what is said as pointing toward unstated assumptions (tacit knowledge), the documentary method enables researchers to examine commonsense or tacit knowledge that is central to the production of mutual understanding.

Garfinkel's emphasis on the routine nature of "seen but unnoticed" procedures for accomplishing normal courses of action (Heritage, 1984) has led more

---

[11]Although Garfinkel's initial focus of analysis was naturally occurring talk in local interactions, nearly any form of data can be treated as an account rather than as a description.

recent ethnomethodologists to draw from Sacks' (1992) work on the use of membership category devices (MCDs) and membership categorizations, to explore and elaborate on accounts. A membership category device is an overarching conceptual frame that reflexively organizes the member categories it contains. For example, in the United States, "family" is an MCD that includes membership categories of parents, children, siblings, cousins, aunts, uncles, and so forth. In this sense, the term *membership category* is phenomenologically based and refers to displays that inform others about the person's social identity; they reveal nothing of the individual character of the person but rather exhibit socially learned, patterned behavior that establishes the terms of interaction (Goffman, 1976).

The MCD in use in an interaction determines which membership categories (and types of behaviors) are potentially accountable. For example, within a family one may be called to account for her or his behavior *as* a parent, or *as* a child, a cousin, and so forth. In interaction, behavior perceived to be appropriate to the membership category in use passes without comment, but breaches may be remarked upon. Within "family" one is potentially accountable for behavior as a cousin but not as a scientist—even though one may be both a cousin and a scientist. The category of "scientist" is not incumbent within the MCD of "family." Situationally relevant membership categories are made salient through the concrete details of the interaction.

Every membership category has category-bound behaviors associated with it and consequently holds the potential for requiring members to be accountable for behavior. This does not mean that actions are subject to oversight (e.g., teachers are accountable to parents or administration). Rather, membership categories make the organization of activities visible and therefore potentially vulnerable to being evaluated by others. One might be visible as a man or woman in an interaction and therefore potentially be held responsible for behavior as a man or as a woman. In environments in which gender is a relevant MCD, boys might be chided to "man up," or girls might be told to "act like a lady" (cf. West & Zimmerman, 1987). Through localized contexts we learn what behaviors are potentially accountable.

ANALYSIS OF NEWSPAPER, TELEVISION, AND INTERVIEW EXEMPLARS

This section uses foundational concepts of ethnomethodology to examine the same exemplars that were used in Chapters 3 and 4: a newspaper excerpt, an excerpt from a television drama, and an interview excerpt. As noted earlier, one might rightly argue that Garfinkel intended ethnomethodology to be used to analyze talk and interaction in natural environments—he did not envision it being used in this way. While some scholars might argue that these data may not best showcase the analytical strengths of Garfinkel's ethnomethodology, it is also true that today scholars use ethnomethodology in a wide variety of ways, and with a range of data, that Garfinkel had not envisioned. My intent is only to demonstrate the ontological and epistemological commitments of the framework and so the exemplars are of value for the following exercises.

Newspaper Analysis

An ethnomethodological analysis of news articles approaches them not as descriptions of events but as accounts that produce what they appear to describe—news. This demands a documentary approach to the analysis in order to get at tacit knowledge.

Newspaper Exemplar

Being a double amputee is not often described as an unfair advantage, but that is the argument made by the governing body of world athletics, the International Association of Athletics Federation (IAAF) in newspaper articles about Oscar Pistorius, a 20-year-old South African runner. Pistorius was born without fibulae in his legs; his parents, on the advice of multiple medical experts, had their son's legs amputated just beneath the knee when he was 11 months old (Philip, 2005). Pistorius has run for many years in the para-Olympics with record performances in this and other events at 100 meters (10.91 seconds), 200 meters (21.58 seconds), and 400 meters (46.34 seconds) (Longman, 2007). While those times do not meet Olympic qualifying standards for men, Pistorius is fast enough that his marks "would have won gold medals in equivalent women's races at the 2004 Athens Olympics" (Longman, 2007).

When the Beijing Games were still 15 months away, Pistorius petitioned the IAAF to run in the 2008 Olympics. I examined newspaper articles about Pistorius's petition and the IAAF administrative response and found that

(Continued)

(Continued)

administrators, athletes, and ethicists argued that Pistorius's prosthetic legs create a potentially unfair advantage for him over runners with biological legs. The following newspaper excerpt is an exemplar of coverage on the issue:

"The rule book says a foot has to be in contact with the starting block," Leon Fleiser, a general manager of the South African Olympic Committee, said. "What is the definition of a foot? Is a prosthetic device a foot, or is it an actual foot?"

I.A.A.F. officials have also expressed concern that Pistorius could topple over, obstructing others or injuring himself and fellow competitors. Some also fear that, without limits on technological aids, able-bodied runners could begin wearing carbon-fiber plates or other unsuitably springy devices in their shoes.

Among ethicists, Pistorius's success has spurred talk of "transhumans" and "cyborgs." Some note that athletes already modify themselves in a number of ways, including baseball sluggers who undergo laser eye surgery to enhance their vision and pitchers who have elbow reconstruction using sturdier ligaments from elsewhere in the body. At least three disabled athletes have competed in the Summer Olympics: George Eyser, an American, won a gold medal in gymnastics while competing on a wooden leg at the 1904 Games in St. Louis; Neroli Fairhall, a paraplegic from New Zealand, competed in archery in the 1984 Olympics in Los Angeles; and Marla Runyan, a legally blind runner from the United States, competed in the 1,500 meters at the 2000 Olympics in Sydney. But Pistorius would be the first amputee to compete in a track event, international officials said.

A sobering question was posed recently on the Web site of the Connecticut-based Institute for Ethics and Emerging Technologies. "Given the arms race nature of competition," will technological advantages cause "athletes to do something as seemingly radical as having their healthy natural limbs replaced by artificial ones?" wrote George Dvorsky, a member of the institute's board of directors. "Is it self-mutilation when you're getting a better limb?" (Longman, 2007).

Pistorius's bid for the Olympics is itself an exercise in breaching that exposes unspoken assumptions about the nature of athletes and athletic competition. In this excerpt, the legitimacy of Pistorius's bid to compete in the Olympics is challenged initially through recourse to a rule book quoted as saying, "A foot must be in contact with the starting block." Leon Fleiser, the general manager of the South African Olympic Committee, appears to take the rule book literally. He is quoted questioning whether or not a prosthetic device could be interpreted as meeting this requirement ("What is the definition of a foot? Is a prosthetic device a foot, or is it an actual foot?"). Yet even a literal reading of the rule book would not leave us with a foot in contact with the starting block but presumably another form of a prosthetic device—a shoe. Fleiser's comments suggest an assumption about runners (as having *feet*, not just shoes) has been breached. Further, this breach provides grounds for dismissing Pistorius for failing to meet the commonsense qualification of an Olympic runner.

The article goes on to construct Pistorius's body as being outside of the bounds of what constitutes an athlete generally and an Olympic runner in particular. Entrance into Olympic competitions would appear to be based on athletic performance. Yet Pistorius's bid for Olympic competition breached commonsense assumptions about the kinds of athletes who are allowed to participate in the Olympics. The organization is not called "the able-bodied Olympics"; instead, ability functions as the unmarked category—that which is presumed. By contrast, consider the athletic competitions called the Paralympics and the Gay Games. This marking constitutes the events and the athletes who compete in them as a special class—something other than "ordinary."

While runners typically are not vetted based on the likelihood of whether or not they might fall, or cause an accident, the article quotes IAAF officials as having "expressed concern" that Pistorius might "topple over." If stumbling or falling is a misfortune that many athletes encounter over the course of a career, it is an experience that seems to be fundamentally different from "toppling over"—which more often is used to refer to human pyramids or physical structures. In this context, the characterization of "toppling over" suggests that Pistorius is precariously balanced, and if he fell, he may not be able to right himself again. Through the possibility of "toppling over," as opposed to falling, his presence is constructed as a threat to the safety of others and hence the integrity of the game. Yet the ability to recover quickly from a potential fall has never been an explicit criterion for vetting athletes.

Newspaper articles generally assemble current events and quotes into a linear narrative that can be recognized by readers as "news"; they less often include historical background. Consequently, it is particularly interesting to examine how the article makes use of historical references to "disabled" athletes that the Olympic committee approved for competition in the past. The article notes three people: George Eyser with a wooden leg competing in gymnastics; Neroli Fairhall, a paraplegic competing in archery; and Marla Runyan, a legally blind runner. In no instance was the athlete characterized as having a prosthetic that could have created a level playing field for their participation in the games. By contrast, at issue seems to be the possibility that Pistorius's prosthetic leg could be as good as—or perhaps better than—biological legs. Pistorius is distinctly different from Eyser, Fairhall, and Runyan in this respect. However, it is important to note that as members of the same membership category (disabled athlete) such arguments *could have been made* about them—like Pistorius they were potentially accountable for their participation in the Olympics *as disabled athletes*. For example, one could have argued that sitting in a wheelchair would enable Fairhall to maintain the bow at a constant, perfect angle or that Eyser's wooden leg might be lighter or less likely to strike a piece of equipment. Such arguments are always available but not always made.[12]

The article constructs Pistorius not as an inspiring athlete who overcomes in the face of adversity but as one who threatens to redefine the meaning of ability—evidenced by the quotes from an ethicist. By quoting an ethicist in this particular way, the article moves center of the apparent controversy from Olympic competition to "talk of 'transhumans' and 'cyborgs.'" It replaces questions about what it means to be an Olympic athlete with questions about what it means to be *human*. Finally the article relies on the common sense of readers to accept the construction/production of news, including the *shift* from athletics to cyborgs, as ordinary and unremarkable.

Analysis of the Analysis

The preceding ethnomethodological analysis of this newspaper excerpt attempts to get at the assumptions underlying the logic of the statements in this article. It takes the linguistic accomplishment of "news" as an analytic

---

[12]I want to acknowledge John Kelly for helping to initiate and develop this line of thinking.

point—although it is not central to the analysis. Indeed from an ethnomethodological perspective there is no such thing as news—only events that are constructed as news. While the preceding analysis fits with those commonly done, it would be possible to create ethnomethodological analyses that focused more on the structure of the article (e.g., it could attend to the organization of paragraphs). Ontologically, the analysis is anchored to phenomenology; hence, it concerns only that which can be observed—the presence of the text. This is consistent with the Cartesian ontological premise of analytic induction. In ethnomethodology, this foundation requires a close reading of a text, evidenced here as a longer and more detailed analysis of the exemplar than in previous chapters. *However, it is important to note that the result is not standard empiricism; the objects of analysis are the assumptions that can be demonstrated to exist through reference to the text.*

In considering the production of news, ethnomethodologists would consider who is quoted, when they are quoted, the relationship of narrative to quotes, how the perception of objective reporting is credibly established, and so forth. My reference to the marked categories of Paralympics and the Gay Games can be justified as explicating the unmarked nature of the Olympics. What I believe to be most distinctive of the ethnomethodological analysis is that it treats the excerpt as an account and uses the documentary method to get at unstated assumptions in the text. So while the analysis doesn't leave the page, neither does it stay at the surface of what is on the page.

In daily life, because people belong to so many membership categories, ethnomethodology requires that the analysis incorporate only those that can be identified in the text. This enables me to analyze "transhumans" and "cyborgs" but not ability, whiteness, wealth, or masculinity—since these are not named. There is no evidence in the article that such categories are relevant. Ethnomethodology's strong commitment to the proof of empirical evidence often leads scholars to erroneously describe it as postpositivist. I say erroneously because "proof" functions differently for ethnomethodologists than it does for postpositivists—because of its ontological commitment. *"Evidence" in an ethnomethodological sense is not proof of how things exist but a gloss to show what things are being assumed and how meaning is being constructed.* Epistemologically, ethnomethodology presents a departure from other forms of empirical study, yet it also is consistent with analytic induction, which constitutes the process of formalization.

The narrow context for analysis provides insight into assumptions, but stripped of broader social contexts, it places the locus of all agency in (and only in) individuals. Experience is always an interpretation and always limited to situated interaction in localized contexts. Ethnomethodology does not take up issues of identity or subjectivity but works with membership categories—which might be conceptualized as the equivalent of subject positions. However, it is important to recall that in ethnomethodology both "man" and "runner" are membership categories—and in this sense, membership categories are quite distinct from subject positions.

Importantly, for ethnomethodologists there is no fundamental difference between the membership categories of man and runner except for the frequency with which these categories are relevant to social interaction. Hence ethnomethodology's ability to get at issues of power that infuse membership categories themselves is severely circumscribed. Further, in ethnomethodology, membership categories are not intersectional—although they could be analyzed as such, it would be unusual.

Ethnomethodology as a qualitative framework is highly specified but largely undertheorized. For example, while ethnomethodology examines the production of an apparently objective social world, this does not mean that everything exists in language. Rather, the material world has its own existence, but the meaning and order of social life are constituted through interaction in ways that make them appear to be objectively real. Like other interpretive strategies, ethnomethodology relies on the logic and method of analytic induction and consequently is grounded to a Cartesian framework. This is apparent in what has become a commonsense assumption for qualitative researchers: Evidence is something that one can literally see and point to.

Television Analysis

Harold Garfinkel certainly had access to television as he developed ethnomethodology, yet it never became a focus for analysis for him. Concerned with naturally occurring interaction, Garfinkel did not take up interviews, much less highly scripted and edited forms of media. Goffman's *Gender Advertisements* (1976) foreshadowed some of the analytical power of treating images as accounts. Given the primary importance of media (new and old) to 21st-century social life, it seems worthwhile to explore the potential of ethnomethodological analyses for media.

Television Exemplar

The ABC drama *Brothers and Sisters* features a white, upper-class family in Southern California involved in the daily dramas of a family-run business—complicated (of course) by interpersonal relationships and family intrigues. The series is unusual in that one of the adult siblings in the Walker family is gay, which makes it a potentially interesting site for examining talk about sexuality. I examined shows from the first season and found two relevant patterns.

First, scenes consistently allowed for multiple and contradictory audience engagements with politically controversial issues related to sexuality. *Brothers and Sisters* commonly dramatizes political issues that affect many families in the United States—particularly with regard to same-sex marriage and the Republican/Democrat partisan divides that characterized the George W. Bush administration.

Second, scenes consistently left disagreements about sexuality unresolved. The show framed these disagreements within the contexts of family intimacy, human frailty, and political aspirations—and typically used humor to drain or divert dramatic tension when very harsh or divisive conflict threatened to break out.

The following excerpt features a scene between siblings Kitty Walker, played by Calista Flockhart, and Kevin Walker, played by Matthew Rhys. Kitty enters this scene having just come from a meeting with Republican Senator Robert McCallister (played by Rob Lowe), who offered her a position as head of communications for his presidential campaign. Their meeting holds particular significance to the following scene for two reasons: Kitty and her deceased father have been the only Republicans in a family with strong Democrat affiliations, and it exposed romantic tension between Kitty and the senator, who is a father of two young children and is in the process of a divorce.

Kitty has just mentioned the job offer to her brother, Kevin, who is an attorney and the only gay primary character in the show in the first season.[13] As the scene opens, Kevin is upset with Kitty because Robert McCallister has voted in favor of a constitutional ban on same-sex marriage. Throughout

(Continued)

---

[13]Subsequent seasons have included several other white gay men.

(Continued)

this scene, Kitty is preoccupied with the mail while Kevin is consumed by the conversation; the camera alternates with the speaker, taking the view of the listener.

Kevin: Well, why *you*?

Kitty: Well, what the hell does that mean?

Kevin: [*stuttering*] Well, c-cause it's completely absurd. You can't work for this guy!

Kitty: Why? [*Kitty laughs.*] Why, Kevin? Because he's a Republican?

Kevin: No, because he's against gay marriage!

Kitty: There are lots of people in the world, Kevin, for instance *me*, who have no problem with gay people but still believe that marriage is fundamentally a religious institution that has nothing to do with the [*camera turns to Kevin who is visibly upset*] state and that does not discount civil unions or domestic partnerships or anything you . . . .

Kevin: [*Voice escalates*] Oh come on! That's just a cover that people like you provide for people like him who hate people like me.

         [*Kitty shakes her head.*]

Kitty: Oh, Kevin! Please, let's not make it personal.

Kevin: Ah, ah . . . [*Raises eyebrows*] Personal? Kitty, in 10 years . . . in 20 years, when I am finally . . . m-mature enough to sustain a committed relationship I would like to settle down and get married. That's personal.

         [*Kitty stops glancing through mail and looks up to speak.*]

Kitty: That's improbable.

Kevin: Don't take this job, Kitty. I'm warning you it will cause a great deal of . . . .

Kitty: Wait a minute. Wait, wait, wait, wait, wait a minute. You're *warning* me?

                         [*Brothers and Sisters,* Episode 11: "Family Day" 1/7/07]

As the scene opens, Kevin's question "Well, why *you*?" can be interpreted in multiple ways—as is evident by Kitty's response. Initially it is not clear if Kevin is asking why McCallister would offer the job to Kitty (challenging her ability) or if he is asking, "Why does it have to be you who does this work?" (challenging her politics, perhaps). It becomes possible to understand Kevin's question "Why you?" as this later formulation, through Kitty's response. Kitty meets Kevin's injunction with sarcasm: "Why Kevin, because he's a Republican?" Her ability to do the work does not appear to be in question.

While Kevin protests that Senator McCallister is against gay marriage, Kitty talks about McCallister's position against same-sex marriage as ordinary— shared by "lots of people" including herself. By constituting McCallister's view as ordinary, Kitty renders it apparently less alarming and less dangerous than it appears to be to Kevin. By locating same-sex marriage as being about religious institutions rather than about gay people, she advocates limiting rights without claiming homophobia. Kevin's response seems to reflect his recognition of this: "That's just a cover that people like you provide for people like him who hate people like me." Further, Kevin's comment produces membership categories (people like me/you) that are less than clear because they rely on knowledge that exceeds the immediate interaction. While it is plausible that the categories refer to gay/straight, they might also refer to people who are pro/anti same-sex marriage, or the membership categories may not be so obviously binary—this could be a reference to a kind of Republican person and gay men. What is clear is that the membership categories Kevin evokes are not brother and sister—if the argument began as a sibling dispute, Kevin has just changed the terms of the conflict.

Kitty's response again fails to take Kevin's concerns seriously and through sarcasm returns the *tone* of the interaction from an emerging political conflict between adults to a familial one between siblings. "Oh, Kevin!" is delivered (and received) as condescending admonishment—her younger brother responds in a childish way intended for comedic effect ("Kitty, in 10 years . . . in 20 years, when I am finally . . . m-mature enough to sustain a committed relationship I would like to settle down and get married. That's personal."). In this conversation, Kevin's ability to sustain a committed relationship is construed as a personal issue of immaturity and unrelated to the broader political issues regarding a society that denies him access to the institution of marriage that helps to sustain such commitment. Yet at a moment when the dramatic tension threatens to bring this issue from subtext to text, the issue is deflected through humor—arguably homophobic humor articulated through a gay character. Kitty delivers the punch line ("That's improbable"). Yet the excerpt closes as it opened, with Kevin attempting to issue an order and Kitty responding both aggressively and defensively.

Analysis of the Analysis

While an ethnomethodological analysis of news articles takes up the construction of events into news, the ethnomethodological emphases on interaction in localized contexts lead to the analysis of a television excerpt as if it was an interpersonal interaction, rather than a scripted scene. The analysis is able to get at the assumptions and interpretations made by "Kitty" and "Kevin" by examining their responses to each other because the excerpt simulates a social interaction. Consequently, it reveals more clearly how ethnomethodology treats empirical evidence as a gloss for something beneath the surface of the interaction. The power of the analysis comes from being able to get at that which is not present in the surface of the talk but which can be shown to be implicit through a close reading of the transcript.

At two places, the analysis presses the boundaries of a strict ethnomethodological analysis. First is the analysis that critiques that Kevin's ability to sustain a committed relationship is construed as a personal issue of immaturity and unrelated to the fact that he is denied access to the institution of marriage. In order to make this point, I went outside the boundary of the show. This occurs again when I interpret Kevin's humor regarding his inability to commit as homophobic. There is nothing in this interaction to indicate that Kitty, as a listener, heard that sarcasm as homophobia. This is a case of bringing my own outside knowledge to the analysis rather than bracketing it as is required of strict ethnomethodological analyses.

Although ethnomethodology would be quite effective for analyzing how audiences talk about the show, it is not grounded to an ontological or epistemological foundation that provides tools for analyzing television as a system of representations. The analytical focus is entirely on the process of meaning-making without regard to the nature of the exchange as between television characters. This does not disrupt a realist ontology embedded in both ethnomethodology and the processes of analytic induction subsumed in this analysis. Ethnomethodology is epistemologically distinct from other qualitative frameworks—how it generates evidence is consistent with other frameworks, while the kind of evidence it seeks and the process of interpretation it applies are different.

As in a realist ontology, agency and experience are just what one sees—even if the meaning of each is constituted in interaction. While our attention is directed to the analytical insights of ethnomethodology, the possibilities for analysis remain shaped and constrained by analytic induction—which is not apparent in the analysis. In this respect, it eludes consideration when critiques consider the strengths and weaknesses of ethnomethodology.

If membership categories might be thought to function as subject positions, they are not anchored to any broad cultural or historical processes and overall less developed theoretically. As in other frameworks, routine relations of privilege cannot be captured because they fall outside the bounds of the localized context—there is no evidence that race, class, gender, or ability is relevant. Although ethnomethodology is concerned with routine interaction, routine relations of power and privilege escape the analytical frame because they are unmarked in interactions.

Interview Analysis

Within an ethnomethodological framework, interviews must be approached as mutually constituted interaction—the interviewer's participation is as much a point of analysis as is that of the interviewee. While interviews are a long way from naturally occurring conversation, they can serve as rich sites of analysis—and at a minimum serve here as a useful basis for the exercise.

Interview Exemplar

While dominant public discourses in the United States construct race as natural, and apparently self-evident, in interviews with Native American Indians, I found that talk about race consistently exposed the social, historical, and legal processes of racialization. The exemplar that follows is from my interview with Tony Romero an Esselen Indian. It is important to note that in the early 1900s, Esselen Indians (indigenous to the land that came to be called California) were declared "extinct" by the U.S. government. The federal government's policy of recognition for Native Americans requires genealogical evidence of unbroken ancestry over

(Continued)

(Continued)

hundreds of years. Indigenous nations unable to provide that evidence were "terminated" by the government—that is to say denied federal recognition that would have entitled them to land and other settlement claims, as well as university scholarships and other forms of affirmative action candidacy. The Esselens, however, were never officially terminated but rather declared "extinct."

The federal declaration of their "extinction" has become part of a dominant cultural discourse. For example, the *Economist* featured an article on the Esalen [*sic*] Institute, and described it as "named after the Esselen, a now-extinct Indian tribe that used the place as their burial ground. In 1910 the Murphy family bought the land from homesteaders" (*The Economist*, 2007). The Esalen Institute is a spa/retreat center that has drawn renowned authors including John Steinbeck, Aldous Huxley, and Henry Miller. In the 1950s, the beat poets visited Esalen, and it later became a home to Alan Watts (*The Economist*, 2007).

In the following excerpt from my interview with Tony Romero in 2000, he talks about growing up in California as an Esselen Indian.

Celine-Marie: I wonder if you could tell me what it was like for you growing up and crossing worlds between your family and your home and the rest of the culture you experienced around you.

Tony: Well grownin' up, uh, growin' up, I remember my mom and dad always told me, "Don't tell anybody you're Indian." Uh, they were scared because I had uncles that were either drug behind horses or hung just 'cause they said they were Native American Indians. I have documentation of that. I had a couple of my relatives that were hung in a barn in Carmel Valley 'cause they wouldn't sell their property.

Celine-Marie: I'm so sorry.

Tony: It's things like that that happened in those days, and you know were talkin' like the '50s—1950s—and things like that were still goin' on like I remember when I was in high school I used to go down Monterey, I used to go to Louis' Bar on Alvarado Street. My uncle used to hang out, and there were two Obispo used to hang out in front of Louis' all the time and sit, they used to have these benches in front of all the pool halls. They were like, I guess there were like 10 or 12 pool halls you know on Alvarado Street and all these bars. So the Indians always used to carry these little pints of whiskey. I'll never forget the whiskey bottles cause they're, they're made in a shape where you can put 'em in your back pocket and they just fit perfect cause they had a little concave, concave shape to 'em.

Celine-Marie: Mmm.

Tony: And, uh, I remember 'em always sippin' out them damn whiskey bottles and, uh, but I remember one time I was comin' out of Louis' pool hall and my uncle was fightin' with these two white guys. He was tellin' how they were on his land, he didn't like it you know, he was feelin' a little tipsy there. So then I just ignored him, went across the street with some friends of mine to another place. And about a half an hour later I came back out and my uncle was sittin' on the same bench but he had a bloody nose, his eye was all black and blue, what they did was, they drug him in the back alley, beat the shit out of him to teach him a lesson, you know, that it wasn't his land anymore, it was theirs. And, uh, it was things like that that happened in Monterey where my mother was scared. She said well don't tell anybody you're Indian, tell 'em you're Spanish. So then when I *did* tell people I was Spanish and Indian, the first thing that came into mind was you're *Mexican.* I said no, no. I said bein' a Spanish Indian didn't make you Mexican. It wasn't the idea that I was ashamed of bein' a Mexican, it was the idea of wanting to be called what I really *was.* And I wasn't a Mexican. And I *knew* that and my parents knew that and, uh, so anyway, I went through that through my whole school years. You know OK, Tony, you're Spanish and Indian but you're Mexican. I says no. So anyway I had to go through this whole thing when I was a kid. I was always, I was always, when I was a kid I was always fightin' to protect my heritage.

(Continued)

(Continued)

Celine-Marie: Mmm.

Tony: Always fightin' you know to show people I was Native
               American Indian and I was proud of it. But then, uh, after
               a while I just, I just ignored the whole thing. But then after
               my mom passed away, I will never forget my mom passed
               away in 1970, she, uh, she looked at me and says you're
               Native American Indian. She said be proud of it. I'll never
               forget that. She says you're Esselen Indian. She said be
               proud of it. And, uh, so ever since then I've been fightin'
               for my recognition as a Native American Indian. I'm doin'
               it not only for her, but for my family, you know my existing
               family I have now, which isn't much.

In this excerpt, I begin as an interviewer with a broad and vague question
that makes sense only to the extent that Tony and I share some understanding
of the cultural environments that shaped his life—it reveals some level of
shared knowledge that was developed outside of this excerpt. Throughout the
interview, Tony identifies one of the "worlds" he crosses between as Esselen
Indian/Native American Indian but never names the other—and never is asked
to do so. Because of this, it appears that both of us assume that we share an
understanding of the nature of the other world that Tony navigated as a child.
Yet he does not assume that his parents' logic ("don't tell anybody you're
Indian") would be clear to me. Instead, he explains their fear with a story of
his uncles being "drug behind horses or hung." In addition, his mention of having "proof" of the murders seems to anticipate disbelief, if not an open challenge. If my interruption ("I'm so sorry") acknowledges the violence, Tony's
response prevents this violence from being seen as an exception. Tony
describes deadly violence as an ordinary part of his life ("It's things like that
that happened in those days and you know were talkin' like the 50s, 1950s and
things like that were still goin' on"). Again Tony never names, and is not asked
to name, the membership category of those who perpetrated the violence.

    It is not clear from the excerpt where this presumption of shared under-
standing comes from; however, what is most important is that Tony does not
need to name the perpetrators of racist violence in order for his narrative to

make sense to me. His narrative unfolds through a series of conflicts as he tells the story of his youth as a constant effort to fight physical and emotional victimization in relationship to his identity as Esselen Indian.

The stories of conflict (internal and external) are interspersed with a bit of nostalgia for the whiskey pints ("I'll never forget the whiskey bottles cause they're, they're made in a shape where you can put 'em in your back pocket and they just fit perfect cause they had a little concave, concave shape to 'em"). Tony's narrative is anchored to a hometown where people congregated at Louis' Bar on Alvarado Street or at the string of bars and pool halls. Tony and I both know this town and its more recent history. In this context, the names of streets and a specific bar can be understood as place markers that make his narrative both more familiar and concrete and therefore, perhaps more real.

Analysis of the Analysis

The analysis is shorter than the previous two because my ability to get the constructed nature of the account is limited and because the interactional exchange is limited. The concept of membership categories was not useful in this particular excerpt although the documentary method for analyzing accounts proved to be especially useful.

The epistemological framework is quite technical and again very narrow— and still grounded to analytic induction. While I am able (compelled) to examine how the interview was mutually produced, whiteness and white racism escaped scrutiny. In addition, my inability to analyze whiteness is compounded because Tony named Indians as being involved in the conflicts (but not whites), and so the conflicts he detailed seems to be "about being Indian" or about being perceived as "Mexican," rather than being about the construction of white racial privilege. Further the narrow frame of analysis makes the conflicts appear to be unrelated to masculinity or poverty—there is no evidence to pursue. Finally, the narrow analytical focus also makes both interviewee and interviewer appear to be sovereign actors, and experience is reduced to interaction. The forces that might constrain or shape agency are not present in the excerpt.

The analysis demonstrates how the interviewer and interviewee mutually produce the interview process—both through questions that are asked and through those that are not asked. Despite a long history of white racism, the analysis does not examine, or even consider, whiteness or racism because these are never named in the interview. Could I have argued there is an assumption of white racism? That becomes possible only if there is something explicit in the interaction (a question, a response, or a statement) that would be concordant with that interpretation. In this excerpt there is none. Similarly there is no analytical avenue that would enable me to explore the implications of Tony's claim to be Spanish and Indian rather than Mexican and Indian. The ontological foundation dictates the narrow focus on the situated interaction; as a researcher, I am asked to bracket my knowledge of broader cultural frameworks for identifying or interpreting the violence that Tony experienced.

To the extent that interviews can appear to be less constructed (there are not hosts of writers, editors, and advertisers that escape the analytical frame) they can seem to be more "objective" forms of social research. Consequently, I believe it is important to notice that Tony's narrative of fights, pool halls, and drinking corresponds with many white racist stereotypes of Native cultures. Therefore, it is important to look carefully to see to what extent my whiteness (the whiteness of the interviewer) in some way produced this *particular* kind of narrative. Consider, for example, the opening question that solicits his childhood stories and implicitly calls forth stories of conflict: "I wonder if you could tell me what it was like for you growing up and crossing worlds between your family and your home and the rest of the culture you experienced around you." To get at the shared knowledge that makes this exchange meaningful, I need to go outside of the text to understand "the worlds" that I asked about as being implicitly white and American Indian. Consequently, the history of genocide by whites against American Indians is also implicit in the opening question.

Without explicitly saying so, I *had asked* Tony to talk about racialized conflicts that existed for him as an Esselen Indian living in a predominantly white society. This is particularly important since on the surface the question might appear to be open rather than directive. It clearly solicits stories of racialized conflict for a white audience. Therefore it is important to ask, To what extent is the violence of white racism reproduced by the interviewer's question? It is a question that needs to be raised, regardless of whether or not it can be answered. It is also a strong argument for providing the broader context of exchanges when analyzing interviews.

IMPLICATIONS FOR SOCIAL RESEARCH

Ethnomethodology focuses on the methods people use to decide what is relevant and meaningful in any specific situation. Because ethnomethodology is interested in order-producing practices, truth and authenticity are never problems for researchers—nor are researchers ever in the position of "knowing better than" the people they study. Garfinkel (1967) focused on the concrete analysis of localized contexts and the routine nature of "seen but unnoticed" procedures for producing courses of action. Since the most *efficient* forms of domination are those that are "seen but unnoticed," ethnomethodology has much to offer potentially liberatory analyses.

In addition, ethnomethodology is especially useful because it suspends notions of a shared culture; rationality and understanding are the *outcome*s of what people do, not the premises (Sharrock & Anderson, 1986). However, ethnomethodology's ontological and epistemological roots in phenomenology and use of analytic induction mean that all social resources that exist outside of the immediate context, even those which enable meaning-making practices, are excluded from analysis. Consequently, its ability to get at relations of routine privilege (arguably exploitation and domination as well) is quite limited. The ontological formulation of experience brackets the unconscious as well as discursive, cultural frames. Ethnomethodology changes the object of analysis and the epistemology (ways of knowing the object) but not the ontological premise—which is rooted to analytic induction.

While ethnomethodology examines the reflexive production of meaning, because it is bound to localized contexts, all discourse appears to emerge as if for the first time. Yet all communication has to have a place in collective memory; it must be repeatable (iterable and anticipatable) in order to be understood. Garfinkel (2002) argued that all phenomenon need to be studied as "another *next first time*"—because the realizations will be different from any other time. This mandate acknowledges, but dismisses, the importance of repetition over time—that we "recognize" phenomenon (including words and images) as meaningful *because* we have encountered them before. However, ethnomethodology delivers analyses devoid of historical contexts.

The use of membership categories in place of a theorization of subjectivity creates some interesting possibilities. Working with the definition of categories as learned, patterned, social behavior, membership categories provide a way of examining the relationships between subject positions and identity-in-use. This seems to me to be a potentially rich site of analysis. Yet the analytical power is radically diminished because ethnomethodological analyses treat all membership categories such as woman, white, cousin, and clerk as equivalent; there is no access to historically constructed relations of power, or social categories of difference, that make membership categories meaningfully different from each other. Such aspects are treated as irrelevant to the interaction unless there is empirical evidence to the contrary. It does not address the problem that one can decide to stop being a clerk, but generally, one does not decide to stop being white or a woman in the same way. Social life is layered in ways that arguably exceed the context and tools of ethnomethodological analysis.

It is important to repeat that ethnomethodology treats empirical evidence as a gloss for something beneath the surface of the interaction. However, while ethnomethodologists *interpret* notions of evidence differently than other frameworks rooted to a Cartesian ontology, they *locate* evidence in the same way. That is to say researchers use analytic induction. Social science has produced multiple challenges to systems of interpretation but not to systems of formalization. Qualitative research relies on analytic induction to locate patterns that can then be interpreted.

Although ethnomethodology levels important and profound charges at Cartesian ontology, ethnomethodological analyses are themselves constrained by the seen but unnoticed influence of a Cartesian paradigm. If a researcher could easily point to an act of violence or oppression in a localized interaction, *routine* relations of power function as such only to the extent that they pass without remark in localized contexts. Hence ability, whiteness, wealth, masculinity, and heterosexuality are never named in any of the three analyses. Ethnomethodologists would argue that each person belongs to numerous membership categories, and we cannot presume that any one of them is relevant but must look for evidence of a category as being in use in the localized context in order to establish its relevance. While a particular strength of ethnomethodology is apprehending the "seen but unnoticed" aspects of daily life, routine relations of privilege largely operate outside of its analytical framework.

While ethnomethodology demonstrates how members actively construct their sense of objective social worlds, the epistemological demand for "evidence" that one can point to in a localized context prevents analyses from examining the processes, events, and relations of power that shape localized contexts. Although social contexts provide the means for interpreting the importance of membership categories in use, relations of power depend on the category's repetition over time in multiple contexts. Meaning is always context bound but contexts themselves are boundless. The historicity of language, talk-in-interaction always exceeds the circumstances of its production.

By placing spatial and temporal limits on the context of talk to be analyzed, researchers make people appear to be sovereign speakers, free of history and discourse.

CONCLUDING THOUGHTS

Ethnomethodology offers interesting and innovative ways to explore processes of meaning-making; however, the analytical constraints lead most often to descriptive, rather than critical, research. This is completely in keeping with the philosophy of ethnomethodology, which would regard any preconceived notion, even that of social justice, an imposition on empirical evidence. Yet it is more than idealistic to imagine that researchers truly could bracket all of their assumptions or that we would be able to make sense of any interaction if we did! While membership categories might appear to be a parallel strategy for getting at subjectivity, they are anchored to a phenomenological account that makes it impossible to get at historical formations that operate through categories.

So while ethnomethodological analyses may be able to get at allusions and assumptions that rest beneath the surface of what is said in a localized context, they cannot apprehend how historical relations of power (such as race and processes of racialization) operate, since these are never fully articulated in any single localized context. This limitation is consistent with, and amplified by, the analytical emphasis on personal agency that cannot adequately address the broader constraining forces of language and culture. As a consequence, while ethnomethodological analyses are said to reveal the practices through which social structures are maintained, they are unable to demonstrate how discursive structures enable and constrain the conditions that constitute the sayable. The latter has never been the mission of ethnomethodology, but it remains an important limitation to consider for social science.

While ethnomethodology, social constructionism, and symbolic interaction each offer substantially different ways of interpreting the three exemplars used in *Cartographies*, they are all consistently constrained by the ontological and epistemological assumptions embedded in analytic induction—the technique of data collection and analysis common to all three forms of analysis. The processes of interpretation have changed, but the process of formalization has remained the same. This illustrates why strengthening qualitative methods through the use of feminist, critical race, and poststructural theories has been both helpful for strengthening qualitative research and also inadequate.

FURTHER READING

Coulon, A. (1995). *Ethnomethodology* (Vol. 36). Thousand Oaks, CA: Sage.

Garfinkel, H. (1967). *Studies in ethnomethodology*. Cambridge, UK: Polity Press.

Handel, W. (1982). *Ethnomethodology: How people make sense*. Englewood Cliffs, NJ: Prentice Hall.

Heritage, J. (1984). *Garfinkel and ethnomethodology*. Cambridge, UK: Polity Press.

Maynard, D., & Clayman, S. (1991). The diversity of ethnomethodology. *Annual Review of Sociology, 17,* 385–418.

Mehan, H., & Wood, H. (1975). *The reality of ethnomethodology*. New York: John Wiley.

Sharrock, W., & Anderson, B. (1986). *The ethnomethodologists*. London: Tavistock Publications.

Smith, D. (1999). *Writing the social: Critique, theory and investigations*. Toronto: University of Toronto Press.

ten Have, P. (2004). *Understanding qualitative research and ethnomethodology*. Thousand Oaks, CA: Sage.

Watson, G., & Seiler, R. (Eds.). (1992). *Text in context: Contributions to ethnomethodology*. Newbury Park, CA: Sage.

CHAPTER SIX

SOCIAL RESEARCH

Drawing New Maps

————◄•◆•►————

INTRODUCTION

Social sciences have much to contribute to public debates regarding changing social landscapes in an increasingly globalized world. Globalization and the internationalization of disciplines are central to our time (Sztompka, 2010), yet exactly what scholars are able to contribute—and how useful those contributions may be—will have much to do with how we think about our research in relationship to narratives of science. "Science" functions as a disciplining force that privileges some modes of inquiry at the expense of others. In a variety of ways, the project of rethinking qualitative inquiry has been underway for decades—and a great deal of change has been accomplished.

Scholars have developed multiple, and more effective, ways of interpreting data than existed a century ago. Yet as Chapters 3, 4, and 5 demonstrated, processes of interpretation operate separately from, but in relationship to, processes of formalization. The analytical styles of social constructionism, symbolic interaction, and ethnomethodology are significantly different from each other. However, each of these frameworks produces analyses that are constrained in similar ways because they share the same process of formalization for generating systematic elaboration.

Researchers, academic institutions, funding institutions, and the state are all intimately involved in the production of valid "science." Even as qualitative research occupies a "mainstream" location in social research, it faces new political challenges in a time of global uncertainty.

> Around the globe, governments are attempting to regulate scientific inquiry by defining what is good science. Conservative regimes are enforcing evidence, or scientifically based, biomedical models of research (SBR). These regulatory activities raise fundamental philosophical, epistemological, political, and pedagogical issues for scholarship and freedom of speech in the academy. (Denzin & Giardina, 2006, pp. ix–x)

Despite these challenges, in recent years there also has been a proliferation of new qualitative journals, books, and conferences that reflect both international and transnational scholarship that actively challenges traditional paradigms of social science. The prominence of this scholarship in relationship to funding and more mainstream research varies in relation to the dominant discourse of science at work in each social science discipline.

All scientific claims are relative to their paradigmatic frameworks—which makes it impossible to verify or falsify any claim from *outside* of the framework (Kuhn, 1970). Science is performative in that the claims of science make sense only within the discourse of science. The continuation of what Kuhn called "normal science" depends upon conducting research and developing findings that do not challenge the parameters of the dominant research paradigms. By endorsing only biomedical models as the gold standard of social research, conservative movements profoundly narrow what we can know about social worlds. Scholars today would not limit social theory to the sweeping narratives of grand theory, yet many continue to use its philosophical counterpart as the sole or primary foundation for empirical research.

Perhaps the best response to the contemporary debates about the meaning of "science" is to refuse the push back to older and narrow definitions of science by moving forward with a broader, more inclusive definition of science that can effectively get at the complexity of 21st-century social worlds. Efforts to expand the discourse of science—to provide what de Certeau (1984) called the as yet undrawn map—have been premised on the understanding that models of the physical science are inadequate for understanding social life and that social life in the 21st century is substantially different from that in other eras.

As previous chapters have illustrated, expanding the discourse of science is essential to developing analytical tools for effectively exploring routine relations of power and privilege, for examining porous relationships among social phenomena, for thinking about the nature of evidence differently, and for situating localized contexts in the broader cultural and historical contexts from which they emerged. Continuing efforts to broaden the paradigms used for social research require that scholars challenge the dominant binaries through which the social sciences have been constructed, including art/science, objective/subjective, theory/method, and scientific/ideological. A more inclusive social science would recognize multiple styles of inquiry that use a variety of processes of formalization for making systematic claims—each best suited to its purpose.

In previous chapters, I demonstrated the need for critically engaging the ontological and epistemological assumptions embedded in qualitative frameworks and the importance of rethinking data collection and interpretation in relationship to each other. This chapter is intended as a kind of provocation toward rethinking social research from the foundations up. It begins with a brief overview that synthesizes arguments made in previous chapters and then explores the imperatives of social research and the production of knowledge in relationship to power, media, ethics, and language. The chapter concludes with consideration of the importance of social epistemologies for social sciences.

THE PROBLEMS OF SOCIAL RESEARCH REVISITED

Bertrand Russell (1938, p. 10) once said the fundamental concept in the social science is power—in the same sense in which energy is the fundamental concept in physics. Like energy, there are many expressions of power, and none of these can be necessarily regarded as subordinate to another; there is no single expression of power from which other forms derive, no stagnant expression of power and no expression of power that exists in isolation. The complex networks of power that infuse social life require specific and diverse methodologies and methods.

As noted at the start of this book, researchers today denounce the colonialist projects of earlier scholarship—and here I use "colonialist" broadly to refer both to the ways that anthropologists have studied so-called primitive nations and peoples and also to the ways that sociologists have studied "the poor and disenfranchised." The ontological and epistemological foundations of Cartesian dualism used to organize and validate colonialist research continue to form the foundations of contemporary scholarship. Individually and collectively, the preceding chapters demonstrated the powerful influence of Cartesian ontology—even in interpretive frameworks that openly *reject* the premise of Cartesian dualism.

Qualitative researchers have made significant efforts to move beyond Cartesian dualism through the use of interpretive frameworks; however, despite these efforts, techniques of valid data collection and analysis have kept the analytical process tethered to a Cartesian paradigm. This has created odd ontological and epistemological crosscurrents in social research that have truncated the ability of interpretive methods to apprehend routine relations of power and privilege, prevented consideration of processes of subjectification (such as those which create race), and profoundly limited the ability to examine contemporary media.

Cartesian ontological and epistemological assumptions pervade scientific research and are used to systematically discredit techniques of knowledge production that fall outside of this paradigm. Indeed research can be discredited simply on the grounds that it falls outside of this paradigm. Although Descartes' epistemology initially was conceptualized in resistance to centralized religious authoritarianism, it has become "a practice of ignorance—a methodological inward-turning, promoting cognitive dismissal of all that lies outside its bounds of sense, and resulting in a highly sophisticated Eurocentrism" (Hoagland, 2007, p. 101). As noted in Chapter 2, ignorance is not simply "not knowing" but an active misapprehension that systematically produces inaccurate information. An epistemology of ignorance is one that uses socially acceptable but faulty systems of justification (Alcoff, 2007; Sullivan & Tuana, 2007).

The epistemic foundations of social research encourage us to see "local contexts" as naturally occurring rather than as socially constructed. In addition, the current epistemic foundations prevent us from addressing the broader cultural conditions that shape localized contexts. This is not an accidental or inadvertent aspect of social research. Since the social sciences have been modeled on the physical sciences, it is illustrative to consider a study by Latour and Woolgar (1986) that sought to sociologically understand what constitutes typical scientific practice. In particular, they were interested in what they took to be a general lack of methodological reflexivity in scientific methods.

Through daily contact over a period of 2 years, they studied the social construction of scientific knowledge by examining the processes through which physical scientists made claims about their research observations. In short, they sought to produce insights into the social construction of scientific claims and disputes of claims. They found that in a scientific laboratory the most commonly used method to dispute a researcher's work was to place his or her findings in a broader social context. Latour and Woolgar (1986) argued that the distinction between technical processes of research and social phenomena meant that researchers introduced broader social analyses only when things had gone wrong in their own work or when they wanted to discredit the work of others.[1] Distinction between the social and the intellectual provided a resource that scientists used to explain error but not knowledge.

The master narratives of science and modernity were constructed through a self-consciously antihistorical, antinarrative, naturalistic conceptual frame (Somers & Gibson, 1996, p. 46). These discourses remain in place today as part of the dominant scientific paradigm and affect the broader legitimacy of qualitative research generally and interpretative research in particular—especially in relation to research funding. However, a great deal of qualitative research continues to challenge and diverge from this conceptualization of science. The commitment among qualitative researchers to transforming the discourse of science is evident as well in critical race and feminist critiques of existing research and in attempts to deepen understandings of reflexive and interpretive repertoires.

Over the years, challenges to hegemonic discourses of science have brought greater inclusivity, both in terms of scholars and fields of interest; they have developed competing notions of objectivity; and elaborated new processes of interpretation including those focused on intersubjectivity. Within qualitative frameworks, many scholars have sought to expand the limitations of analytical frameworks by incorporating poststructural discourse analysis, psychoanalytic literature, and cultural studies.[2]

In addition, there has been a growing interest in critical methodologies that challenge the epistemic frameworks of social research (cf. Harding, 2008; Sandoval, 2000; Smith, 2004; Zuberi & Bonilla-Silva, 2008). This literature is theoretically driven and generally provides frameworks for

---

[1]"For example, the assertion that X observed the first pulsar can be severely undermined by use of the following formulation: x thought he had seen the first optical pulsar, having stayed awake three nights in a row and being in a state of extreme exhaustion" (Latour & Woolgar, 1986, p. 21).

[2]"The analytics of interpretive practice has benefited from drawing together ethnomethodology and Foucauldian sensibilities. This is not simply another attempt at bridging the so-called macromicro divide . . . . [T]hose who consider ethnomethodology and Foucauldian analytics to be parallel operations focus their attention instead on the interactional, institutional, and cultural variability of socially constituting discursive practice or discourses-in-practice, as the case might be" (Holstein & Gubrium, 2005, p. 492).

interpreting data—not methods for collecting it. There is also a small but growing body of new methods (including performance and autoethnography), which are very useful yet fairly limited without the broad coherence associated with social science. The impulse for change has been both clear and highly controversial.

With that said, as we have seen in previous chapters, as long as researchers remain (consciously or unconsciously) committed to Cartesian presuppositions, the most profound changes in social research methodologies and methods remain trapped by the entropy of 19th-century philosophy of science. In a Cartesian framework, epistemology is individualistic; it concerns the ability of subjects to know objects. This epistemological compulsion to individuate is a naturalistic and historical creation of modernity (Somers & Gibson, 1996). However, knowledge is never an individual enterprise as the Cartesian framework insists. Knowledge, cognition, and perception must always be cultural productions as well as individual ones. Even the internal landscape of thought comes to us through language—the premier signifying system of culture. Consider how the cultural force of language shapes perception and experience.

> "Savages" tend to do certain things and to be unable to do others; these go with the conceptual territory. Thus the term itself encourages if not quite logically determines particular conclusions. . . . In the classic period of European expansionism, it then becomes possible to speak with no sense of absurdity of "empty lands" that are actually teeming with millions of people, of "discovering" countries whose inhabitants already exist. (Mills, 2007, p. 27)

To the extent that Cartesian dualism is a philosophical foundation for research that regards *individual* practices of knowing in localized contexts, it denies the cultural relationality of knowledge production. By its own self-validating standards, a Cartesian foundation actively prevents researchers from being able to apprehend and examine the cultural relationality of knowledge production. While analyses of localized practices can document meaning-making practices in interaction, the demands of science force these practices to stand apart from the cultural discourses that make them possible.

The principles of science make it possible to study inequality without ever exploring who benefits from the impoverishment of others; they also make it possible to "study up" without connecting wealth and power to the daily lives of those who are marginalized and oppressed. The principles of science also make it possible to study how people are oppressed without also considering how they are *simultaneously* oppressors; they encourage an understanding of the world that is divided into victims and aggressors. Further, the principles of scientific discourse create frameworks that are not capable of effectively exploring the presence of absence: what is not said and who is not present in a localized context. Recall that whiteness generally passes without remark in conversation and in media. As noted earlier, the routine and privileged subject position of whiteness is accessible through standard empirical analyses only in very limited ways. The power of whiteness, particularly for white people, works through virtue of its invisibility.

In order for whiteness to be effective as a routine relation of power and privilege, it must flourish beneath the surface of interaction, at the level of commonsense knowledge. That is to say through the ability of common sense to erase the presence and meaning of white racial identities while producing all other racial identities as apparently inherently meaningful—even if the meanings of those racialized identities is unclear or contradictory. This is true for all unmarked categories of social experience and is particularly critical in sustaining social hierarchies of race, gender, ability, sexuality, and class. Like all relations of power, the *meaning* of these categories exceeds any local context. Hegemonic hierarchies arise only through repetition over time in multiple contexts. Scholars can never fully examine the production of routine relations of power and privilege if we attend only to a localized context of interaction—regardless of whether we attend to that interaction through interpretive or positivist methods. The production of unmarked social categories exceeds our ability to critically examine them through conventional tools of social science. Routine relations of power and privilege escape existing social research paradigms.

Consider also that standard social research methods make it virtually impossible to analytically include people who are physically absent from the research setting. Indeed the concept of including people who are absent from a research site flies against commonsense knowledge in the sciences so forcefully that it may be difficult to consider seriously. The needs and perspectives of those "not in the room" cannot be evidenced through the procedures of science. On one hand, it might seem unreasonable to be asked to address every possible absence. On the other hand, there is not reason to include every possible absence—only those with theoretical and practical relevance. As researchers, our failure to acknowledge the importance of people who are absent from the localized context naturalizes exclusionary environments as ordinary environments. By normalizing localized contexts that exclude, researchers perpetuate and ingrain a naturalistic view of historical relations of power. To account for absence as a *meaningful social production* involves epistemic and ethical shifts that foreground interdependent relationality in data collection and analysis as well as self-reflexivity by the researcher. Localized contexts exist as they do because they are shaped by broader cultural imperatives including relations of power and privilege.

Some scholars might argue that their purpose is not to *presume*, or reveal, relations of power and privilege but rather to examine lived experience in relation to social interactions and social structures. This raises key questions for scholars working in qualitative methods generally, as well as for those working in interpretive methods in particular. Of what use is an understanding of agency in local interaction that does not account for broader relations of power that shape and constrain agency? Without an understanding of subjectivity, how are we to understand the relationship between social categories (such as race, gender, ability, sexuality, and class) and personal identities? Who is served by research on oppression that does not demonstrate how such exploitation benefits "ordinary" others?

Mining New Media With an Old Tool

The philosophical foundations of social research methods shape and constrain both what counts as techniques for analysis and as data. *The Polish Peasant in Europe and America* (Thomas & Znaniecki, 1918) once broke historic ground in the social sciences by broadening the notion of evidence to include life history. Today life histories, interviews, and archives are mainstream sources of social science data; in addition, media have become more accepted as sources of data for social research. Pragmatist Charles Sanders Peirce, who pursued semiotics, and Herbert Blumer, who approached media as iconic signs, significantly influenced early media studies in the social sciences. Their media scholarship paved the way for notable studies such as Howard Becker's (1974) research on photography and Erving Goffman's (1976) study of gender in advertisements.

More recently, scholarship on media has begun to bend the parameters of science by drawing from a variety of disciplines in the humanities including cultural studies, media studies, discourse studies, and communication studies. While such interdisciplinary research has been quite useful, it fits only marginally within the social sciences. Unfortunately, within the social sciences, techniques for studying media have not kept pace with the expanding presence and forms of media—largely because the 19th-century philosophical *premises* of social research restrict the ability to study 21st-century media. For example, without recourse to methods of other disciplines, researchers are left to approach film, television, and newspapers with the same analytical frameworks used for interviews or ethnography. Consequently, researchers pursue cinematic realism—or at the very least to treat film, television, and newspapers just as they would interview transcripts.[3] A focus on localized contexts leads interpretive researchers to "recognize" the indexicality of meaning—that is to say the way that the meaning of any words depends on its context for sense. Yet both indexical and iconic systems of representation are limited. Media are not the same as the situated interaction of daily life; nor are they a second-order mirror that reflects daily life.

In the example of television drama in this book, qualitative frameworks blurred distinctions between production and consumption. Focused on the immediacy of a localized context, how does one make sense of editors, writers, producers, advertisers, designers, and so forth? Ethnomethodologists would argue that this is exactly why they focus only on naturally occurring talk-in-interaction. If this once seemed a reasonable way to understand social life, the explosion and pervasion of media calls such a narrow scope into question today.

Not only is there a massive proliferation of media in the 21st century, there is also a "media convergence" as media content crosses multiple platforms, genres, industries, and audiences (Jenkins, 2008). Changes in media are simultaneously technological, industrial, cultural, and social; media convergence "alters the logic by which media industries operate and by which media consumers process news and entertainment" (Jenkins, 2008, pp. 15–16). However, the research paradigms of the social sciences have not adjusted to be able to effectively address the complex issues of representation in the proliferation of media and its porous relationships with arguably all aspects of social life. The complexities of 21st-century media demonstrate the limitations of social science.[4]

---

[3]At the same time, the approach of cinematic realism dialogically supports the discourse on participant observation, establishing it as an empirical scientific methodology (Clough, 1992, p. 27).

[4]"Mass media have enframed configurations of the subject (psychic structure), have regulated what will be constituted for that subject as reality (objects of knowledge), and have established the distribution of persons, places, events, and perspectives in relations of knowledge production (rules of knowledge formation), these effects have been produced through adjustments between realist narrativity and mass media communication technologies. These adjustments, I would argue, serve to maintain empirical sciences's hegemony. Thus science, nearly identical with writing technologies of the subject, is, as Bruno Latour (1983) describes it, a site for the production of knowledge/power, aligning itself with political, economic arrangements or what Aronowitz (1988) refers to as the capital/state/axis (p. 300)" (Clough, 1992, p. 8).

Daily life is mediated by technology in unprecedented ways; indeed, media have a broad range of possibilities for constructing meaning. Even television has become less a singular text and more a technological movement and mediation of culture; the extension and intensification of "teletechnology" has moved television well beyond a broadcast model (Clough, 2000, p. 96). "[T]elevision shows repeat over and again through various forms of syndication" (Pascale, 2007, p. 20). Shows can be viewed online, on DVD, through Wii, or downloaded onto iPods and iPads. Soundtracks for television shows have moved from the background to center stage; popular music now has a regular and important place in the soundtracks of primetime network television as well as in film. Indeed, shows such as *Glee* foreground music and the soundtracks for this and many other television shows are available on iTunes. Yet perhaps more consequentially, television provides, and draws upon, cultural resources for more than immediate audiences. In this sense, television collapses distinctions between production and reproduction, between production and circulation, and between text and context (Clough, 2000).

All media are intertextual—the meanings of any one image or text depend on the meanings carried by other images and texts (Rose, 2007, p. 142); however, new technologies, marketing strategies, and social relations converge in the production of transmedia texts. Consider that *The Matrix* opened in theaters but also became available on DVD, on television, online, and through downloads onto iPods and iPads; in addition, it comes in two different game forms (*Enter the Matrix* and *The Matrix*), a series of comics, and several animated videos, all of which textually interact with the film. Changes in media content and circulation embody processes that are simultaneously technological and social. Yet social science research remains constrained by a philosophy of science that cannot begin to address intertextuality, the changing nature of social interaction, or the porousness of mediated relationships. Further, technology alone, no matter how sophisticated, cannot account for the shifts in production and consumption that occur in and through a variety of forms of media. "The circulation of media content—across different media systems, competing media economies, and national borders—depends heavily on consumer's active participation" (Jenkins, 2008, p. 3). Qualitative researchers need specific capacities for deciphering the layers of media intertextuality (cf. Fornäs, Becker, Bjurstöm, & Ganetz, 2007), new forms of sociality, and the complexities of mediated social interaction.

The advent of TiVo and other similar recording devices are contributing to the decreasing value of 30-second commercials and causing marketing strategists to rethink possibilities for generating media that blur the lines between marketing and entertainment. Beyond the most obvious product placement techniques, MTV videos, *American Idol*, and Virgin Media come immediately to mind as new genres created by this blurring of advertising and entertainment. In an ever-increasing media landscape, with new forms of media constantly emerging, former distinctions among culture, politics, and economics come to seem less relevant than they once were. Consider that what first started as a campy joke in Dino Ignacio's bedroom as he assembled a collage combining *Sesame Street*'s Bert with Osama bin Laden (to "prove" that Bert was truly evil) quickly became part of an international controversy when the collage appeared on thousands of posters across the Middle East—some of which appeared in anti-American protests (Jenkins, 2008, pp. 1–2). New media, including wikis, blogs, vlogs, videoconferencing, text messaging, Facebook, and Twitter have shifted the meaning of interaction itself. Arguably, they have completely collapsed what has been imagined historically as a local interactional context. From the privacy of our homes, we can enter an endlessly public space. Truth, authenticity, and reality are no longer easily assumed or clearly apparent.

If audiences were once understood as passive spectators of television, film, or other forms of media, today audiences must be understood as participatory cultures. Increasingly, youth are not only consuming media but also producing it. An elementary school child being homeschooled began *The Daily Prophet*, a student written and run newsletter dedicated to bringing the world of Harry Potter to life; the paper now has a staff of 102 children around the world who have never met face-to-face but who form a community that writes, edits, and reads the paper (Jenkins, 2008). This is not to say that all participatory cultures are equal—certainly the ability to participate varies dramatically. Corporations still exert far greater power in this participatory culture than do any individuals or smaller groups. Yet it does indicate how quickly social interactions and social relations are transforming in important ways that pose profound problems of data collection and analysis for the social sciences.

In the 21st century, social research must be able to consider the technological mediation of social relationships. While many scholars would argue the physical sciences never presented a good model of social research, the complexities of social life in the 21st century render the model of the physical science even less useful. Not only do changes in media content and circulation embody processes that are simultaneously technological and social but changes in technology and computerization blur the distinction between manual labor and mental activity.

Consider that consumers have always purchased not just products but also symbolic value. However, in the 21st century, the symbolic value of products seems strikingly disproportionate. The increased symbolic value of products has come to erode obvious distinctions among economic processes, consumer products, and systems of representation. If this seems implausible, consider how the presence (or absence) of a Nike "Swoosh" affects the price of running shoes. Even on otherwise identical shoes, the Swoosh can increase the market value of a pair of shoes five times; clearly we are not buying the physical characteristics of the Nike symbol but its symbolic effect, its meaning (Ives, 2004, p. 13). It is impossible to separate the value of the Nike Swoosh from the advertisements that give it social value. Yet the research paradigms of the social sciences have not adjusted to be able to effectively address the complex issues of representation in the proliferation of media, social relationships, and economic processes.

The philosophical foundations of social research methods make it impossible to effectively examine 21st-century media using only social science methods. While interpretivist frameworks can get at meaning-making processes in various ways, they also bind us to a narrow context of analysis— the demands of formalization make it difficult to do effective and credible studies of representation.[5] A Cartesian ontology directs *techniques* of data collection and analysis—even if another ontology, such as pragmatism, directs the interpretive process. The demands for empirical evidence necessitate an epistemological focus on localized contexts, which precludes intertextual and generally broader cultural analyses.

To call social life into question without also calling into question our conception of an adequate explanation of social life makes research vulnerable to intensely ideological and unconscious conclusions. A philosophy of science must question the presuppositions that constitute both apparent problems and the methods to address them. What is the value of a social science that cannot meaningfully apprehend and account for technological mediation, symbolic value, and intertexuality of social relationships? Is this ineffectiveness a reasonable price to pay to maintain the boundary of "science"? Should social sciences continue to concede media studies to the humanities? Clearly the answer to these last two questions is "no," *if* we believe that all experience is intensely personal, profoundly intersubjective, and culturally mediated. However,

---

[5]Tools (such as psychoanalytic, poststructural, and semiotic frameworks) that are commonly used to apprehend the productive power of media stand outside the parameters of social sciences.

before a more substantial response can be offered, it's important to take up consideration of ethics and subjectivity, since these are fundamental to how we understand the production of knowledge.

A MATTER OF ETHICS:
THE MAKING OF A SOCIAL SCIENTIST

Feminist criticisms regarding the inadequacy of prevailing standards of research within the social sciences have focused on notions of objectivity, as well as on the assumptions, practices, and philosophies of science (Harding, 2008, p. 7). In addition, feminists have engaged related discussions of ethical responsibilities with respect to insider/outsider research (Zinn, 1979) and ethnography (Rosaldo, 1993; Smith, 1999), as well as more generally with respect to the construction of feminist methods (DeVault, 1999; Harding, 1991; Naples, 2003; Ramazanoğlu & Holland, 2002; Reinharz, 1992; Stanley & Wise, 1983). These important and relevant feminist innovations in social research ethics have not yet made it into the foundations of mainstream social research, which remain primarily concerned with institutional review board (IRB) procedures. Indeed even having to designate practices as "feminist" points to their distance from hegemonic practices. Feminist analyses linger at the periphery of social sciences to such an extent that they are underdeveloped by new generations of scholarship. "Objectivity, rationality, good method, real science, social progress, civilization—the excellence of these and other self-proclaimed modern achievements are all measured in terms of their distance from whatever is associated with the feminine and the primitive" (Harding, 2008, p. 3). From this perspective, even in the 21st century, feminism is still one more barbarian at the gate of science.

What does it mean to speak of research ethics beyond the demands of IRBs? To what extent must the historical relationship between objectivity and research ethics continue to change? The concept that a researcher needs to establish a strong boundary between oneself and interviewees, that a scholar must protect her- or himself from the problems of strangers, is the product of an enlightenment notion of objectivity based upon a subject/object dichotomy. In this framework, emotional distance is thought to provide the needed objectivity for evaluating the truth or falsity of the information our interviewees offer to us. It protects researchers from becoming "lost in the stories" and hence vulnerable to distorted or inaccurate data. Consequently, there appears to be no middle ground: no opportunities between doing nothing (as an objective scholar) and attempting a total rescue (as "not objective" activist). This logic alleviates a sense of responsibility and nearly compels inaction—it is both presumptuous and impossible to rescue people from their own lives. It is important to pay attention to the premise of a *social* science.

> The social sciences are strongest where the natural sciences are weakest: just as the social sciences have not contributed much to explanatory and predictive theory, neither have the natural sciences contributed to the reflexive analysis and discussion of values and interests, which is the prerequisite for an enlightened political, economic and cultural development in any society. (Flyvbjerg, 2001, p. 3)

Exploration of social values, interests, and meanings form the core of social sciences; such exploration *requires* a critical intersubjectivity. If empathy (the ability to relate compassionately to another) is one of our greatest pathways to interpersonal relationships, it is also one of our greatest resources in social research. Empathy and compassion form a bridge between the interviewer and the interviewee—not a bridge that allows one to cross over and share an experience but a bridge that makes shared understanding more likely.

Empathy is a very powerful point of human connection that can help researchers to better understand people whose experiences and values were very different from our own. For example, in interviews, empathy helped me to understand how multimillionaires might truly think of themselves as belonging to the middle class. It also helped me to understand how white people—who did not identify as racists and would never have sanctioned racism—routinely expressed racist views. Yet by suspending my own views to see the world through the eyes of those I interviewed, I often found myself implicated in both bigotry and human suffering in ways I had not anticipated.

As researchers, we become intimately acquainted with the suffering of others—suffering that we cannot resolve. This is why social researchers are often trained, as I was, "to not think about it." Circumstances such as these form the very conditions of our research, and for that reason, it seems to me to be of critical importance that we reflect carefully on them. Witnessing the effects of 3 days of unrelenting rain on people living without housing gave me a visceral understanding of why it is important never to look away from suffering and never to forget. Especially when we are powerless to change the circumstances we face, it is important to bear witness and through witnessing and remembering to deepen our commitment and to sharpen our strategies for enacting meaningful social change. This is the place from which we can begin to rethink the meaning of social research and the ethics of knowledge production.

To develop research methods that are able to effectively apprehend both routine relations of power and media in the 21st century, it will be necessary to draw theory and method into more integrated frameworks than currently exist in the social sciences. Many important issues in the social sciences, such as the nature of agency, subjectivity, and experience, can only be solved by conceptual analysis, not empirical research (cf. Winch, 1958). Experience does not consist of discrete moments, like frames in a film. Experience is a complex, multidimensional web in which all moments are related to others. Of course, all research requires temporal limits, yet how scholars envision appropriate limits is as much a political process as a research one. This is one reason why it is important to write about *localized* contexts rather than local contexts.

The ability to set temporal limits relies on the self-reflexive skills of the researcher; what we bring to the study enables us to make sense (or prevents us from making sense) of what we observe. For example, a racial slur is recognizable as a slur only because it has been used as such in the past—it connects us to a cultural history of racism (Butler, 1997b). Without the broader social and historical context, it is not possible to understand a slur *as* a slur. Yet the demand for analyses of localized contexts ignores the cultural contexts that make a slur meaningful and reduce it to an individual act. As de Certeau (1984) reminds us, words are tools marked by their use. Yet ethically and intellectually we are accountable only for the knowledge produced within a very narrow temporal frame. This is precisely how research reproduces dominant cultural ideologies.

REVISITING SUBJECTIVITY, AGENCY, AND EXPERIENCE

Problems of subjectivity are at the heart of all questions about human existence. While such problems may be taken up in courses on methodology, they appear only superficially, if at all, in discussions of research methods. Robust distinctions between social theory and social science have prevented social scientists generally, and sociologists in particular, from taking up issues of subjectivity, agency, and experience. At the start of the 21st century, efforts to understand human interaction must call into question the usefulness of the theory/method binary. While researchers once studied subject locations such as race, gender, sexuality, class, and ability as if they were the essential and fixed natures of persons, today our positionalities along these lines are understood more commonly as *subject locations* that become part of individual identity (Althuser, 1971; Hall, 1997b, 1997c).

The tension and interplay between the social, symbolic, and imaginary *processes of identification* defy any simple notion of distinctly separate selves. However, within the common sense of Cartesian dualism, "identity" is who we know ourselves to be. Identity is believed to express an essential or authentic core of "self-ness" (cf. Minh-ha, 1989). Identity is what Minh-ha referred to as "a continuing me" while "difference" is the boundary that distinguishes me from not me. In this sense, identity refers to "the whole pattern of sameness" within a human life (Hall, 1997a; Minh-ha, 1989). Certainly, the reification of an objective social world presupposes a persistent self as its subject.

> Much of what we in sociology treat as abstract or presuppositional categories—subject and object, agent and structure for example—carry within them "frozen" historical arguments, which have been abstracted into our familiar general categories. To "unfreeze" requires "undoing" and that requires history. Taking a look at the historicity of apparently presuppositional categories of social thought also involves asking how the historical construction and transformations of a concept shaped and continue to shape its logical dimensions and its social meanings. (Somers & Gibson, 1996, p. 44)

If we accept that people are brought into being through social interaction, there is no identity (no me, or I) that can stand outside of the conditions of its emergence. Experience then is not what one has but the processes through which one is constituted. Every "I" is implicated in a social context that exceeds its own existence (Butler, 2005, p. 7). The only way to know oneself is through a mediation that takes place outside of oneself.[6]

It is one thing to accept that social categories such as race are socially constructed and quite another to examine *the processes of subjectification*—the processes through which people become bearers of social structures. Processes of subjectification give researchers access to ways of thinking and writing about categories such as race, gender, sexuality, and ability without reifying them and without divesting them of the historical relations of power through which they are produced. Analyses and narratives about who people are, and the lives they

---

[6]To an important extent, identity categories are both reductive (essentialist) and productive (as political dispositions); any use of them must be self-reflexive, self-conscious, and strategic in order to maximize their productive usefulness and minimize their essentialist reductions.

have lived, will always be incomplete if we cannot see the processes of social formation through which they became inaugurated as subjects.

The "frozen historical arguments" of ontological and epistemological assumptions have particular consequences for marginalized subjectivities. For example, if we no longer accept a fixed or reified notion of race, sexuality, or ability, it becomes incumbent upon researchers to understand the social conditions through which people come to occupy related subject positions. This would demand that we broaden the analytical focus of research methods to include cultural knowledge as well as local practices. Localized contexts of data collection do not provide a broad enough lens for generating insights into processes of subjectification. "Material conditions are the necessary but not sufficient condition of all historical practice" (Hall, 1996, p. 147). Social science has much to gain by bringing empirical, theoretical, and historical lenses together in order to effectively make sense of social life.

In the social sciences, there is little agreement about the ontology of the subject (how subjects exist) or about the epistemology of the subject (how the subject can be known). Contemporary researchers have argued that the notion of a persistent subject is itself incoherent. For example, in order to conduct statistical analyses of race, researchers must assume that people have a single constant racial identification over the course of their lives: This assumes that a multiracial person will always identify as such and not as a black person in one context and multiracial in another. Indeed, the notion of a persistent subject over time is untenable, because it requires researchers to ignore the ontological conditions of knowledge.

Changing conceptions of subjectivity demand a concomitant reexamination of notions of agency. What does it mean to speak of agency? To a commonsense attitude, agency might be as simple as the ability to affect some aspect of our environment. Yet as noted in Chapter 2, social research demands a more complicated question: Where is the *locus* of the action that affects our environment? Notions of agency derived from Cartesian (body/mind) dualism are associated with consciousness and the mind: Agency begins with a thought or intention that directs our action. In Cartesian dualism, bodies emerge either as the *conditions* of social action or as objects that are acted upon. Commonsense attitudes and much of social research reflect this orientation to agency.

At the heart of issues of agency are ontological narratives regarding the nature of the world and epistemological narratives about how that world can be apprehended or known. In the social sciences, the practice of conceptualizing agency as a personal quality is related to the concomitant conceptualization of constraint as the consequence of social structures. This binary framing of agency and constraint comes from, and perpetuates, a Cartesian paradigm that continues to preclude certain forms of knowledge. Recall from Chapter 2 that if we challenge the notion of gender and sex as natural essences, we necessarily complicate understandings of agency. If gender is socially constructed, people need to learn to put some measure of effort into making ourselves recognizable as gendered beings. This is not only a matter of hairstyle and clothing but one that also includes body language, demeanor, interactional styles, and so forth. From this perspective, how do we locate the source of agency behind the accomplishment of gender? If gender is not an individual choice, to what extent is gendered demeanor—hegemonic or subversive—a matter of individual agency?

To the extent that scholars believe that gender and sex are socially constructed, we must consider bodies not as natural but as processes of subjectification—that is to say, as the result of social processes of embodiment. Scholars then must reconsider both the meanings of bodies and the locus of agency. From this perspective, the humanist conception of agency is decentered: Agency is no longer centered in, or emanating from, an individual. In this sense, agency is understood as a nonlinear process with no single point of origin. Agency and constraint are expressions of the complex conditions of their constitution.

Tradition, norms, and roles, along with more theoretically driven concepts of false consciousness and discursive formations, have at various times emerged as focal points for understanding social constraint. Gramsci's notion of hegemony provides a rich example of how seemingly private lives are infused in politically important ways with cultural relations of power. Indeed the institutions responsible for the creation of "civil society" (schools, churches, temples, mosques, news media, and so forth) are hegemonic forces of the state that are intimately involved in processes of coercion and consent. For Gramsci, consent always implies both coercion and constraint—and coercion and constraint always imply some level of consent. These concepts cannot be separated meaningfully from each other. However, in the social sciences the analytic tension between free will and the forces of social control that constrain free will has been institutionalized through macro/micro divides in social research.

Empirical analyses typically pursue either macro analyses of constraining structures or micro analyses that foreground the agency of personal action. Yet agency is always situated in, and to some extent determined by, specific historical, political, structural, and social factors. Agency is never entirely free nor is it entirely constrained. From this perspective, the work of social research becomes, at least in part, understanding agency as neither fully determined nor fully free but produced paradoxically through a struggle with constraining forces—the "unchosen" conditions of our lives (Butler, 2005).

Social research that seeks to fully understand processes of social change must resist the dualistic impulse to explain constraint and agency as dichotomous binaries. This would lead us not only to examine the compromised nature of agency, but also to examine the compromised nature and inherent vulnerability of social structures. To refuse a dichotomous framing of agency and constraint would direct social research—not to studies of people, places, times, events, or contexts—but to the *relations* that bind people, places, times, events, and contexts.

I want to underscore the point that in order to develop non-reifying empirical knowledge of domination, we need to examine *the determining force of relationships of domination*, as well as its effects. If we understand that material conditions are not fixed absolutes, we must consider the range of conditions that give rise to them. From this starting point, social research shifts from being solely (or primarily) about *exposing* exploitation to making power and privilege as visible as oppression and exploitation. Of course, in order to make this starting point possible, scholars need to explore and reconceptualize both processes of formalization and interpretation in social research. It would require exploring more fully how philosophical foundations, as well as technical procedures, can work to prevent relations of power and privilege from fully appearing in analyses of disenfranchisement.

ENVISIONING SOCIAL EPISTEMOLOGIES

How might the philosophical roots of qualitative analysis be transformed? How might future research reframe and broaden social science research? At present, the strong investment in a Cartesian philosophy of science makes it difficult to account for layers of interpretation in the research process without appearing to compromise the very name of science. Producing knowledge is always a political act—one in which ideologies are both rationalized and naturalized. The more effective scholars become at revealing the processes and terms of knowledge production, the foundation of cognitive authority, the more effective we will be at minimizing the effects of ideologies.

Research will never be an ideal process, but it can be a more accountable one. Recall from Chapter 2 that social science research is charged with two overarching tasks: formalization and interpretation. Formalization regards the processes for systematizing knowledge production. To varying degrees, all research draws from deductive, abductive, and inductive *logics*. However, qualitative research relies most strongly on both the principles of inductive *logic* and generally on the *method* of analytic induction. Grounded theory and analytic induction, as commonly practiced today, vary in the mechanics of coding, in the processes of sampling, and arguably in reliance on analytic abduction; however, they both rest on inductive strategies for identifying themes and variations in empirical data from a localized context.

In qualitative research, principles of analytic induction provide the scientific rationale and technical parameters for systematic qualitative data collection and analysis—the process of formalization. The ability to identify/produce empirical data and to generate findings from data is the cognitive condition of social science; researchers make their case through warranted interpretations of themes and exceptions. To the extent that theory and method are treated as binaries, the logics of historicism, deconstruction, or genealogy have no place in social science. Indeed, within the cognitive space of social *science*, it is impossible to critique processes such as reification and hegemony. Formalization seems possible only if evidence is understood as a thing to which one can physically point, rather than as a heuristic for investigation. Operationally, social science has depended upon realism. We might speak of multiple realities, but the techniques of qualitative research redirect us to a Cartesian construct. Constrained by ontological and epistemological foundations, interpretive research is compelled to operate in reified modes of thought—yet researchers lose sight of this by focusing on the second task of social research: processes of interpretation.

The second task of social research is to provide systems of interpretation—hermeneutics for apprehending social processes. Realism, social constructionism, symbolic interaction, and ethnomethodology each offer different interpretive strategies for making sense of social life. Where qualitative research is concerned, we have developed far more strategies for interpretation than we have for formalization. Since the development of "modified analytic induction" and grounded theory, nearly all challenges to the natural science model have regarded processes of interpretation, not processes of formalization.[7] Consequently the effectiveness of interpretive research is both limited and fragmented. Utilizing,

---

[7]The two exceptions are autoethnography and performance scholarship, and these remain quite marginal to the social sciences precisely because they eschew processes of systematization that distinguish science from other modes of inquiry. Institutional ethnographies are well positioned to challenge processes of formalization but do not always do so.

indeed requiring historical procedures of formalization for social science research, has profound consequences for conducting social research that is truly capable of advancing social justice. To the extent that the social sciences remain exclusively bound to empirical evidence in localized contexts, we will fall short of our abilities to analyze power, privilege, culture, and knowledge. To repeat an old adage introduced in Chapter 2, if we do not see the big picture, "we 'look' but never 'see'" (Steinberg, 2007, p. 11).

Any adequate epistemology must account for the inseparability of knowledge and social organization. Epistemic communities are not groups of individuals; they are interdependent relationships. Social sciences need *social epistemologies*. Where individualistic epistemologies are concerned with truth and error, social epistemologies are concerned with social practices in relation to knowledge production. There are myriad ways of conceptualizing social epistemologies that have a broad range of political effects (cf. Clarke, 2009; Goldman, 2002; Lynch & McNally, 1999; Smith, 1990a, 1990b, 1999; Weinstein & Stehr, 1999). Of particular relevance here are those that best support the production of knowledge in ways that are consistent with efforts to apprehend the intertextuality of socialities: specifically, the historicity of localized contexts, the technological mediation of culture, and the subjective processes of social research. With *relationality* as an ontological premise, social epistemologies demand that we pursue knowledge about the social world by examining social routes to knowledge. Narratives must be understood both in relationship to each other and to broader discursive systems. In addition, social epistemologies refuse the possibility of conceptualizing identity or subjectivity as fixed. All identities and subject locations would need to be analyzed in the relational contexts that make them possible and which give them meaning.

Many scholars seeking to pursue more social epistemologies than currently exist in the social sciences have drawn from poststructural discourse analysis (Charmaz, 2009; Clarke, 2009; Denzin, 1992; Holstein & Gubrium, 2000; Pascale, 2007; Saukko, 2003; Scheurich, 1997; St. Pierre & Pillow, 2000). Although the use of poststructural discourse analysis does not provide simple answers to social problems, it does enable close analysis of the operations of power. "It enables us to examine how power operates to construct our desires, our thoughts, our ways of being in the world—our subjectivities—in ways that can make us unconsciously complicit in our own oppression" (Gannon & Davies, 2007, p. 91). If this seems a long way from the charge of social sciences, consider Adele Clarke's (2005) elaborated technique of situational analysis as a means to examine empirical data, while disrupting the illusion that

coherent meaning exists in isolated moments. Working with a social epistemology, situational analysis seeks to integrate symbolic interaction, constructivist grounded theory, and poststructural discourse (Clarke, 2009).

Discourse, understood as the intersection of text and context, provides an
important analytical resource for developing social epistemologies.[8] Systems
of representation, particularly narratives and discourse, are the basic concepts
of a social ontology and a social epistemology. Through narratives we come
to know and make sense of the social world, and through narratives we constitute social research. Yet narratives can never be entirely of our own making,
they are the products of broader cultural discourses. In a social ontology,
events and phenomena exist as constellations of relationships—not singular or
isolated moments—that are discerned in temporal and spatial relationship to
other events and phenomena. Ontological narratives dialogically define who
we are and what course of action to pursue—these are socially constituted, not
individual, narratives. In this sense, ontological narratives are fundamental to
conceptions of agency and constraint. Indeed, agency and constraint are possible only through the narratives in which they are embedded.

Challenging the limited notion of localized contexts necessarily disrupts the
theory/method binary. It also expands the presence and need for analyses that in
the social sciences have not traditionally been considered empirical, or even relevant to the empirical. Practically speaking, there are at least two ways to transform the notion of empirical evidence to create more fully developed social
epistemologies. One way of moving forward is to expand the notion of empirical contexts by situating localized interactions in broader cultural/historical
contexts. As noted earlier, some qualitative scholars are pursuing this route. In
education, scholars such as Patti Lather (1991), and Elizabeth St. Pierre and
Wanda Pillow (2000) challenge both research and writing practices; in cultural
studies, Paula Saukko (2003) and Johnson, Chambers, Raghuram, and Tincknell
(2004) propose cultural studies analyses that refuse the notion of localized contexts; and Patricia Clough (1992, 2000, 2008) includes a psychoanalytic perspective that pushes the boundaries of sociological research. Dorothy Smith's
(1990b, 1999) work on the social organization of knowledge demonstrates the
usefulness and need for apprehending the conceptual organization of power as
it functions in daily lives. There are many scholars, often working at the margins
of their disciplines, to transform the practices of social research.

---

[8]I want to acknowledge Ezerbet Barat for this particular framing of discourse.

A second way of cultivating social epistemologies emerges through a focus on language as an organic connection between local and cultural contexts. By language, I do not refer to the study of grammar or syntax but to a range of disciplinary approaches that get at the discursive production of meaning and knowledge in local and cultural contexts. Consider, for example, the range of disciplines in which researchers are attempting to expand analyses of the localized context associated with social constructionism, symbolic interaction, and ethnomethodology through the incorporation of more theoretical tools such as deconstruction, psychoanalysis, Foucauldian discourse analysis, and genealogy. "Some of the most influential intellectual movements of the 20th century—including psychoanalysis, structuralism, postmodernism, deconstruction, and discourse analysis—have focused on language" (Ives, 2008, p. 3).

A short list of scholars who have made substantial contributions to cultural analyses of language include Roland Barthes, Ferdinand de Saussure, Louis Althusser, Antonio Gramsci, Walter Benjamin, Jurgen Habermas, Mikhail Bakhtin, Valentin Volosinov, Ludwig Wittgenstein, Monique Wittig, Michel Foucault, Pierre Bourdieu, Jacques Derrida, Jacques Lacan, Judith Butler, Michael Billig, Norman Faircough, Teun van Dijk, Margaret Wetherell, and Ruth Wodak. Notably, however, these are largely theorists in the social sciences or scholars in the humanities. Perhaps because language is the premiere signifying system of cultures, studies of language have been regarded as something other than the basis of scientific investigation. Glyn Williams (1999) argued that

> Sociology's emergence as a feature of modernism was responsible for the separation of language, mind and reality. This meant that it was possible to study reality without reference to language. It also meant that reality was reflected in language and that a consideration of evidence, as language, implied an introduction to truth. In the same manner, language and nature were separated, involving the separation of representation and fact. This meant that society could become something to study as something separate from language. In a sense, language was excluded from proto-sociology. (p. 294)

The need for social epistemologies in the 21st century points to the importance of reclaiming the study of language (in many variations) as integral to the study of social life. This might mean broadening conceptions of "mixed methods" to also refer to efforts to combine interpretive and critical qualitative strategies of empirical analysis with more theoretical strategies such as deconstruction, genealogy, and poststructural discourse analysis. Or it might mean developing sociological studies of language that are empirically and theoretically rich and tethered to a pragmatist ontology and epistemology. There are many possibilities.

If we accept that Max Weber had it right when he said that people are suspended in webs of significance that we ourselves have spun, then social analysis must be understood not as an experimental search for laws but an interpretive search for meaning (Geertz, 1973). Our most private experiences are narratively constructed through the cultural framework of language. The ability to distinguish among truth, illusion, and falsity is dependent upon language—upon culture. All classificatory systems are narratively produced; even the individual, as such, does not exist as such prior to language. Without language there is no social interaction; without social interaction there is no social structure, no culture. Language, broadly construed as systems of representation, is arguably the foundation of shared culture. Consequently, it offers an effective means for developing social epistemologies that link together structure and agency, history and local interaction.

Linguistic turns have occurred in social, political, and economic contexts because there are commonalities among these contexts including an emphasis on the interrelated character of phenomena, the idea that the source of knowledge does not reside in individuals or objects but in relationships among individuals and objects, and an appreciation of language as actively contributing to our lives and our choices (Ives, 2004, p. 16). Perhaps one of the most common frameworks for analyzing social relationships in terms of language is critical discourse studies (CDS).

CDS, often referred to as critical discourse analysis (CDA), draws from a wide array of sampling procedures, theories, and analytic frameworks (cf. Wodak & Meyer, 2009). Some researchers readily make use of strategies that are strongly bound by the discipline of linguistics, such as corpus linguistics and sociolinguistics, yet others use analytic frameworks associated with Foucauldian discourse analysis, social psychology, or rhetoric studies. Under the broad umbrella of CDS, theories and methods are contingent upon the kind of intellectual problem being explored. Issues taken up by scholars in CDS, such as cognition, critical transmedia analysis, social interaction, and cultural texts, all require different analytic tools. Perhaps what most binds the variety of research together is an interest in looking at language and a commitment to understanding intertextuality. In this sense, the field is congruent with Gramsci's (1995) assertion that every process of inquiry needs to be congruent with its own particular purpose.

However, while CDS may provide a conceptual model for how many analytic frameworks might form a broad umbrella of qualitative methodologies/ methods, it has not been well defined empirically or theoretically. As a consequence, CDS can appear to lack a coherent, disciplinary center; there may be as many ways of conducting CDS as there are scholars working in the field. Indeed from a social science perspective, the multitude of approaches would benefit from more coherence, particularly greater clarification and elaboration of processes of formalization.

Within the social sciences, sociology has developed studies of language that focus on highly technical aspects of conversation and sociolinguistics in an effort to reconcile the importance of language and the demands of science. However, with changing and contested notions of what constitutes a social science, and deeper appreciation for the inseparability of symbolic practices and material realities, more sociologists are turning to a broader range of methods and theories for apprehending the sociological importance of language. For example, Steinberg (1999) demonstrated how material and discursive forces conjoin in shaping inequalities. Similarly, Bourdieu (2003) argued that the potency of symbolic power is the capacity of systems of meaning and signification to strengthen relations of oppression and exploitation. In the Research Committee on Language and Society of the International Sociological Association (ISA), scholars whose research ranges from sociolinguistics to poststructural discourse analysis are united by the desire to look at rather than through systems of communication. Moving away from a technical focus commonly associated with conversation analysis and sociolinguistics, sociologists are increasingly concerned about the ability of studies of language to effectively apprehend routine relations of power and privilege—to get at the reproduction of power and the intertextuality of ordinary life.

IMPLICATIONS FOR SOCIAL RESEARCH

Scientific rationality was established and enabled through historically specific power relations. One consequence has been that Western science has been produced through narratives of achievement that actively disassociate science from disasters such as the Tuskegee syphilis experiment, Hiroshima, environmental degradation, global militarism, entrenched racism, and other forms of systemic social and economic inequalities (Harding, 2008). Yet a strong commitment to challenging hegemonic science and to advancing social justice is clear in much of qualitative research. Scholars continue to address the limitations of qualitative frameworks, particularly through incorporating poststructural and psychoanalytic analyses. While this has created some improvements, it still leaves the field with philosophical crosscurrents that make it difficult (if not impossible) to examine routine power and privilege, intertextuality, and contemporary media. Our efforts can be made more effective.

Throughout this book I have attempted to demonstrate that there are real limits to the amount and kind of change that can be produced within the current social science paradigms. We need new techniques for analyzing data and new standards for empirical analysis that will enable us to legitimately ask (and answer) different kinds of questions. While the social sciences have changed dramatically in the past 50 years, our transformation is incomplete—indeed precisely because it can never *be* complete, scholars must continue to examine the theoretical foundations of research methodologies that determine what counts as valid knowledge and consequently limit what can be known.

The social sciences have been predicated on "an epistemology of ignorance," a state of "unknowingness," in relationship to routine relationships of power and privilege—indeed our identities as social researchers are forged through institutional processes that simultaneously construct and obfuscate our own privileged positions of power. We should not and cannot trust that research methodologies created by the most privileged, during eras of great oppression, will serve as the basis of socially just research. It is not a matter of good methods applied to bad uses but rather academia's ignorance of its own processes of reproduction. Opacity seems to be built into our own formation as we construct "others" who are knowable.

To the extent that social researchers assume, rather than account for, the ontological and epistemological commitments of social research, social scientific knowledge is bound to an unacknowledged, ideologically determined, and culturally biased production of knowledge. Both the practices and representations of the social sciences are constitutive of epistemic realities. As researchers, we know that "knowledge" and "truth" are polemical, strategic relations of power—our efforts to create just social research paradigms will always be imperfect, but we can do better.

Social research has served (and arguably continues to serve) as a powerful marginalizing force. More recently, however, scholars have come to argue that social research, as well as all of social life, is *storied*; "narrative is an *ontological condition of social life*" (Somers & Gibson, 1996, p. 38). Stories, in this sense, are not objects of knowledge. Rather, they are practices that constitute what they intend to mean. All representations of empirical realities, even statistical representations, are narratively constructed; this is true as well for the construction of factuality at the heart of all dominant forms of mass media communication technologies (Clough, 1992, p. 2).[9] Indeed all observations of social life and all data require narratives that enable us to recognize what we see and to make comparisons.

The incompleteness of narratives, and of interpretation, is inevitable because everything is already an interpretation; there is no primary moment that stands apart from the chain of interpretation. There is always a strategic place where the chain of interpretations is cut off from its origins in order to be analyzed. In social sciences, the chain of interpretation has been cut off at a localized context, which prevents any complex analysis of the phenomenon's conditions of emergence. Yet language itself is *epistemic*: language makes "reality" real. How we relate to ourselves and to each other is dependent upon not only the words we exchange but also upon the conceptualization that language makes possible.

Meaning is only possible through language; our conversations are always constructed through systems of representation that preceded us and will go on well past us. Consider, for example, that in the search for intellectual autonomy in West Africa, many scholars find it important to deconstruct the narratives of science and society that have been inherited from colonial regimes (Ocha, 2005; Sall & Quedraogo, 2010). Without doubt, "under colonialism, social science became a science in service of the colonial order" (Sall & Quedraogo, 2010, p. 226). Unfortunately, this practice of deconstruction has been limited; many countries around the globe still practice social sciences as they were constructed by empire.

The diversity of methods that could place the empirical findings of localized contexts in broader social and historical contexts are crushed by demands for more "evidence-based" research and the declaration of methods of the physical sciences as the "gold standard" of social research. The current Western social science paradigm demands that we treat language as a transparent bearer

---

[9]In the 21st century, interpretivism can no longer be juxtaposed against realism. Realism in science and in media must be understood as an *unconscious* construction of "empirical reality" that attempts to prevent the narrative construction of empiricism and factuality from becoming visible (Clough, 1992, p. 6).

of information, devoid of history, which can be understood through examination of a very narrow context of use. This practice speaks to one of the most profound and lasting binaries in social research—that of theory and method. The distinction has been maintained, in part, through the construction of positivist conceptions of evidence. In the face of ever-narrowing conceptions of evidence, it is critical to explore broader social and historical contexts—not as a search for origins but as an effort to identify and understand rhizomatic connections to events beyond the immediacy of what can be seen at a particular time, in order to generate an understanding of the multiple, intersecting forces that produce the meaning of a particular phenomenon or practice. In this sense, expanding what counts as legitimate evidence would constitute what Foucault (1972) and Nietzsche (1994) referred to as a genealogy—a kind of topology of social practices.

CONCLUDING THOUGHTS

In the 21st century, social sciences require techniques of data collection, analysis, and interpretation that can apprehend the tensions between personal agency and social constraints while accounting for relative consistency in contexts of multiplicity, contingency, and difference. Around the globe there are multiple traditions and practices that may be of core relevance for rethinking social science. At a minimum, reconceptualizing discourses of science to account for routine relations of power, contemporary media, and intertextuality requires a more integrated and flexible relationship between theory and method.

The social sciences need processes of formalization that can draw from both empirical data and logical warrants in order to situate localized practices in broader cultural contexts. A more integrated, less dualistic approach to theory and method would not generate limitless relativism. Rather, it would provide an intellectual framework that is capable of addressing issues of formalization and interpretation in scholarship that would make social research more accountable, and more relevant, to contemporary social life. At present, the complexities of routine relations of power, media convergence, and the intertextuality of social life demand that researchers rethink the philosophical foundations of social science. In addition, I have underscored the importance of a broader conception of social ethics based on principles of intersubjectivity. Social sciences are distinctively positioned to draw from interpersonal strengths of critical empathy and compassion to cultivate a deeper self-reflexive awareness of intersubjectivity in scholarship.

The work of rethinking social sciences has been in process for decades, although it exists at the margins of disciplines. It is past time for these lines of inquiry to become part of mainstream discussion and debate. The strength of future social science research depends upon the abilities of scholars to rethink the very foundations of scientific assumptions that define our work. This book concludes by returning to the initial provocation to rethink both the philosophical foundation and methodological techniques of qualitative research. If the mark of a mature science is its ability to generate new paradigms for research, social sciences are coming of age. It is both possible and necessary to move social research toward a coherent, 21st-century ontological and epistemological foundation expressed not only in data collection and interpretation but also in ethics and social justice. Changing the way we conduct research is both impossible and necessary.

FURTHER READING

Butler, J. (2005). *Giving an account of oneself.* New York: Fordham University Press.

Clarke, A. (2005). *Situational analysis: Grounded theory after the postmodern turn.* Thousand Oaks, CA: Sage.

Clough, P. T. (2000). *Autoaffection: Unconscious thought in the age of teletechnology.* Minneapolis: University of Minnesota Press.

Cruz, C. (2006). Toward an epistemology of a brown body. In D. D. Bernal, C. A. Elenes, F. E. Godinez, & S. Villenas (Eds.), *Chicana/Latina education in everyday life: Feminista perspectives on pedagogy and epistemology* (pp. 59–75). Albany: State University of New York Press.

Denzin, N. K., Lincoln, Y. S., & Smith, L. T. (Eds.). (2008). *Handbook of critical and indigenous methodologies.* Thousand Oaks, CA: Sage.

Foucault, M. (1994). *Aesthetics, method, and epistemology* (R. Hurley, Trans.). New York: The New Press.

Harding, S. (2008). *Sciences from below.* Durham, NC: Duke University Press.

Ladson-Billings, G. (2003). Racialized discourses and ethnic epistemologies. In N. K. Denzin & Y. S. Lincoln (Eds.), *The landscape of qualitative research* (pp. 398–432). Thousand Oaks, CA: Sage.

REFERENCES

Addelson, K. P. (2007). Knowers/doers and their moral problems. In L. M. Alcoff & E. Potter (Eds.), *Feminist epistemologies* (pp. 265–295). New York: Routledge.

Alcoff, L. M. (2007). Epistemologies of ignorance: Three types. In S. Sullivan & N. Tuana (Eds.), *Race and epistemologies of ignorance* (pp. 39–58). Albany: State University of New York Press.

Althuser, L. (1971). *Lenin, philosophy, and other essays.* London: New Left Books.

Baert, P. (2005). *Philosophy of the social sciences.* Cambridge, UK: Polity Press.

Barrotta, P., & Dascal, M. (2005). Introduction. In P. Barrotta & M. Dascal (Eds.), *Controversies and subjectivity* (pp. 1–30). Amsterdam/Philadelphia: John Benjamins Publishing Company.

Becker, H. S. (1974). Photography and sociology. *Studies in the Anthropology of Visual Communication, 1,* 3–26.

Behar, R., & Gordon, D. (1995). *Women writing culture.* Berkeley: University of California Press.

Berger, P., & Luckmann, T. (1966). *The social construction of reality: A treatise in the sociology of knowledge.* Garden City, NY: Doubleday.

Bernal, D. D. (2002). Critical race theory, Latino critical theory, and critical race-gendered epistemologies: Recognizing students of color as knowledge holders. *Qualitative Inquiry, 8*(1), 105–126.

Best, J. (1993). But seriously folks: The limitations of strict constructionist interpretation of social problems. In J. Holstein & G. Miller (Eds.), *Reconsidering social constructionism* (pp. 129–147). New York: Aldine de Gruyter.

Bjelic, D., & Lynch, M. (1992). The work of a (scientific) demonstration: Respecifying Newton's and Goethe's theories of prismatic color. In G. Watson & R. Seiler (Eds.), *Text in context: Contributions to ethnomethodology* (pp. 52–78). Newbury Park, CA: Sage.

Blumer, H. (1933). *Movies and conduct.* New York: Macmillan.

Blumer, H. (1941). Critiques of research in the social sciences, vol. I: An appraisal of Thomas and Znaniecki's "The Polish Peasant in Europe and America." *The Journal of American Sociology, 46*(6), 903–906.

Blumer, H. (1986). *Symbolic interactionism: Perspective and method.* Berkeley: University of California Press.

Blumer, H. (2004). *George Herbert Mead and human conduct.* Walnut Creek, CA: AltaMira Press.

Boden, D. (1990). People are talking: Conversation analysis and symbolic interaction. In H. S. Becker & M. McCall (Eds.), *Talk and social structure* (pp. 244–273). Chicago: University of Chicago Press.

Boden, D., & Zimmerman, D. H. (1991). Structure-in-action: An introduction. In D. Boden & D. H. Zimmerman (Eds.), *Talk and social structure: Studies in ethnomethodology and conversation analysis* (pp. 3–21). Berkeley: University of California Press.

Bonilla-Silva, E. (2003). *Racism without racists: Color-blind racism and the persistence of racial inequality in the United States.* Lanham, MD: Rowman & Littlefield.

Boothman, D. (1995). Introduction. In D. Boothman (Ed.), *Further selections from the prison notebooks.* Minneapolis: University of Minnesota Press.

Bourdieu, P. (2003). *Language and symbolic power.* Cambridge, MA: Harvard University Press.

Burke, P. J. (1980). The self: Measurement implications from a symbolic interactionist perspective. *Social Psychology Quarterly, 43*, 18–29.

Butler, J. (1993). *Bodies that matter.* London: Routledge.

Butler, J. (1997a). *Excitable speech: A politics of the performative.* New York: Routledge.

Butler, J. (1997b). Gender is burning: Questions of appropriation and subversion. In A. McClintock, A. Mufti, & E. Shohat (Eds.), *Dangerous liaisons: Gender, nation and postcolonial perspectives* (pp. 381–395). Minneapolis: University of Minnesota.

Butler, J. (2005). *Giving an account of oneself.* New York: Fordham University Press.

Cahill, S. (1987). Directions for an interactionist study of gender development. In M. J. Deegan & M. Hill (Eds.), *Women and symbolic interaction* (pp. 81–98). Boston: Allen and Unwin.

Cannella, G., & Lincoln, Y. S. (2004). Epilogue: Claiming a critical public social science— Reconceptualizing and redeploying research. *Qualitative Inquiry, 10*(20), 298–309.

Charmaz, K. (2001). Qualitative interviewing and grounded theory analysis. In J. F. Gubrium & J. A. Holstein (Eds.), *Handbook of interview research: Context & method* (pp. 675–694). Thousand Oaks, CA: Sage.

Charmaz, K. (2006). *Constructing grounded theory: A practical guide through quali- tative analysis.* Thousand Oaks, CA: Sage.

Charmaz, K. (2009). Constructivist grounded theory methods. In J. M. Morse (Ed.), *Developing grounded theory: The second generation* (pp. 127–154). Walnut Creek, CA: Left Coast Press.

Clarke, A. (2005). *Situational analysis: Grounded theory after the postmodern turn.* Thousand Oaks, CA: Sage.

Clarke, A. (2009). From grounded theory to situational analysis. In J. M. Morse (Ed.), *Developing grounded theory: The second generation* (pp. 194–235). Walnut Creek, CA: Left Coast Press.

Clough, P. T. (1988). The movies and social observations: Reading Blumer's movies and conduct. *Symbolic Interaction*, *11*(1), 85–97.

Clough, P. T. (1989). Letters from Pamela: Reading Howard S. Becker's writing(s) for social scientists. *Symbolic Interaction*, *12*, 159–170.

Clough, P. T. (1992). *End(s) of ethnography*. Thousand Oaks, CA: Sage.

Clough, P. T. (2000). *Autoaffection: Unconscious thought in the age of teletechnology*. Minneapolis: University of Minnesota Press.

Clough, P. T. (2008). Celebrating work. In N. K. Denzin (Ed.), *Studies in symbolic interaction* (Vol. 30, pp. 37–44). Bingley, UK: Emerald Group Publishing Ltd.

Code, L. (1993). Taking subjectivity into account. In L. M. Alcoff & E. Potter (Eds.), *Feminist epistemologies* (pp. 15–48). New York: Routledge.

Collins, P. H. (1993). Black feminist thought in the matrix of domination. In C. Lemert (Ed.), *Social theory: The multicultural & classical readings*. San Francisco: Westview Press.

Collins, P. H. (2000). *Black feminist thought: Knowledge, consciousness, and the politics of empowerment* (2nd ed.). New York: Routledge.

Connell, R. (2010). Learning from each other: Sociology on a world scale. In S. Patel (Ed.), *The ISA handbook of diverse sociological traditions* (pp. 40–51). Thousand Oaks, CA: Sage.

Coulon, A. (1995). *Ethnomethodology* (Vol. 36). Thousand Oaks, CA: Sage.

Cruz, C. (2006). Toward an epistemology of a brown body. In D. D. Bernal, C. A. Elenes, F. E. Godinez, & S. Villenas (Eds.), *Chicana/Latina education in everyday life: Feminista perspectives on pedagogy and epistemology* (pp. 59–75). Albany: State University of New York Press.

Cuff, E. C., Sharrock, W. W., & Francis, D. W. (2006). *Perspectives in sociology* (5th ed.). New York: Routledge.

Daly, K. (2007). *Qualitative methods for family studies and human development*. Thousand Oaks, CA: Sage.

de Certeau, M. (1984). *The practice of everyday life* (S. Rendall, Trans.). Berkeley: University of California Press.

della Porta, D., & Keating, M. (2008). Introduction. In D. della Porta & M. Keating (Eds.), *Approaches and methodologies in the social sciences: A pluralist perspective* (pp. 1–16). Cambridge, UK: Cambridge University Press.

Denzin, N. K. (1970). Symbolic interaction and ethnomethodology. In J. Douglas (Ed.), *Understanding everyday life* (pp. 261–286). Chicago: Aldine.

Denzin, N. K. (1978). The research act. In J. Manis & B. N. Meltzer (Eds.), *Symbolic interaction: A reader in social psychology* (3rd ed., pp. 58–68). Boston: Allyn & Bacon.

Denzin, N. K. (1992). *Symbolic interactionism and cultural studies*. New York: Blackwell.

Denzin, N. K. (2002a). The cinematic society and the reflexive interview. In
    J. Gubrium & J. Holstein (Eds.), *Handbook of interview research: Context and
    method* (pp. 833–848). Thousand Oaks, CA: Sage.

Denzin, N. K. (2002b). *Reading race.* Thousand Oaks, CA: Sage.

Denzin, N. K. (2003a). Cultural studies. In L. T. Reynolds & N. J. Herman-Kinney
    (Eds.), *Handbook of symbolic interactionism* (pp. 997–1019). Walnut Creek, CA:
    AltaMira Press.

Denzin, N. K. (2003b). The call to performance. *Symbolic Interaction, 26*(1), 187–207.

Denzin, N. K., & Giardina, M. D. (2006). Introduction: Qualitative inquiry and the con-
    servative challenge. In N. K. Denzin & M. D. Giardina (Eds.), *Qualitative
    research and the conservative challenge* (pp. ix–xxxi). Walnut Creek, CA: Left
    Coast Press, Inc.

Denzin, N. K., Lincoln, Y. S., & Smith, L. T. (Eds.). (2008). *Handbook of critical and
    indigenous methodologies.* Thousand Oaks, CA: Sage.

DeVault, M. (1999). *Liberating method: Feminism and social research.* Philadelphia:
    Temple University Press.

Dillard, C. B., & Dixson, A. D. (2006). Affirming the will and the way of the ances-
    tors: Black feminist consciousness and the search for "good"[ness] in qualitative
    science. In N. K. Denzin & M. D. Giardina (Eds.), *Qualitative research and the
    conservative challenge* (pp. 227–254). Walnut Creek, CA: Left Coast Press.

The Economist. (2007, December 19). Where "California" bubbled up: Esalen, birth-
    place of the New Age, is a victim of its own success. *The Economist.* Retrieved
    from http://www.economist.com/displayStory.cfm?Story_ID=10278745

Ellis, C., & Bochner, A. P. (Eds.). (1996). *Composing ethnography: Alternative forms
    of qualitative writing.* Walnut Creek, CA: AltaMira Press.

Essed, P., & Goldberg, D. T. (Eds.). (2002). *Race critical theories.* New York:
    Blackwell.

Feldman, M. (1995). *Strategies for interpreting qualitative data* (Vol. 33). Thousand
    Oaks, CA: Sage.

Flyvbjerg, B. (2001). *Making social science matter: Why social inquiry fails and how
    it can succeed again.* Cambridge, UK: Cambridge University Press.

Fornäs, J., Becker, K., Bjurstöm, E., & Ganetz, H. (2007). *Consuming media:
    Communication, shopping and everyday life.* New York: Oxford University Press.

Foucault, M. (1972). *The archeology of knowledge* (A. M. S. Smith, Trans.). New York:
    Pantheon Books.

Foucault, M. (1977). *Discipline and punish: The birth of the prison* (A. Sheridan,
    Trans.). New York: Vintage Books.

Fuss, D. (1989). *Essentially speaking: Feminism, nature & difference.* New York:
    Routledge.

Gannon, S., & Davies, B. (2007). Postmodern, poststructural and critical theories. In
    S. N. Hesse-Biber (Ed.), *Handbook of feminist research: Theory and praxis*
    (pp. 71–106). Thousand Oaks, CA: Sage.

Garfinkel, H. (1967). *Studies in ethnomethodology.* Cambridge, UK: Polity Press.

Garfinkel, H. (2002). *Ethnomethodology's program: Working out Durkheim's aphorism*. Lanham, MD: Rowman & Littlefield.

Geertz, C. (1973). Thick description: Toward an interpretive theory of culture. In C. Geertz (Ed.), *The interpretatin of cultures: Selected essays* (pp. 3–30). New York: Basic Books.

Glaser, B., & Strauss, A. (1967). *The discovery of grounded theory: Strategies for qualitative research*. New York: Aldine de Gruyter.

Glenn, E. N. (2002). *Unequal freedom*. Cambridge, MA: Harvard University Press.

Goffman, E. (1959a). *Asylums: Essays on the social situation of mental patients and other inmates*. New York: Anchor Books.

Goffman, E. (1959b). *The presentation of self in everyday life*. New York: Anchor Books/Doubleday.

Goffman, E. (1963). *Stigma: Notes on the management of spoiled identity*. New York: Simon & Schuster.

Goffman, E. (1967). *Interaction ritual: Essays on face-to-face behavior*. New York: Pantheon Books.

Goffman, E. (1976). *Gender advertisements*. New York: Harper Torchbooks.

Goldman, A. (2002). *Pathways to knowledge*. Oxford, UK: Oxford University Press.

Gordon, A. (1997). *Ghostly matters: Haunting and the sociological imagination*. Minneapolis: University of Minnesota Press.

Gramsci, A. (1995). *Further selections from the prison notebooks* (D. Boothman, Trans.). Minneapolis: University of Minnesota Press.

Gubrium, J., & Holstein, J. (1997). *The new language of qualitative method*. Oxford, UK: Oxford University Press.

Gubrium, J., & Holstein, J. (2003). The life course. In L. T. Reynolds & N. J. Herman-Kinney (Eds.), *Handbook of symbolic interactionism*. Walnut Creek, CA: AltaMira Press.

Gusfield, J. R. (2003). A journey with symbolic interaction. *Symbolic Interaction, 26*(1), 119–139.

Hak, T. (1992). Psychiatric records as transformations of other texts. In G. Watson & R. Seiler (Eds.), *Text in context: Contributions to ethnomethodology* (pp. 138–155). Newbury Park, CA: Sage.

Hall, D. E. (2004). *Subjectivity*. New York: Routledge.

Hall, S. (1996). On postmodernism and articulation: An interview with Stuart Hall. In D. Morely & K.-H. Chen (Eds.), *Stuart Hall: Critical dialogues in cultural studies* (pp. 131–150). New York: Routledge.

Hall, S. (1997a). Introduction. In S. Hall (Ed.), *Representation: Cultural representations and signifying practices* (pp. 1–11). Thousand Oaks, CA: Sage.

Hall, S. (1997b). The spectacle of the "Other." In S. Hall (Ed.), *Representation: Cultural representations and signifying practices* (pp. 223–290). Thousand Oaks, CA: Sage.

Hall, S. (1997c). The work of representation. In S. Hall (Ed.), *Representation: Cultural representations and signifying practices* (pp. 13–74). Thousand Oaks, CA: Sage.

Hammersley, M. (1981). Using qualitative methods. *Social Science Information Studies*, *1*, 209–220.

Handel, W. (1982). *Ethnomethodology: How people make sense*. Englewood Cliffs, NJ: Prentice Hall.

Haraway, D. (1991). *Simians, cyborgs, and women: The reinvention of nature*. New York: Routledge.

Harding, S. (Ed.). (1987). *Feminism and methodology*. Bloomington: Indiana University Press.

Harding, S. (1991). *Whose science? Whose knowledge? Thinking from women's lives*. Ithaca, NY: Cornell University Press.

Harding, S. (2007). Rethinking standpoint epistemology: What is "strong objectivity"? In L. M. Alcoff & E. Potter (Eds.), *Feminist epistemologies* (pp. 49–82). New York: Routledge.

Harding, S. (2008). *Sciences from below*. Durham, NC: Duke University Press.

Hartsock, N. (1987). The feminist standpoint: Developing the ground for a specific feminist historical materialism. In S. Harding (Ed.), *Feminism and methodology* (pp. 159–166). Bloomington: Indiana University Press.

Hawkesworth, M. (2007). Truth and truths in feminist knowledge production. In S. N. Hesse-Biber (Ed.), *Handbook of feminist research: Theory and praxis* (pp. 469–491). Thousand Oaks, CA: Sage.

Helle, H. J. (2005). *Symbolic interaction and verstehen* (Vol. 4). New York: Peter Lang.

Hendry, P. M. (2007). The future of narrative. *Qualitative Inquiry*, *13*, 487–498.

Heritage, J. (1984). *Garfinkel and ethnomethodology*. Cambridge, UK: Polity Press.

Herman-Kinney, N. J., & Verschaeve, J. M. (2003). Methods of Symbolic Interactionism. In L. T. Reynolds & N. J. Herman-Kinney (Eds.), *Handbook of symbolic interactionism* (pp. 213–252). Walnut Creek, CA: AltaMira Press.

Hernstein, R., & Murray, C. (1994). *The bell curve: Intelligence and class structure in American life*. New York: Free Press.

Hesse-Biber, S. N. (2007). Feminist research: Exploring the interconnections of epistemology, methodology and method. In S. N. Hesse-Biber (Ed.), *Handbook of feminist research: Theory and praxis* (pp. 1–28). Thousand Oaks, CA: Sage.

Hesse-Biber, S. N., & Leavy, P. (2006). *Emergent methods in social research*. Thousand Oaks, CA: Sage.

Hoagland, S. L. (2007). Denying relationality: Epistemology and ethics and ignorance. In S. Sullivan & N. Tuana (Eds.), *Race and epistemologies of ignorance* (pp. 95–118). Albany: State University of New York Press.

Holstein, J., & Gubrium, J. (1998). Phenomenology, ethnomethodology, and interpretive practice. In N. K Denzin & Y. S. Lincoln (Eds.), *Strategies of qualitative inquiry* (pp. 262–272). Thousand Oaks, CA: Sage.

Holstein, J., & Gubrium, J. (2000). *The self we live by: Narrative identity in a postmodern world*. Oxford: Oxford University Press.

Holstein, J., & Gubrium, J. (2005). Interpretive practice and social action. In N. K. Denzin & Y. Lincoln (Eds.), *The Sage handbook of qualitative research* (3rd ed., pp. 483–505). Thousand Oaks, CA: Sage

Holstein, J., & Miller, G. (1993). Social constructionism and social problems work. In J. Holstein & G. Miller (Eds.), *Reconsidering social constructionism* (pp. 151–172). New York: Aldine de Gruyter.

Hruby, G. (2001). Sociology, postmodern, and new realism perspectives in social constructionism: Implications for literacy research. *Reading Research Quarterly, 36*(1), 48–62.

Husband, R., & Foster, W. (1987). Understanding qualitative research: A strategic approach to qualitative methodology. *Journal of Humanistic Education and Development, 26*(2), 50–63.

Husserl, E. (1960). *Cartesian meditations: An introduction to phenomenology* (D. Cairns, Trans.). The Hague: Martinus Nijhoff.

Husserl, E. (1964). *The idea of phenomenology* (W. P. Alston & G. Nakhnikian, Trans.). The Hague: Martinus Nijhoff.

Husserl, E. (1970). *Logical investigations.* New York: Humanities Press.

Ibarra, P. (2008). Strict and contextual constructionism in the sociology of deviance and social problems. In J. Holstein & J. Gubrium (Eds.), *Handbook of constructionist research* (pp. 355–369). New York: Guilford Press.

Ibarra, P., & Kitsuse, J. (1993). Vernacular constituents of moral discourse. In J. Holstein & G. Miller (Eds.), *Reconsidering social constructionism* (pp. 25–58). New York: Aldine de Gruyter.

Iser, W. (2006). *How to do theory.* New York: Blackwell.

Ives, P. (2004). *Language and hegemony in Gramsci.* London: Pluto Press.

Ives, P. (2008). *Gramsci's politics of language: Engaging the Bakhtin Circle and the Frankfurt School.* Toronto: University of Toronto Press.

Jackson, P. T. (2010). *The conduct of inquiry in international relations.* New York: Routledge.

James, W. (1902). *Varieties of religious experience.* New York: Longmans, Green & Company.

James, W. (1948). *Essays in pragmatism.* New York: Hafner Publishing Company.

James, W. (1971). *The moral equivalent of war and other essays and selections from some problems of philosophy.* New York: Harper Torchbooks.

Jenkins, H. (2008). *Convergence culture: Where old and new media collide.* New York: New York University Press.

Johnson, P. (1998). Analytic induction. In G. Symon & C. Cassell (Eds.), *Qualitative methods and analysis in organizational research: A practical guide* (pp. 29–50). Thousand Oaks, CA: Sage.

Johnson, R., Chambers, D., Raghuram, P., & Tincknell, E. (Eds.). (2004). *The practice of cultural studies.* Thousand Oaks, CA: Sage.

Katovich, M. A., Miller, D. E., & Hintz, R. A. (2002). Empiricism on the prairie: Four waves of the new Iowa School. *Studies in Symbolic Interaction, 25,* 5–23.

Katovich, M. A., Miller, D. E., & Stewart, R. L. (2003). The Iowa school. In L. T. Reynolds & N. J. Herman-Kinney (Eds.), *Handbook of symbolic interactionism* (pp. 119–139). Walnut Creek, CA: AltaMira Press.

Kincheloe, J., & McLaren, P. (1998). Rethinking critical theory and qualitative research. In N. K. Denzin & Y. S. Lincoln (Eds.), *The landscape of qualitative research* (pp. 260–299). Thousand Oaks, CA: Sage.

Korth, B. (2002). Critical qualitative research as consciousness raising: The dialogic texts of researcher/researchee. *Qualitative Inquiry, 8*, 381–403.

Kuhn, T. (1970). *The structure of scientific revolutions.* Chicago: University of Chicago Press.

Ladson-Billings, G. (2003a). It's your world, I'm just trying to explain it: Understanding our epistemological and methodological challenges. *Qualitative Inquiry, 9*(1), 5–12.

Ladson-Billings, G. (2003b). Racialized discourses and ethnic epistemologies. In N. K. Denzin & Y. S. Lincoln (Eds.), *The landscape of qualitative research* (pp. 398–432). Thousand Oaks, CA: Sage.

Lal, J. (2008). On the domestication of American public sociology: A postcolonial feminist perspective. *Critical Sociology, 43*(2), 169–191.

Lather, P. (1991). *Getting smart: Feminist research and pedagogy with/in the postmodern.* New York: Routledge.

Lather, P. (2001). *Getting lost: Feminist efforts toward a double(d) science.* Albany: State University of New York Press.

Latour, B. (1993). *We have never been modern.* Cambridge, MA: Harvard University Press.

Latour, B., & Woolgar, S. (1986). *Laboratory life: The construction of scientific facts* (2nd ed.). Princeton, NJ: Princeton University Press.

Lincoln, Y., & Guba, E. (1985). *Naturalistic inquiry.* Thousand Oaks, CA: Sage.

Longino, H. E. (2007). Subjects, power and knowledge: Description and prescription in feminist philosophies of science. In L. M. Alcoff & E. Potter (Eds.), *Feminist epistemologies* (pp. 101–120). New York: Routledge.

Longman, J. (2007, May 16). *An amputee sprinter: Is he disabled or too-abled? New York Times.* Retrieved from http://www.nytimes.com/2007/05/15/sports/othersports/15runner.html

Lynch, M., & Bogen, D. (1994). Harvey Sacks's primitive natural science. *Theory Culture and Society, 11*(4), 65–104.

Lynch, M., & McNally, R. (1999). Science, common sense and common law: Courtroom inquiries and the public understanding of science. *Social Epistemology, 13*(2), 183–196.

Maines, D. R. (1977). Social organization and social structure in symbolic interactionist thought. *Annual Review of Sociology, 3*, 325–359.

Mansfield, N. (2000). *Subjectivity: Theories of the self from Freud to Haraway.* New York: New York University Press.

Maynard, D., & Clayman, S. (2003). Ethnomethodology and conversation analysis. In L. T. Reynolds & N. J. Herman-Kinney (Eds.), *Handbook of symbolic interactionism* (pp. 173–202). Walnut Creek, CA: AltaMira Press.

Mead, G. H. (1962). *Mind, self and society: From the standpoint of a social behaviorist.* Chicago: University of Chicago Press.

Memmi, A. (2000). *Racism* (S. Martinot, Trans.). Minneapolis: University of Minnesota Press.

Miller, S. I. (1982). Quality and quantity: Another view of analytic induction as a research technique. *Quality & Quantity, 16*, 281–295.

Millman, M., & Kanter, R. (Eds.). (1975). *Another voice: Feminist perspectives on social life.* New York: Anchor Books.

Mills, C. W. (2007). White ignorance. In S. Sullivan & N. Tuana (Eds.), *Race and epistemologies of ignorance* (pp. 11–38). Albany: State University of New York Press.

Minh-ha, T. T. (1989). *Woman, native, other.* Bloomington: Indiana University Press.

Mitchell, P. (2007). *Cartographic strategies of postmodernity: The figure of the map in contemporary theory and fiction.* London: Routledge.

Moerman, M. (1992). Life after CA: An ethnographer's autobiograpy. In G. Watson & R. Seiler (Eds.), *Text in context: Contributions to ethnomethodology* (pp. 20–34). Newbury Park, CA: Sage.

Morse, J. M., & Mitcham, C. (2002). Exploring qualitatively derived concepts: Inductive–deductive methods. *International Journal of Qualitative Methods, 1*(4), Article 3. Retrieved from http://www.ualberta.ca/~ijqm

Musolf, G. R. (2003). The Chicago school. In L. T. Reynolds & N. J. Herman-Kinney (Eds.), *Handbook of symbolic interactionism* (pp. 91–117). Walnut Creek, CA: AltaMira Press.

Naples, N. (2003). *Feminism and method.* New York: Routledge.

Nietzsche, F. (1994). *On the genealogy of morality* (C. Diethe, Trans.). Cambridge, UK: Cambridge University Press.

Northcutt, N., & McCoy, D. (2004). *Interactive qualitative analysis: A systems method of qualitative inquiry.* Thousand Oaks, CA: Sage.

Olesen, V. (1994). Feminisms and models of qualitative research. In N. K. Denzin & Y. S. Lincoln (Eds.), *Handbook of qualitative research* (pp. 158–174). Thousand Oaks, CA: Sage.

Osha, S. (2005). *Kwasi Wiredu and beyond: The text, writing and thought in Africa.* Dakra, Senegal: Council for the Development of Social Science Research in Africa.

Parsons, T. (1970). *Social structure and personality.* New York: The Free Press.

Pascale, C.-M. (2007). *Making sense of race, class, and gender: Commonsense, power, and privilege in the United States.* New York: Routledge.

Philip, R. (2005, April 27). Pistorius masters quick step. *Telegraph.* Retrieved from www.telegraph.co.uk/philip

Pidgeon, N., & Henwood, K. (2004). Grounded theory. In M. Hardy & A. Bryman (Eds.), *Handbook of data analysis* (pp. 625–648). Thousand Oaks, CA: Sage.

Platt, J. (1996). *A history of sociological research methods in America, 1920–1960.* Cambridge, UK: Cambridge University Press.

Pollock, G. (2008). Feminism and culture: Theoretical perspectives. In T. Bennett & J. Frow (Eds.), *The Sage handbook of cultural analysis* (pp. 249–270). Thousand Oaks, CA: Sage.

Prasad, A., & Prasad, P. (2002). The coming of age of interpretive organizational research. *Organizational Research Methods, 5*(1), 4–11.

Prasad, P. (1993). Symbolic processes in the implementation of technological change: A symbolic interactionist study of work computerization. *Academy of Management Journal, 36*(6), 1400–1429.

Prasad, P. (2005). *Crafting qualitative research: Working in the postpositivist traditions.* New York: M.E. Sharpe.

Ragin, C. (1994). *Constructing social research.* Thousand Oaks, CA: Pine Forge Press.

Ramazanoğlu, C., & Holland, J. (2002). *Feminist methodology: Challenges and choices.* Thousand Oaks, CA: Sage.

Ratcliff, D. E. (2006). *Analytic induction as a qualitative research method of analysis.* Retrieved from http://www.vanguard.edu/uploadedFiles/faculty/dratcliff/qualresources/analytic.pdf

Reason, P., & Bradbury, H. (2008). Introduction. In P. Reason & H. Bradbury (Eds.), *The Sage handbook of action research: Participative inquiry and practice* (2nd ed., pp. 1–9). Thousand Oaks, CA: Sage.

Reinharz, S. (1992). *Feminist methods in social research.* New York: Oxford University Press.

Rettig, K. D., Tam, V. C.-W., & Magistad, B. M. (1996). Using pattern matching and modified analytic induction in examining justice principles in child support guidelines. *Marriage & Family Review, 24*(1/2), 193–222.

Reynolds, L. T. (2003a). Early representatives. In L. T. Reynolds & N. J. Herman-Kinney (Eds.), *Handbook of symbolic interactionism* (pp. 59–81). Walnut Creek, CA: AltaMira Press.

Reynolds, L. T. (2003b). Intellectual precursors. In L. T. Reynolds & N. J. Herman-Kinney (Eds.), *Handbook of symbolic interactionism* (pp. 39–58). Walnut Creek, CA: AltaMira Press.

Reynolds, L. T., & Herman-Kinney, N. J. (Eds.). (2003). *Handbook of symbolic interactionism.* Walnut Creek, CA: AltaMira Press.

Richardson, L. (2004). *Travels with Ernest: Crossing the literary/sociological divide.* Walnut Creek, CA: AltaMira Press.

Robinson, W. S. (1951). The logical structure of analytic induction. *American Sociological Review, 16*(6), 812–818.

Rosaldo, R. (1993). *Culture and truth: The remaking of social analysis.* Boston: Beacon Press.

Rose, G. (2007). *Visual methodologies: An introduction to the interpretation of visual materials* (2nd ed.). Thousand Oaks, CA: Sage.

Rousseau, N. (2002). *Self, symbols, and society: Classic readings in social psychology.* Lanham, MD: Rowman & Littlefield.

Russell, B. (1938). *Power: A new social analysis.* New York: Routledge.

Sacks, H. (1992). *Lectures on conversation* (Vol. 1). Oxford, UK: Basil Blackwell.

Sall, E., & Ouedraogo, J.-B. (2010). Sociology in West Africa: Challenges and obstacles to academic autonomy. In S. Patel (Ed.), *The ISA handbook of diverse sociological traditions.* Thousand Oaks, CA: Sage.

Sandoval, C. (2000). *Methodology of the oppressed.* Minneapolis: University of Minnesota.

Saukko, P. (2003). *Doing research in cultural studies.* Thousand Oaks, CA: Sage.

Scheff, T. J. (2005). Looking-glass self: Goffman as symbolic interactionist. *Symbolic Interaction, 28*(2), 147–166.

Scheurich, J. (Ed.). (1997). *Research methods in the postmodern*. London: Falmer Press.

Schutz, A. (1970). *On phenomenology and social relations*. Chicago: University of Chicago Press.

Schwandt, T. A. (1994). Constructivist, interpretivist approaches to human inquiry. In N. K. Denzin & Y. S. Lincoln (Eds.), *Handbook of qualitative research* (pp. 118–137). Thousand Oaks, CA: Sage.

Scott, J. W. (1991). The evidence of experience. *Critical Inquiry, 17*(4), 773–797.

Searle, J. (2003). *Minds, brains, and science*. Cambridge, MA: Harvard University Press.

Sharrock, W., & Anderson, B. (1986). *The ethnomethodologists*. London: Tavistock Publications.

Smelser, N. J., & Baltes, P. B. (2001). International encyclopedia of the social and behavioral sciences. Retrieved from http://www.sscnet.ucla.edu/soc/faculty/katz/pubs/Analytic_Induction.pdf

Smith, D. (1990a). *Texts, facts, and femininity: Exploring the relations of ruling*. New York: Routledge.

Smith, D. (1990b). *The conceptual practices of power*. Boston: Northeastern University Press.

Smith, D. (1999). *Writing the social: Critique, theory and investigations*. Toronto: University of Toronto Press.

Smith, L. T. (2004). *Decolonizing methodologies: Research and indigenous peoples*. London: Zed Books Ltd.

Smith, R. W., & Bugni, V. (2006). Symbolic interaction theory and architecture. *Symbolic Interaction, 29*(2), 123–155.

Somers, M. R., & Gibson, G. D. (1996). Reclaiming the epistemological "other": Narrative and the social constitution of identity. In C. Calhoun (Ed.), *Social theory and the politics of identity* (pp. 35–99). Cambridge, MA: Blackwell Publishers.

St. Pierre, E., & Pillow, W. (2000). *Working in the ruins: Feminist poststructural theory and methods in education*. New York: Routledge.

Stanfield, J. H., II. (1993). Methodological reflections: An introduction. In J. H. Stanfield II & R. M. Dennis (Eds.), *Race and ethnicity in research methods* (pp. 3–15). Newbury Park, CA: Sage.

Stanley, L., & Wise, S. (1983). *Breaking out: Feminist consciousness and feminist research*. London: Routledge and Kegan Paul.

Steinberg, M. (1999). *Fighting words: Working-class formation, collective action, and discourse in early 19th century England*. Ithaca, NY: Cornell University Press.

Steinberg, S. (2007). *Race relations: A critique*. Palo Alto, CA: Stanford University Press.

Strauss, A., & Corbin, J. (1998). *Basics of qualitative research: Techniques and procedures for developing grounded theory* (2nd ed.). Thousand Oaks, CA: Sage.

Stryker, S. (1980). *Symbolic interactionism: A social structural version*. Menlo Park, CA: Benjamin Cummings.

Sullivan, S., & Tuana, N. (Eds.). (2007). *Race and epistemologies of ignorance*. Albany: State University of New York Press.

Sztompka, P. (2010). One sociology or many? In S. Patel (Ed.), *The ISA handbook of diverse sociological traditions* (pp. 21–39). Thousand Oaks, CA: Sage.

ten Have, P. (2004). *Understanding qualitative research and ethnomethodology.* Thousand Oaks, CA: Sage.

Thomas, W. I., & Znaniecki, F. (1918). *The Polish peasant in Europe and America.* Boston: The Gorham Press.

Travers, M. (2001). *Qualitative research through case studies.* Thousand Oaks, CA: Sage.

Twine, F. W., & Warren, J. W. (Eds.). (2000). *Racing research, researching race: Methodological dilemmas in critical race studies.* New York: New York University Press.

Van Dijk, T. A. (1993). Analyzing racism through discourse analysis: Some methodological reflections. In J. H. Stanfield II & R. M. Dennis (Eds.), *Race and ethnicity in research methods* (pp. 92–134). Newbury Park, CA: Sage.

Watson, G., & Goulet, J.-G. (1998). What can ethnomethodology say about power? *Qualitative Inquiry, 4*(1), 96–114.

Watson, G., & Seiler, R. (Eds.). (1992). *Text in context: Contributions to ethnomethodology.* Newbury Park, CA: Sage.

Weber, M. (1978). *Economy and society: An outline of interpretive sociology* (G. Roth & C. Wittich, Eds.). Berkeley: University of California Press.

Weinstein, J., & Stehr, N. (1999). The power of knowledge: Race science, race policy, and the Holocaust. *Social Epistemology, 13*(1), 3–36.

West, C., & Zimmerman, D. H. (1987). Doing gender. *Gender & Society, 1*(2), 125–151.

Williams, G. (1999). *French discourse analysis: The method of post-structuralism.* New York: Routledge.

Willis, J. W. (2007). *Foundations of qualitative research: Interpretive and critical approaches.* Thousand Oaks, CA: Sage.

Winch, P. (1958). *The idea of a social science and its relationship to philosophy.* London: Routledge & Kegan Paul.

Wodak, R., & Meyer, M. (Eds.). (2009). *Methods of critical discourse analysis* (2nd ed.). Thousand Oaks, CA: Sage.

Young, K. (1941). Critiques of research in the social sciences, vol. I: An appraisal of Thomas and Znaniecki's "The Polish Peasant in Europe and America" by Herbert Blumer, William I. Thomas, Florian Znaniecki, Read Bain. *American Journal of Sociology, 46*(6), 903–906.

Zinn, M. B. (1979). Field research in minority communities: Ethical, methodological and political observations by an insider. *Social Problems, 27*(2), 209–218.

Znaniecki, F. (1934). *The method of sociology.* New York: Farrar & Rinehart.

Zuberi, T. (2001). *Thicker than blood: How racial statistics lie.* Minneapolis: University of Minnesota Press.

Zuberi, T., & Bonilla-Silva, E. (Eds.). (2008). *White logic, white methods: Racism and methodology.* Lanham, MD: Rowman & Littlefield.

INDEX

SAGE Research Methods Online

The essential tool for researchers

Sign up now at www.sagepub.com/srmo for more information.

An expert research tool

- An **expertly designed taxonomy** with more than 1,400 unique terms for social and behavioral science research methods
- **Visual and hierarchical search tools** to help you discover material and link to related methods

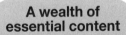

- Easy-to-use navigation tools
- Content organized by complexity
- Tools for citing, printing, and downloading content with ease
- Regularly updated content and features

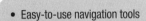

A wealth of essential content

- The most comprehensive picture of quantitative, qualitative, and mixed methods available today
- More than **100,000 pages of SAGE book and reference material** on research methods as well as editorially selected material from SAGE journals
- More than **600 books** available in their entirety online

Launching 2011!

⑤SAGE research methods online